Toni Morrison's
Song of Solomon

A CASEBOOK

CASEBOOKS IN CRITICISM

General Editor, William L. Andrews

TONI MORRISON'S

Song of Solomon

◆ ◆ ◆

A CASEBOOK

Edited by
Jan Furman

OXFORD
UNIVERSITY PRESS

2003

OXFORD
UNIVERSITY PRESS

Oxford   New York

Auckland   Bangkok   Buenos Aires   Cape Town   Chennai
Dar es Salaam   Delhi   Hong Kong   Istanbul   Karachi   Kolkata
Kuala Lumpur   Madrid   Melbourne   Mexico City   Mumbai   Nairobi
São Paulo   Shanghai   Taipei   Tokyo   Toronto

Published by Oxford University Press, Inc.
198 Madison Avenue, New York, New York 10016

www.oup.com

Oxford is a registered trademark of Oxford University Press

Library of Congress Cataloging-in-Publication Data
Toni Morrison's Song of Solomon : a casebook / edited by Jan Furman.
p. cm. — (Casebooks in criticism)
Includes bibliographical references.
ISBN 0-19-514634-4; 0-19-514635-2 (pbk.)
1. Morrison, Toni. Song of Solomon.   2. African American families in literature.   3.
African Americans in literature.   4. Michigan—In literature.   I. Title: Song of Solomon.   II.
Furman, Jan.   III. Morrison, Toni. Song of Solomon.   IV. Series.
PS3563.O8749 S64 2003
813'.54—dc21   2002193006

1 3 5 7 9 8 6 4 2

Printed in the United States of America
on acid-free paper

Credits

Contents

Part II Myth and Folklore

Part III Narrative Influence

Part IV Historical Perspectives

Part V An Interview

.

Toni Morrison's
Song of Solomon

A CASEBOOK

Introduction

JAN FURMAN

❖ ❖ ❖

TONI MORRISON'S *Song of Solomon* appeared in 1977 to a
standing ovation. Anne Tyler of the *Washington Post* called it
"a stunningly beautiful book." "Morrison dazzles," declared the
Nation. The *Philadelphia Enquirer* described Morrison as "the most
sensible lyrical writer around today." John Leonard, writing in the
New York Times, considered it his honor to review *Song of Solomon*.
Cataloging his reviewer's canon of admirable books—among
them Nabokov's *Lolita*, Heller's *Catch-22*, Lessing's *The Golden Note-
book*, Grass's *The Tin Drum*, Cheever's *Bullet Park*, García Márquez's
One Hundred Years of Solitude, and Kingston's *The Warrior Woman*—
Leonard added Morrison's novel to the list. "The first two-thirds
of *Song of Solomon* are merely wonderful," he wrote. "The last 100
pages are a triumph." The year following its publication, *Song of
Solomon* won both the National Book Critics Circle Award and the
American Academy and Institute of Arts and Letters Award and
was also chosen as a Book-of-the-Month Club selection.

More than twenty-five years later, *Song of Solomon*'s audience is
still expanding. In a second burst of popularity, largely inaugu-

3

rated by Oprah Winfrey's Book Club endorsement in 1996, *Song of Solomon* came to the attention of Oprah's viewers, receiving generous appreciation from a new throng of earnest readers. Morrison has remarked, in a sporting spirit, that the novel has had more celebrity during this second lifetime than it had during the first. Indeed, before Oprah announced her selection of *Song of Solomon* on October 18, approximately thirty-three hundred copies had sold so far that year. During the week after the announcement, as hundreds of thousands of books were printed to meet the expected demand, its sales exceeded forty thousand copies.

While the critical and popular praise of *Song of Solomon* has been exuberant, Morrison herself has soberly referred to the novel as "a very simple story . . . [about] a young man who seeks his fortune" (LeClair 26). In less capable hands, this might have been the formula for a weary cliché, but in Morrison's imagination, cliché is converted to fabulous narrative. Morrison admits that she likes to "treat old ideas, old situations" and offer them as tales for modern life. At the same time, she "makes them mean whatever they may have meant originally" (LeClair 26), suggesting that a common storytelling trope can be used inventively to construct a new and vital narrative. Morrison's familiar trope in *Song of Solomon* is the heroic quest, which might predictably begin with a young man, once upon a time, traveling far from home in search of gold. The narrative of *Song of Solomon* is, however, much more complex than most storybook versions of this theme. Yet it is also true that Milkman Dead is after his fortune, and the adventure of his pursuit gives the novel its structure. Milkman at age thirty-two is disaffected and isolated, desiring escape from the entanglements of family and community. He believes he can only achieve such freedom by recovering the gold he thinks is hidden in a Pennsylvania cave. Because the gold does not exist, the focus of Milkman's quest shifts to the richer vein of his acquiring virtue and heroic stature through a series of trials. By water, land, and air, Milkman slays the dragons of greed and selfishness. Cleansed in body and spirit, he returns home, bringing with him a rejuvenating harmony. Remarkably, in a single day and night, he transforms himself from callow and unthinking to generous and intuitive.

Milkman's path turns out not to be material, as he imagines it, but spiritual, as Morrison imagines. His is a timeless human tale based on the premise that every purposeful endeavor is a search for vitality. Joseph Campbell, in his writings on heroes and mythic journeys, makes the case for this perspective. "What we're seeking," he writes, is not, as many believe, the meaning of life but "an experience of being alive, so that our life experiences on the purely physical plane will have resonance within our own innermost being and reality, so that we actively feel the rapture of being alive" (Campbell 3). Campbell's idea points toward an interesting interpretation of the meaning of Milkman's venture. Macon conceives a dead world for his son, where all relationships are inert and the day-to-day life occupied by collecting rents is stagnant. As a result, Milkman possesses no love, empathy, or deep understanding. He lacks compassion for or connection to anyone. The clever recitation, "My name is Macon; I'm already dead," is his unrecognized truth. Fortunately, both Milkman's perceptions of himself and his involvement with others change as his adventure comes to its end in Shalimar, Virginia. His intellect and passion engaged by the cultural and familial significance of Solomon's flight to freedom, Milkman comes to life. For the first time, "he is exhilarated by simply walking the earth. Walking it like he belonged on it; like his legs were stalks, tree trunks, a part of his body that extended down down down into the rock and soil, and were comfortable there—on the earth and on the place where he walked" (Morrison 284). In this awakened state, Milkman is poised to realize his potential as a man.

While Milkman's story is relatively straightforward, *Song of Solomon*'s interweaving of many additional narratives is exquisitely complex. Milkman's development, for example, is impossible without Pilate, whose life is so authentic and commanding that Morrison has claimed she threatened to make the novel her own. By the time Milkman meets her at the commencement of his restless manhood, the neither conventional nor conformist Pilate has already defined her priorities: family and relationships are important, while money and manners are not. Over time, Milkman acquires a similar understanding, but ultimately his achievement is possible only because of Pilate's example.

Guitar assists Milkman as well, at least for a while. Throughout Milkman's extended adolescence, Guitar continually taps both rural values and urban savvy to usher Milkman patiently toward an honorable adulthood. Guitar's function as a mentor is compromised, however, as he is gradually overwhelmed by the violence of a black man's life in America. In yet another story line, Macon, in contrast to Pilate, elevates the acquisition of property above love of family. Over the course of their long marriage, he condemns Ruth to a loveless existence. She is complicit in her own abuse, and neither is redeemed. Milkman does the same to Hagar but, unlike his father, he repents and becomes a better man. The backdrop to all of these dramas is the black community of history. Beginning with slavery, the narrative presents every major era and circumstance, including Reconstruction in the South, segregation in the North, racial brutality on the eve of the Civil Rights movement, and the black nationalists' equally brutal response. At the same time, *Song of Solomon* examines the nature of individual identity and its relationship to community, past and present. While dramatizing the benefits and risks of female empowerment, it also delves deeply into male consciousness, discovering that men learn what is useful from women and not often from other men. These themes recur often in Morrison's treasury of works.

Song of Solomon is Toni Morrison's third novel. Her first, *The Bluest Eye*, published in 1970, is set in Lorain, Ohio, a small midwestern town marked by self-hatred and intraracial bigotry. Morrison's central character is a little girl named Pecola who is driven to madness by the dysfunctions of the community that must bear the burden of blame for her fate. Although Morrison exposes the moral culpability of an American society that codifies blue eyes and blond hair as the standard of beauty against which all others are unfavorably compared, her primary interest is in exploring the painful acceptance of that standard by Lorain's black community.

Toni Morrison grew up in Lorain, a coal-mining town on Lake Erie, twenty-five miles west of Cleveland. Born Chloe Anthony Wofford on February 18, 1931, Morrison was the second of four children. Her parents, George and Ramah Wofford, were, like many African Americans in northern cities, transplanted southerners. George Wofford had come from Georgia and Ramah from Alabama. Morrison has described her childhood as rich with the culture of black folk traditions, including her grandmother's interpretation of dream symbols from a book she kept for that purpose, her mother's constant singing, and both parents' stories of the supernatural. As one might expect, these familiar rituals of African-American life resonate in the characters and stories of Morrison's fiction.

After completing high school in 1949, Morrison attended Howard University, graduating in 1953 with a degree in English. Two years later, she earned a master of arts degree from Cornell University and spent the next several years teaching. From 1955 to 1957, she was an English instructor at Texas Southern University in Houston, and from 1957 to 1964, she taught English at Howard University. During this period, she married Harold Morrison, a young architect from Jamaica. In 1964, after six years of marriage and two sons, the couple divorced, and Morrison subsequently went to work at Random House, first as an editor at its textbook subsidiary in Syracuse and two years later as a trade book editor in New York City. Morrison remained at Random House for nearly twenty years, becoming a senior editor who counted Toni Cade Bambara, Gayle Jones, Angela Davis, Leon Forrest, and Andrew Young among the writers whose work she published.

While Morrison edited the work of other writers, she was also working on her own fiction. Her first four novels were written during this period. *The Bluest Eye* was followed by *Sula* (1973), whose predominant subjects are women's lives and friendships, their freedom and courage. *Sula* explores the question of whether childhood friends with opposite sensibilities can remain friends as adults, even after one or both betray the other's trust. *Song of Solomon*, which came after *Sula*, marked a change in Morrison's narrative perspective and sense of place as a fiction writer: for the first time, her work began to scrutinize male consciousness. Instead of writing mostly about women's relationships, she began to focus on men's concerns. Her fictional setting shifted as well. Before *Song of Solomon*, her stories and her narrative point of view were set in the state of Ohio, with *The Bluest Eye* set in her own hometown. *Sula* takes place in the fictional town of Medallion, Ohio. Morrison does not distinguish her towns by particular topographical characteristics and in fact once described *Sula* as a " 'moveable feast'—you could take it anywhere and you didn't have to identify geographically with anything because it was all there" (Denard 4). Yet despite the limitless possibilities, she chose to call the place Ohio, perhaps in recollection of her earliest experience of community, the reassuring place of memory she refers to as "the neighborhood" and "the yard."

With *Song of Solomon*, Morrison left the yard for the first time, placing the action in another state and, significantly, in the same instance, making "a serious attempt . . . not to write in a hermetic, closed way" (Bakerman 58) by adopting a panoramic and sweepingly historical style. Morrison's storytelling process unfolded along with her settings as she "moved out" of the neighborhood. Morrison likens the gesture to a train "revving up, then moving out as he does, and then sort of highball[ing] and leav[ing] you sort of suspended" (Schappell 116). The familiar community in *The Bluest Eye* and *Sula* gave way in *Song of Solomon* to urban Michigan; Danville, Pennsylvania; and Shalimar, Virginia. The village as a repository of cultural values remained intact only as an ideal. Her characters no longer needed to live in that intimate place to be defined by village values and measured against them.

In the fourth novel, *Tar Baby* (1981), Morrison left not just the neighborhood but the United States in order to set her story on L'Arbe de la Croix, a remote Caribbean island. Featuring white characters—a first for Morrison—*Tar Baby* examines the complex loyalties and resentments of a benevolent employer and his long-time servants. The novel explores another of Morrison's continuing interests: competing definitions of female authority. To what extent must a woman honor her cultural ancestors? How far can she travel from the neighborhood and the black women who live there and still claim to be authentic?

Although *Tar Baby* was not unconditionally praised by critics and reviewers,[1] following its publication *Newsweek* featured Morrison on its cover, thereby signaling her importance on the national literary landscape. The magazine's lengthy and revealing look at her life and career, entitled "Toni Morrison's Black Magic," credits her with presiding over a "cultural awakening" of black women writers. Noting her increasing success, which spiked with *Song of Solomon*, *Newsweek* described Morrison as a literary genius, "uncanny in her ability to immerse . . . [readers] totally in the world she creates," and as a risk taker "trying something bigger with each new book" (Strouse 57).

In the ten years following *Tar Baby*, Morrison wrote three novels: *Beloved* (1987), which won the 1988 Pulitzer Prize for fiction, *Jazz* (1992), and *Paradise* (1998). Each of these works received the critical attention accorded to major literary novels. *Beloved* began as the first volume in a trilogy whose center of interest would be the murdered daughter of a slave woman. Morrison thought she might follow this young girl, Beloved, through successive phases of her life in various locations; instead, she wrote three stories connected only in a loosely thematic way in that they all examine the consequences of obsessive love. In *Beloved*, the escaped slave Sethe insists that her maternal love—and not the slave-master's claim—will determine her children's lives and their deaths. In an audacious exercise of that love, she kills her crawling baby just as the master tries to recapture child and mother. In *Jazz*, middle-aged Joe Trace, married and living in New York during the 1920s and 1930s, shoots his teenaged girlfriend, Darcy, when he sees her dancing with another man. Darcy loves Joe more than she does her own life and will not call for medical help until Joe is able to escape. She bleeds to death. *Paradise*, set in an all-black Oklahoma town in the 1970s, opens with the information, "They shoot the white girl first." Nine watchful men from town see the assorted women who have taken refuge in a nearby convent as a threat to the community's uncompromising religious codes. To kill the women is to protect that way of life. Morrison has said her aims in all of these novels is to illustrate the "complexity, profundity and size of human life" (Book TV).

From *Sula* to *Paradise*, Morrison's novels span (though not in chronological order) a century and a half of the black experience in America. Reading her fiction affords an evocative encounter with American history. The same is true of her nonfiction. As a woman, an African American, a professor, a reader, and a thinker, she says much about the politics of race in society and in literature. Her most comprehensive analysis of the way race and gender define the American literary canon, *Playing in the Dark: Whiteness and the Literary Imagination*, was published in 1992. During the same year, she assembled an anthology of essays on race and politics called *Rac(ing) Justice, (En)gender(ing) Power: Essays on Anita Hill, Clarence Thomas and the Construction of Social Reality*. In her introduction, Morrison contends that black male/black female stereotypes infect matters of public policy, such as the Thomas U.S. Supreme Court confirmation hearings, all too often. She has also coauthored (with Claudia Brodsky) a collection of essays entitled *Birth of a Nation'hood: Gaze, Script and Spectacle in the O. J. Simpson Case* (1997). As the title suggests, the essays in the volume examine not the matter of guilt or innocence but rather what the trial spectacle revealed about the way Americans perceive race. Unafraid to take on urgent issues, Morrison has continued to navigate a provocative and thoughtful path to truth.

Morrison's literary success has come with many national and international honors. In 1980, she was appointed to the National Council on the Arts, and the following year she was elected to the American Academy and Institute of Arts and Letters. She is also a member of the American Academy of Arts and Sciences. In 1984, Morrison became the Albert Schweitzer Professor of the Humanities at the State University of New York at Albany, and in 1989, she was named the Robert F. Goheen Professor of Humanities at Princeton University, where she continues to teach. Finally, as the culmination of recognition for her literary achievement, Morrison was awarded the 1993 Nobel Prize for literature.

In awarding the Nobel Prize, the Swedish academy praised Morrison as one "who, in novels characterized by visionary force and poetic import, gives life to an essential aspect of American reality." While the academy's recognition encompassed all of Morrison's fictional works, its description of her achievement is especially pertinent to *Song of Solomon*, a novel that honors the brilliant resilience of successive generations of black community and confirms the subtle, elegant power of cultural myths to seduce and transform the individual spirit. This casebook is a tribute to *Song of Solomon*'s force, impact, and status—achieved in little more than two decades—as a classic literary text.

The selections in this volume begin with one of several versions of "People Who Could Fly," the folktale that spiritually grounds *Song of Solomon*. As most commonly rendered, the tale of flight depicts a mass exodus that delivers an entire community from slavery back home to Africa. In Morrison's version, only the individual who possesses knowledge of Africa is able to fly; all the others are left behind to suffer in slavery. Michael Awkward's essay, " 'Unruly and Let Loose': Myth, Ideology, and Gender in *Song of Solomon*," examines the reasons for Morrison's decision to revise the traditional communal basis of the story.[2]

The nine critical essays that follow this folktale, while not arranged chronologically, mirror the course of twenty years of *Song of Solomon* scholarship. Moving away from an early focus on folklore, African-American history, gender representation, and myth, more recent criticism explores the narrative strategies Morrison employs, her use of language, and her place in literary history.[3] Reflecting these various scholarly trends, this collection presents the four dominant critical approaches to the novel.

Part I. Quest for Identity

Song of Solomon as a type of *Bildungsroman* is this volume's lead topic of critical inquiry. All of the essays included here address this subject in some measure, although the two in this part make it a focal point. "The Quest for and Discovery of Identity in Toni Morrison's *Song of Solomon*" is Valerie Smith's exploration of the underlying theme of *Song of Solomon*. Smith reads the characters and story for what they reveal about progress toward a radical transformation of the self. She identifies in Morrison's work an important thesis which assumes that authentic identity is communal and not individualistic. Smith argues that "Milkman bursts the bonds of the Western, individualistic conception of self, accepting in its place the richness and complexity of a collective sense of identity." Positioning *Song of Solomon* in contrast to the two novels preceding it, Smith observes that the central characters in *The Bluest Eye* and *Sula* also pursue selfhood, but they do so without hope of success, as these texts thwart the aspirations of their characters. Their defeat sets Milkman's triumph in bold relief while also representing a larger shift in Morrison's literary themes.

Catherine Carr Lee's "The South in Toni Morrison's *Song of Solomon*: Initiation, Healing, and Home" is one of many studies that explore the underlying trope of the quest. Lee focuses on the geography of Milkman's journey to reveal the novel's revisionist ideology of North and South. As Milkman travels from indifference and egotism in urban Michigan to empowerment and community in Virginia, Morrison simultaneously rewrites two literary traditions: the classic American initiation story and the African-American narrative. In the former, the protagonist typically travels from the rural safety of family and community to the competitive isolation of urban life. In African-American narratives, characters often escape from an "enslaving agrarian South to an enabling, industrial North." For Milkman's healing, the South is essential as the only place he can find a name that brings him pride of ancestry and the sense of a community that shares his cultural heredity. In the end, Milkman leaps not into the void, as some critics have claimed, but into the arms of his brother, thereby affirming and embodying the surrounding community. This conclusion, in Lee's view, is a rejection of postmodernist fragmentation and despair in favor of hope.

Part II. Myth and Folklore

Investigation of myth in Morrison's work often explores the relation of African-American oral traditions to the paradigms of classical mythology; typically, these studies interpret the folkloric orientation of *Song of Solomon* as a foil to the classical heroic epic.

Michael Awkward in " 'Unruly and Let Loose': Myth, Ideology, and Gender in *Song of Solomon*" reads the novel as Morrison's radical revision of classical male myth. In contrast to the dominant critical focus on male consciousness, Awkward shows that Morrison is really just as interested in a female perspective that calls attention to women's exclusion from traditional male narrative. Awkward borrows the phrase "unruly and let loose" from an interview in which Morrison used the term to describe female imagination. In Morrison's words, when the imagination "is unruly and let loose, it can bring things to the surface that men—trained to be men in a certain way—have difficulty getting access to." This, Awkward maintains, is the gender ideology informing *Song of Solomon*. Aware of mythology's power to shape cultural values and beliefs, Morrison uses the legend of African flight to call the attention of recent generations to black people's forgotten magic and transcendence. While creating a story in which men soar as women languish, Morrison also undermines gender stereotypes. Awkward's "Afrocentric feminist reading" pinpoints Morrison's intentions of celebrating (black) male flight but also of rejecting the consequences of female grounding.

In "*Song of Solomon*: Rejecting Rank's Monomyth and Feminism," Gerry Brenner describes Morrison's adroit construction of a classical hero in the tradition of Moses, Oedipus, Perseus, and many others. Milkman meets every requirement of Otto Rank's monomyth of the birth of a hero. But despite this heroic blueprint, the novel is satiric, since "beneath all these [valorous] episodes resonates a malice-tinged chuckle, delight in humbling the hero." Brenner interprets the ending as proof of Morrison's "disdain" for Milkman. Far from achieving spiritual transcendence and flight in his final leap toward Guitar, Milkman is instead merely flying away from responsibility while harboring the "illusion" that he will ride the air.

For Brenner, the true hero of the novel is Pilate, although her virtues are the opposite of those characteristic of traditional heroes. Her life is a repudiation of the greed, hypocrisy, obsessiveness, and selfishness of the novel's other characters. Yet Brenner only allows a qualified feminist reading: Pilate is exceptional rather than representative of her gender. For, just as all the men are fatally flawed, all the other women fail to live up to Pilate's example.

Part III. Narrative Influence

Morrison is often compared to Faulkner, Joyce, García Márquez, and other great writers. In response, Morrison has said, "I am not *like* James Joyce; . . . I am not *like* Faulkner. . . . My effort is to be *like* something that has probably only been fully expressed in music" (McKay 426). Yet comparisons persist, as Morrison's commanding narrative style continues to invite serious studies of its sources and its place in the canon of Western fiction. In this volume, John Duvall examines Morrison's dialogue with Faulkner. Gay Wilentz describes Morrison's narrative technique not as a conversation with other writers but as a reflection of the multiple storytelling traditions of her African and African-American roots. Joyce Wegs interprets the novel as a blues song. Finally, Lucinda MacKethan places Morrison's treatment of names and identity in the broader historical context of black writers who use naming to define and affirm the self.

In "Doe Hunting and Masculinity: *Song of Solomon* and *Go Down, Moses*," Duvall directs attention to the (perhaps unintentional) cultural implications inherent in discussions that compare Morrison to Faulkner. Working against those critics who see Morrison as indebted to Faulkner for both her themes and style, Duvall dismisses that stance as reductive, suggesting as it does that Faulkner's is the master narrative against which Morrison's storytelling is to be measured. Perhaps a more useful and less presumptuous way to speak of Morrison's work is to say that it "engages" Faulkner's.[4] Morrison knows Faulkner's novels, having written about them in her graduate thesis, and Duvall sees many similarities in the two writers; but he also sees important differences that reflect opposing perspectives and cosmologies. Specifically, *Song of Solomon* engages *Go Down, Moses* by calling into question the masculine world of the hunt, which is present in both novels. Doe hunting is a powerful metaphor for male aggression against women, and Guitar seems to understand this concept as he tells Milkman that it is all right to protect his mother from Macon's assaults. As an adolescent, Guitar learned to feel remorse after killing a doe during a hunting incident, and he later tells Milkman that "a man shouldn't do that" (*Song* 86). Duvall argues, however, that despite this compassion for the female, Guitar ultimately represents misguided male authority. After all, it is Guitar who delivers the speech to Milkman about a black woman's need to destroy a black man's dreams. Focusing on *Song of Solomon* and using Faulkner's text only as a point of reference, Duvall examines Milkman's near-appropriation by both his father and Guitar and his eventual rejection of masculine possession. Pilate's way is the one he comes to value. Duvall sees no such transcendence in Faulknerian characters, who appear doomed to perpetuate the ways of the father; Morrison, on the other hand, refuses this "gambit of tragedy."

As the title "Civilizations Underneath: African Heritage as Cultural Discourse in Toni Morrison's *Song of Solomon*," suggests, Gay Wilentz gives little more than a respectful nod to Faulkner's influence on Morrison. Such comparisons to other writers may be valid, but the magnificent complexity of Morrison's work comes from the historical roots of "her mother's stories, her tribe, and her ancestors—African and African American." Wilentz makes salient Morrison's intention that her fiction approximate the luxurious power of black oral narrative; her desire is to restore the language of black people and bring back "that civilization that existed underneath the white civilization."

Wilentz tracks this repressed civilization to its African roots and finds it unambiguously present in *Song of Solomon*. Pilate emerges as a woman with strong connections to her African ancestry. She is a culture bearer in the African village tradition. The supernatural, ancestor worship, the importance of a name to identity, and—of course—flying Africans are all representative of the novel's Africanisms. Morrison is a masterful storyteller, composing in the mode of an "African dilemma tale," searching out the community's folk roots, and bringing the people back to themselves through her privileging of African heritage and cultural perceptions over Western epistemology.

Joyce Wegs's "Toni Morrison's *Song of Solomon*: A Blues Song" discusses the novel as a drama of black village life. Morrison absorbs the people's experience, giving it coherent expression. She is a blues lyricist, and her characters fulfill the traditional roles of blues people: the men give in to life's frustrations and leave home, while the women stay put and lament. Throughout the novel, men and women depart and sing, enacting a familial pattern. Solomon flies out of slavery, leaving behind twenty-one children and a wailing wife. Milkman, like his great-grandfather, abandons his cousin Hagar, leaving her to complain. Jake and Sing are exceptions in this generational hierarchy: Jake remains on the ground with his family, and Sing dies in childbirth, not of a broken heart. Wegs interprets Jake as a model patriarch who, for Morrison, embodies "the ideal aspects of traditional male traits." Enterprising enough to insist on farming his own land, he is bold enough to defend his right to do so.

Morrison is, however, critical of lesser mortals. Dominating men and emotionally dependent women come in for harsh scrutiny. Morrison, Wegs writes, "excoriates male arrogance, selfishness, isolation, and immaturity," but her women are imperfect too, in their "smothering possessiveness." Milkman rejects his mother and Hagar, the two women intent on owning him, but Pilate is a different sort. She flies and sings, though her flight is not the flight of male abandonment and her song is not of the female blues variety. Pilate reflects Morrison's fundamental ambivalence toward conventional gender scripts. Morrison is fascinated by traveling men, but she also insists on personal responsibility. Women who sing the blues also exercise a right of heritage, yet they too must be self-reliant. This tension resolves itself in Pilate, a woman willing to fly like any man but who loves without condition or possession. In the end, Milkman must learn Pilate's way.

In "Names to Bear Witness: The Theme and Tradition of Naming in Toni Morrison's *Song of Solomon*," Lucinda MacKethan situates Morrison's emphasis upon owning one's name within the black autobiographical tradition. Beginning with narratives of escaped slaves and continuing throughout the literary tradition, the power of a name to invoke history, define the self, and inspire a transformation of consciousness is a dominant theme in African-American writing. From Frederick Douglass to Malcolm X, the act of naming is a gesture of emancipation. Morrison improvises on earlier writers' contempt for continental names. For her, a name cannot diminish an individual life; it bears witness to that life. MacKethan surmises that Milkman's assignment is not to free himself of his father's name but to learn "what it truly means to be one of the living Deads."

Part IV. Historical Perspectives

Song of Solomon covers more than a century of African American history, reflecting Morrison's pedagogy, her manner of teaching cultural knowledge through her fiction. In "Dead Teachers: Rituals of Manhood and Rituals of Reading in *Song of Solomon*," Linda Krumholz argues that, over the entire course of the narrative, Milkman is in search of black history. Unless he acquires cultural literacy, he will be unable to move from self-destruction, cynicism, and isolation to compassionate engagement. Morrison's pedagogy invites the reader, along with Milkman, to achieve cultural awareness and understanding. Readers initially encounter an urban black ethic, shaped by "jaded" sociological and political perspectives, which eventually gives way, as the novel proceeds, to the inspiriting visionary discourse of "southern rural African folk culture." In representing this transformation, Morrison's form mirrors her theme: tone and content shift to reflect the shift in

Milkman's psychology as his lessons unfold. *Song of Solomon*, Krumholz concludes, is a black historical text whose language and form initiate readers and characters into an essential knowledge of a past that validates the individual's identity and ensures the survival of the community.

Part V. An Interview

The last selection is Elissa Schappell's "Toni Morrison: The Art of Fiction." In this conversation with Schappell, Morrison speaks at length and in detail concerning her progress as a novelist, her motivations to write, her development of characters, and the meaning and design in her books, including *Song of Solomon*.[5] "The Art of Fiction" provides, as do most of Morrison's interviews, a provocative tutorial on her life and her fiction.

The essays collected in this casebook represent major currents in critical thinking about *Song of Solomon*, yet they are merely a sampling of the research. The notes and bibliography following each essay and the selected bibliography at the end of the volume provide additional resources to direct the way to the variety of thoughtful scholarship available.

Notes

1. Some critics found *Tar Baby* flawed. See, for example, John Irving's review in the *New York Times*, March 29, 1981, p. 1, sec. 7. See also Robert G. O'Meally, "Review of *Tar Baby*," *Callaloo* (Feb.–Oct. 1981): 193.

2. For variations on the flying theme, see Mason Brewer, *American Negro Folklore* (Chicago, Ill.: Quadrangle, 1972); Richard Dorson, *American Negro Folktales* (Greenwich, Conn.: Fawcett, 1956); Virginia Hamilton, *The People Could Fly: American Black Folktales* (New York: Knopf, 1985); Langston Hughes and Arna Bontemps, eds. *The Book of Negro Folklore* (New York: Dodd, Mead, 1958).

3. The four essays in *New Essays on "Song of Solomon,"* edited by Valerie Smith (1995), illustrate the focus on narrative and language.

4. Writing six years later in "Toni Morrison and the Anxiety of Faulk-

nerian Influence," Duvall is skeptical of Morrison's effort to distance herself from Faulkner, even as she demonstrates, in her scholarship and commentary, a thorough knowledge of his work. An intertexual dynamic is evident and perhaps inevitable, Duvall suggests. Faulkner influences Morrison. But the reverse is also true in that Morrison's fiction and criticism provoke fundamental reconsiderations of Faulkner.

5. In addition to those already cited here, see the following selected Morrison interviews for commentary on *Song of Solomon*: Cecil Brown, "Interview with Toni Morrison," *Massachusetts Review* 36 (Autumn 1995): 455–73; Rosemarie K. Lester, "An Interview with Toni Morrison, Hessian Radio Network, Frankfurt, West Germany," in *Critical Essays on Toni Morrison*, ed. Nellie Y. McKay (Boston: Hall, 1998), 47–54; and Robert B. Stepto, "Intimate Things in Place: A Conversation with Toni Morrison," *Massachusetts Review* 18 (Autumn 1977): 473–89. Morrison writes about the novel, in some detail, in two essays: "Rootedness: The Ancestor as Foundation," in *Black Women Writers (1950–1980)*, ed. Mari Evans (New York: Doubleday, 1984), 339–45, and "Unspeakable Things Unspoken: The Afro-American Presence in American Literature," *Michigan Quarterly Review* 28 (Winter 1989): 1–34.

Works Cited

Bakerman, Jane. "The Seams Can't Show: A Conversation with Toni Morrison." *BALF* 12, no. 2 (1978): 56–60.

Book TV. "In Depth: Toni Morrison." C-SPAN2, February 4, 2001.

Campbell, Joseph. *The Power of Myth.* Garden City, N.Y.: Doubleday, 1988.

Denard, Carolyn. "Blacks, Modernism, and the American South: An Interview with Toni Morrison." *Studies in the Literary Imagination* 31, no. 2 (Fall 1998): 1–16.

Duvall, John N. "Toni Morrison and the Anxiety of Faulknerian Influence." In *Unflinching Gaze: Morrison and Faulkner Re-envisioned*, edited by Carol Kolmerten, Stephen M. Ross, and Judith Bryant Wittenberg, 3–16. Jackson: University Press of Mississippi, 1997.

LeClair, Thomas. " 'The Language Must Not Sweat': A Conversation with Toni Morrison." *New Republic* 18 (March 21, 1981): 25–30.

McKay, Nellie Y. "An Interview with Toni Morrison." *Contemporary Literature* 24 (Winter 1983): 413–39; reprinted in *Toni Morrison: Critical Perspectives Past and Present*, edited by Henry Louis Gates and K. A. Appiah. New York: Amistad, 1993.

Morrison, Toni. *Song of Solomon.* New York: Knopf, 1977.

Schappell, Elissa, with Claudia Brodsky Lacour. "Toni Morrison: The Art of Fiction." *Paris Review* 128 (Fall 1993): 83–125.

Smith, Valerie. *New Essays on "Song of Solomon."* New York: Cambridge University Press, 1995.

Strouse, Jean. "Toni Morrison's Black Magic," *Newsweek*, March 30, 1981, pp. 52–57.

People Who Could Fly

JULIUS LESTER

◆ ◆ ◆

IT HAPPENED LONG, LONG ago, when black people were taken from their homes in Africa and forced to come here to work as slaves. They were put onto ships, and many died during the long voyage across the Atlantic Ocean. Those that survived stepped off the boats into a land they had never seen, a land they never knew existed, and they were put into the fields to work.

Many refused, and they were killed. Others would work, but when the white man's whip lashed their backs to make them work harder, they would turn and fight. And some of them killed the white men with the whips. Others were killed by the white men. Some would run away and try to go back home, back to Africa where there were no white people, where they worked their own land for the good of each other, not for the good of white men. Some of those who tried to go back to Africa would walk until they came to the ocean, and then they would walk into the water, and no one knows if they did walk to Africa through the water or if they drowned. It didn't matter. At least they were no longer slaves.

Now, when the white man forced Africans onto the slave ships, he did not know, nor did he care, if he took the village musicians, artists, or witch doctors. As long as they were black and looked strong, he wanted them—men, women, and children. Thus, he did not know that sometimes there would be a witch doctor among those he had captured. If he had known, and had also known that the witch doctor was the medium of the gods, he would have thought twice. But he did not care. These black men and black women were not people to him. He looked at them and counted each one as so much money for his pocket.

It was to a plantation in South Carolina that one boatload of Africans was brought. Among them was the son of a witch doctor who had not completed by many months studying the secrets of the gods from his father. This young man carried with him the secrets and powers of the generations of Africa.

One day, one hot day when the sun singed the very hair on the head, they were working in the fields. They had been in the fields since before the sun rose, and, as it made its journey to the highest part of the sky, the very air seemed to be on fire. A young woman, her body curved with the child that grew deep inside her, fainted.

Before her body struck the ground, the white man with the whip was riding toward her on his horse. He threw water in her face. "Get back to work, you lazy nigger! There ain't going to be no sitting down on the job as long as I'm here." He cracked the whip against her back and, screaming, she staggered to her feet.

All work had stopped as the Africans watched, saying nothing.

"If you niggers don't want a taste of the same, you'd better get to work!"

They lowered their heads and went back to work. The young witch doctor worked his way slowly toward the young mother-to-be, but before he could reach her, she collapsed again, and the white man with the whip was upon her, lashing her until her body was raised from the ground by the sheer violence of her sobs. The young witch doctor worked his way to her side and whispered something in her ear. She, in turn, whispered to the person beside her. He told the next person, and on around the field it went. They did it so quickly and quietly that the white man with the whip noticed nothing.

A few moments later, someone else in the field fainted, and, as the white man with the whip rode toward him, the young witch doctor shouted, "Now!" He uttered a strange word, and the person who had fainted rose from the ground, and moving his arms like wings, he flew into the sky and out of sight.

The man with the whip looked around at the Africans, but they only stared into the distance, tiny smiles softening their lips. "Who did that? Who was that who yelled out?" No one said anything. "Well, just let me get my hands on him."

Not too many minutes had passed before the young woman fainted once again. The man was almost upon her when the young witch doctor shouted, "Now!" and uttered a strange word. She, too, rose from the ground and, waving her arms like wings, she flew into the distance and out of sight.

This time the man with the whip knew who was responsible, and as he pulled back his arm to lash the young witch doctor, the young man yelled, "Now! Now! Everyone!" He uttered the strange word, and all of the Africans dropped their hoes, stretched out their arms, and flew away, back to their home, back to Africa.

That was long ago, and no one now remembers what word it was that the young witch doctor knew that could make people fly. But who knows? Maybe one morning, someone will awake with a strange word on his tongue and, uttering it, we will all stretch out our arms and take to the air, leaving these blood-drenched fields of our misery behind.

Part I

◆　◆　◆

QUEST FOR IDENTITY

The Quest for and Discovery of Identity in Toni Morrison's *Song of Solomon*

VALERIE SMITH

◆ ◆ ◆

I N   H E R   F I R S T   T H R E E   N O V E L S , *The Bluest Eye* (1970), *Sula* (1973), and *Song of Solomon* (1977), Toni Morrison explores the interplay between self-knowledge and social role. Her characters, like Ralph Ellison's Invisible Man, inhabit a world where inhospitable social assumptions obtain. But Morrison does not provide her people with the option of living underground, in isolation, beyond community. Those whom social relations exclude (like Pecola Breedlove of *The Bluest Eye* or Sula) lack self-knowledge and are destroyed by themselves or by others. My analysis here centers on *Song of Solomon*, the only one of Morrison's novels in which her protagonist completes successfully his or her search for psychological autonomy. Yet, no discussion of the search for identity in *Song of Solomon* would be complete without some mention of Morrison's two earlier novels. The structure and thematic concerns of these two works establish a framework in terms of which we may understand the meaning and status of Milkman's discovery.

I

The black characters in Morrison's early novels are especially vulnerable to the defeats that accompany isolation; in *The Bluest Eye* and in *Sula*, she examines the complex economic, historical, cultural, and geographic factors that problematize their relations within the black community and with the world beyond. Pecola Breedlove, on whom *The Bluest Eye* centers, typifies Morrison's outsiders. Her story illustrates the destructive potential of a culture that recognizes only one standard of physical beauty and equates that standard with virtue. Ostensibly, Pecola is driven mad by her inability to possess blue eyes. But her insanity really results from the fact that she serves as the communal scapegoat, bearing not only her own self-loathing, but that of her neighbors and family as well. Soaphead Church's failure to provide her with blue eyes is thus simply the proverbial back-breaking straw.

The Bluest Eye does not address the hard questions directly. The book does not undertake to explain, for example, why black Americans aspire to an unattainable standard of beauty; why they displace their self-hatred onto a communal scapegoat; how Pecola's fate might have been averted. The metaphors of Claudia MacTeer that frame and image Pecola's story, and the very structure of the novel itself, suggest that such considerations are irresolvable. "This soil is bad for certain kinds of flowers," Claudia remarks. "Certain seeds it will not nurture, certain fruit it will not bear." Claudia accepts as a given the fact that certain "soils" will reject both marigolds and plain black girls. To her, the reasons for this incompatibility are structural, too intricately woven to distinguish. She therefore believes that any attempt to explain Pecola's deterioration will be fruitless and concludes, *"There is really nothing more to say—except why. But since why is difficult to handle, one must take refuge in how."*[1]

I would argue that not only Claudia, but the novel itself, avoids "why," taking refuge instead in "how." Claudia, the narrator of the primer, and the ostensibly omniscient narrator all tell stories—tell "how" fast and furiously. These stories, in gen-

eral, demonstrate what it means to find inaccessible the possessions and attributes that one's culture values. Their thematic similarity reveals the representative nature of Pecola's story:
self-loathing leads inevitably to some form of destruction. Perhaps
more important the remarkable number of stories symbolizes the
complex sources and effects of this cycle of self-loathing. The
form is therefore a figure for the cultural condition the novel
addresses.

The structure of *The Bluest Eye* underscores the proliferation of
stories and of narrative voices within the novel. The body of the
text is divided into four chapters, which are, in turn, subdivided.
Each begins with an episode, usually involving Pecola, told from
the point of view of Claudia the child but shaped by her adult
reflections and rhetoric. Claudia's stories then yield place to one
or two stories told by an apparently objective, omniscient narrator. This narrator usually recalls information to which Claudia
would not have had access: he or she tells stories from Pecola's
life that involve other characters and weaves flashbacks from the
lives of these other characters (Polly or Cholly Breedlove, Ger-
aldine, or Soaphead Church, for example) into Pecola's story. In
addition, in each chapter, several garbled lines from the primer
separate Claudia's voice from that of the omniscient narrator.

The chapters counterpoint three moments in time: a past before the narrative present (the flashbacks), the eternal present of
the primer, and the narrative present of Pecola's story as told by
Claudia. The different narratives in each chapter provide variations on a specific theme. This technique demonstrates here and
throughout Morrison's fiction the interconnectedness of past and
present. The form implies that the meaning of Pecola's story may
only be understood in relation to events that predated her birth.

The cacophony of voices in *The Bluest Eye* demonstrates that
Pecola is inextricably linked to the linguistic community that
forms the novel. Yet she is clearly denied a place in the world
the text purports to represent; her involuntary isolation from
others leads to her psychological disintegration. *Sula* as well features a scapegoat-protagonist, although Sula clearly cultivates
those qualities that distinguish her from her neighbors. Here, too,

Morrison's plot relies on a multiplicity of narratives to implicate Sula in the very community from which she is alienated. Although Sula, unlike Pecola, chooses her isolation, it is precisely that distance that destroys her.

Sula centers on a character who believes that she can create for herself an identity that exists beyond community and social expectations. "An artist with no art form," Sula uses her life as her medium, "exploring her own thoughts and emotions, giving them full reign, feeling no obligation to please anybody unless their pleasure pleased her."[2] She thus defies social restraints with a vengeance. She disavows gratuitous social flattery, refusing to compliment either the food placed before her or her old friends gone to seed, and uses her conversation to experiment with her neighbors' responses. As the narrator remarks: "In the midst of pleasant conversation with someone, she might say, 'Why do you chew with your mouth open?' not because the answer interested her but because she wanted to see the person's face change rapidly" (103). Worst of all in her neighbors' judgment, she discards men, black and white, as rapidly as she sleeps with them, even the husband of her best friend, Nel.

There are moments when the text seems to validate Sula's way of life; the narrator suggests, for example, that Sula's independence has bestowed upon her a kind of immortality:

> Among the weighty evidence piling up was the fact that Sula did not look her age. She was near thirty and, unlike them, had lost no teeth, suffered no bruises, developed no ring of fat at the waist or pocket at the back of her neck. It was rumored that she had had no childhood diseases, was never known to have chicken pox, croup or even a runny nose. She had played rough as a child—where were the scars? (99–100)

But by interweaving Sula's story with Shadrack's and Nel's, Morrison demonstrates structurally the collective nature of human identity.

Sula's story stands in analogous relation to Shadrack's, symbolic evidence that her situation, like Pecola's, is hardly unique.

The communal response to Sula is identically Shadrack's response to the unexpected. Shadrack, the insane World War I veteran whose story opens the novel, exemplifies in the extreme this need to explain or find a place for the inexplicable. By creating National Suicide Day, he finds a way of controlling his fear: "If one day a year were devoted to [death], everybody could get it out of the way and the rest of the year would be safe and free" (12).

The people of the Bottom of Medallion, Ohio, ridicule Shadrack's holiday, but their survival, like his, depends upon finding ways of controlling their terrors. Superstitions, which recur in the narrative and in their collective discourse, help them explain disturbing disruptions. When Hannah, Sula's mother, dies suddenly, Eva, Sula's grandmother, reflects that she would have been prepared for the tragedy if she had read properly the omens she had received. Likewise, the denizens of the Bottom remark that they should have anticipated Sula's deleterious effect on their community, because her return was accompanied by a plague of robins. Like Eva, the townspeople find a sign or a reason for their trouble after the fact. Their retrospective justifications are finally no different from Shadrack's.

And just as they must find a way of controlling the unexpected evils that beset them, so do they find a place for Sula. Since they do not understand her, they call her evil and hold her responsible for the injuries and deaths that befall their community. As the narrator notes, the townspeople actually become more generous when they shun Sula because they assign to her their own baser impulses. For all her efforts to transcend the community, then, Sula remains an integral part of it.

Morrison also undercuts Sula's aspirations to originality by characterizing her as only half a person. As several critics have argued, Sula and Nel complement each other psychologically, and neither is fully herself after geography and Sula's relation to Jude separate them.

Sula and Nel are products of two different styles of childrearing: their friendship grows out of their fascination with their dissimilarities. Sula's family is the source of her independence of mind and sexual nonchalance. Her mother is known especially for her sexual generosity; her grandmother Eva for selling her leg to support her children. Eva's home provides a figure for her family, replete with an ever-changing cast of boarders, gentleman callers, and foundlings:

> Sula Peace lived in a house of many rooms that had been built over a period of five years to the specifications of its owner, who kept on adding things: more stairways—more rooms, doors and stoops. There were rooms that had three doors, others that opened out on the porch only and were inaccessible from any other part of the house; others that you could get to only by going through somebody's bedroom. (26)

Nel, on the other hand, is raised in a well-ordered but repressive household and is thus prepared to choose a life of limited options, such as the one she shares with Jude. Haunted by the image of her own mother, a prostitute, Nel's mother tries to launder the "funk" out of her daughter's life. During their childhood and adolescence, Nel provides Sula with restraints, and Sula offers Nel license. More important, they offer each other a kind of security that neither finds in her own family. Together, they begin to discover the meaning of death and sexuality. As the narrator remarks:

> Because each had discovered years before that they were neither white nor male, and that all freedom and triumph were forbidden to them, they had set about creating something else to be. Their meeting was fortunate, for it let them use each other to grow on. Daughters of distant mothers and incomprehensible fathers (Sula's because he was dead; Nel's because he wasn't), they found in each other's eyes the intimacy they were looking for. (44)

Their relationship is permanently destroyed when Sula sleeps with Jude, although Sula reflects that she never intended to cause Nel pain. Without Nel, "the closest thing to both an other and a self" (103), Sula is cut off from the only relation that endowed her life with meaning, and she drifts to her death. Nel, too, is rendered incomplete when her friendship with Sula ends. She may think that her inescapable grief is the result of having lost her husband but, as she realizes at the end of the novel, what she has missed for so many years is not Jude, but Sula.

The descendant of a line of relatively autonomous women, Sula attempts to go them one better and create herself outside of the collective assumptions of women's behavior. Morrison denies the feasibility of such a choice most obviously by killing off her protagonist. But the narrative structures she employs in *Sula* further undercut Sula's aspirations. By characterizing her as both a scapegoat and the second self of her more conventional best friend, Morrison denies Sula the originality she seeks.

II

Song of Solomon centers on Milkman Dead's unwitting search for identity. Milkman appears to be doomed to a life of alienation from himself and from others because, like his parents, he adheres to excessively rigid, materialistic, Western values and an attendant linear conception of time. During a trip to his ancestral home, however, Milkman discovers his capacity for emotional expansiveness and learns to perceive the passage of time as a cyclical process. When he incorporates both his familial and his personal history into his sense of the present, he repairs his feelings of fragmentation and comprehends for the first time the coherence of his own life.

Milkman's father, Macon Dead, Jr., is a quintessential self-made man. Orphaned and disinherited in his adolescence, he wheeled and dealed his way into his position as the richest black man in town. Milkman can therefore brag about his father's houses, cars, assets, and speculations, to the delight of the Reverend Mr. Cooper and his Danville companions. The avid materialism and rugged individualism that made Macon financially successful have exacted their price from him in other ways, however. Macon has come to believe that money, property, and keys are what is real in the world; his financial success has thus cost him his capacity for communication and emotion. As he advises his son:

> "Come to my office; work a couple of hours there and learn what's real. Let me tell you right now that one important thing you'll ever need to know: Own things. And let the things you own own other things. Then you'll own yourself and other people too."[3]

The Macon Deads exemplify the patriarchal, nuclear family that has been traditionally a stable and critical feature not only of American society, but of Western civilization in general. The primary institution for the reproduction and maintenance of children, ideally it provides the individual with the means for understanding his place in the world. The degeneration of the Dead family and the destructiveness of Macon's rugged individualism symbolize the invalidity of American, indeed Western, values. Morrison's depiction of this family demonstrates the incompatibility of received assumptions and the texture and demands of life in black American communities.

Macon Jr. believes that a successful businessman cannot afford to be compassionate. Reflecting that his first two keys to rental units would never have multiplied had he accommodated delinquent accounts, he sees his tenants as only so much property. Moreover, he objectifies his family. He brutalizes his wife, Ruth, both subtly and overtly because he suspects her of incestuous relations with her father and son. Despite his concern for Milkman, he only speaks to him "if his words [hold] some command or criticism." And by refusing to acknowledge Pilate as his sister, Macon denies her humanity as well. His resentment is based in part on his belief that she stole the gold that the two of them should have shared. More significantly, though, he eschews her company because he considers her deportment to be socially unacceptable. He fears that the white bankers will cease to trust him if they associate him with a woman bootlegger.

Weak and pathetic as she is, Ruth finds subtle methods of objectifying the members of her family as well. She retaliates against her husband's cruelty by manipulating him. Since she cannot attract his attention in any other way, she demeans herself until, out of disgust, he lashes out at her. Similarly, she remarks that her son has never been "a person to her" (131). Before he was born, Milkman was "a wished-for bond between herself and Macon, something to hold them together and reinstate their sex lives" (131). After she realizes that her husband will never again gratify her sexually, she uses Milkman to fulfill her yearnings by breast feeding him until he is old enough to talk, stand up, and wear knickers.

Pilate Dead, Macon's younger sister, provides a marked contrast to her brother and his family. Like Macon, Pilate presides over a household which is predominantly female. But while Macon's love of property and money determines the nature of his relationships, Pilate's sheer disregard for status, occupation, hygiene, and manners enables her to affirm spiritual values such as compassion, respect, loyalty, and generosity.

If the Macon Deads seem barren and lifeless, Pilate's family bursts with energy and sensuality. Pilate, Reba, and Hagar engage ceaselessly in collective activity, erupting spontaneously into harmonious song. On his way to his own emotionally empty house one evening, Macon Jr. peeks through the window of his sister's home in search of spiritual nourishment. He hears the three women sing one song, Pilate stirring the contents of a pot, Reba paring her toenails, and Hagar braiding her hair. Macon is comforted both by the soothing and unending motion of each character in the vignette and by the harmony and tranquillity of the music they make together.

As Pilate introduces vitality into her brother's life, so does she introduce a magical presence into the otherwise spiritually lifeless world of part I of the novel. The circumstances of her birth make her a character of larger-than-life dimensions—one who has transcended the limitations of her historical moment and milieu. Pilate delivered herself at birth and was born without a navel. Her smooth stomach isolates her from society, since those who know of her condition shun her. Moreover, her physical condition symbolizes her thorough independence of others; even as a fetus she did not need to rely on another person for sustenance. Her isolation and self-sufficiency enable her to "throw away every assumption she had learned and [begin] at zero" (149). She is therefore neither trapped nor destroyed by decaying values as her brother's family is. Like Macon, she is self-made, but her self-creation departs from, instead of coinciding with, the American myth. Pilate decides for herself what is important to her, and instead of appropriating collective assumptions, she remakes herself accordingly. After cutting her hair:

> [Pilate] tackled the problem of trying to decide how she wanted to live and what was valuable to her. When am I happy and when am I sad and what is the difference? What do I need to stay alive? What is true in the world? (149)

Quintessential self-made man that he is, Macon predicates his behavior on a linear conception of time. To his mind, future successes determine identity and justify one's actions in the past and in the present. Macon's futuristic, linear vision of time and of identity is displayed by his failure to consider his past as part of himself. He denies the importance of his relationship with his sister and of their shared past. Moreover, as he remarks while telling Milkman about his days in Lincoln's Heaven, he does not even allow himself to think about his past:

> He had not said any of this for years. Had not even reminisced much about it recently. . . . For years he hadn't had that kind of time, or interest. (51)

Macon's linear vision of time is also partly responsible for his sense of family and of morality. Because he believes that the coherence and significance of his identity lie in his future, he cares only about his relationship to his son. To his patriarchal mind, it is in that connection that the most important genealogical transfer occurs. But Macon has no time whatsoever for any connection that would cause him to exercise his capacity for horizontal or (what would be to him) peripheral vision.

Macon's ability to see the world only in linear, exclusive terms explains his lack of sympathy in yet other ways. He believes that the ends justify any means; as a result, he excuses his own corruption by considering only the financial profits it brings him. He feels no need to offer Mrs. Bains (one of his tenants) charity because charity will not increase his wealth. And he encourages Milkman and Guitar to steal what he thinks is Pilate's gold, despite the kindness she has shown them all.

In contrast to Macon's, Pilate's vision of time—indeed, of the world—is cyclical and expansive. Instead of repressing the past, she carries it with her in the form of her songs, her stories, and her bag of bones. She believes that one's sense of identity is rooted in the capacity to look back to the past and synthesize it with the present; it is not enough simply to put it behind one and look forward. As she tells Macon:

> You can't take a life and walk off and leave it. Life is life. Precious. And the dead you kill is yours. They stay with you anyway, in your mind. So it's a better thing, a more better thing to have the bones right there with you wherever you go. That way it frees up your mind. (210)

Before Milkman leaves Michigan, he perceives the world in much the same way that his father does. His steadiness of vision and lack of compassion allow him to abuse remorselessly and unself-consciously the people around him. For instance, his letter to Hagar reveals his inability to understand her feelings and psychology despite their years of intimacy. He fails to accept responsibility for ending their relationship; instead, he writes little more than a business letter suggesting that he leave her for her own best interest. Moreover, his sister Lena tells him that he has "urinated" on the women in his family. That is, he has demanded their service and shown them no consideration. He has presumed to know what is best for them without knowing them at all.

Milkman's search for gold indicates further the similarity between his father's vision of the world and his own. He thinks that leaving his hometown, his past, and his responsibilities will guarantee him a sense of his own identity. As he becomes increasingly implicated in the scheme to retrieve Pilate's gold, Milkman acquires a clearer but equally false sense of what freedom means. He believes that gold will provide him with a "clean-lined definite self," the first sense of identity he has ever known.

Milkman's assumption that the key to his liberation may be found in Danville and Shalimar is correct, although it is not gold that will free him. In his ancestors' world, communal and mythical values prevail over individualism and materialism; when he adopts their assumptions in place of his own, he arrives at a more complete understanding of what his experience means. When Milkman arrives in the South, he wears a "beige three-piece suit, button down light-blue shirt and black string tie, [and] beautiful Florsheim shoes" (229). He ruins and loses various articles of clothing and jewelry as he looks first for gold and then for the story of his people. Indeed, just before his epiphanic moment in the forest, he has changed from his cosmopolitan attire to overalls and brogans. Similarly, the people he meets in Shalimar force him to throw off his pretenses before they offer him the help and information he needs. Only when he ceases to flaunt his wealth and refer to their women casually do they admit him into their community. Until he sheds the leaden trappings of materialism, Milkman is like the peacock he and Guitar see: too weighted down by his vanity to fly.

While in Michigan, Milkman believes that when he finally achieves his freedom, he will no longer need to submit to the claims of others. In the woods, away from the destructive effects of "civilization," he realizes that human connection—horizontal vision—is an inescapable part of life:

It sounded old. Deserve. Old and tired and beaten to death. Deserve. Now it seemed to him that he was always saying or thinking that he didn't deserve some bad luck, or some bad treatment from others. He'd told Guitar that he didn't "deserve" his family's dependence, hatred, or whatever. That he didn't even "deserve" to hear all the misery and mutual accusations his parents unloaded on him. Nor did he "deserve" Hagar's vengeance. But why shouldn't his parents tell him their personal problems? If not him, then who? (279–80)

While previously he had dehumanized his friends and relations, he now empathizes with his parents and feels shame for having robbed Pilate:

The skin of shame that he had rinsed away in the bathwater after having stolen from Pilate returned. But now it was as thick and as tight as a caul. How could he have broken into that house—the only one he knew that achieved comfort without one article of comfort in it. No soft worn-down chair, not a cushion or a pillow.... But peace was there, energy, singing, and now his own remembrances. (304)

In keeping with this new awareness of others and of his personal past, Milkman, insensitive to Hagar and unwilling to accept responsibility for her in life, understands her posthumously and assumes the burden of her death. He acknowledges the inappropriateness of his letter to her and realizes that he has used her. Moreover, he knows without being told that she has died and he is to blame. As Pilate has carried with her the bones of the man she believes she has murdered, so too does Milkman resolve to carry with him the box of Hagar's hair: a symbol of his newly acquired cyclical vision of a past he no longer needs to escape.

Macon Sr., Milkman's grandfather, was an American Adam, a farmer who loved the land and worked it profitably. Moving north cost Macon Jr. some of the talent he had inherited from his father; still able to manipulate cold cash, he lost his father's organic connection to the soil. In the South, Milkman, too, seems disconnected from nature. Graceful in the "civilized" world, he is clumsy and obtuse when he enters the wilderness. However, he becomes increasingly attuned to nature's rhythms as he grows in self-awareness. During the bobcat hunt, he senses through the contact between his fingertips and the ground beneath him that someone is about to make an attempt on his life. And as he returns to the town, Milkman feels as if he is part of the "rock and soil" and discovers that he no longer limps.

Finally, however, Milkman's discovery of his identity lies not so much in his connection with the earth or in his ability to understand his own past; these accomplishments only attend his greater achievement—learning to complete, to understand, and to sing his family song. Milkman comes to know fully who he is when he can supply the lyrics to the song Pilate has only partially known. Throughout his life, Milkman has had an inexplicable fascination with flight. Robert Smith's abortive attempt to fly from the hospital roof precipitated his birth. Riding backward makes him uncomfortable because it reminds him of "flying blind, and not knowing where he [is] going" (31). And as he approaches Circe's house, he recalls his recurring childhood fantasy of being able to take flight. When Milkman knows the entire song, however, and can sing it to Pilate as she has sung it to others, he can assume his destiny. Flight is no longer a fancy that haunts him, appearing unsummoned in his consciousness. He now understands it as a significant action from his ancestral past. Indeed, the ultimate sign of his achievement of identity is his ability to take flight in the way his grandfather did. In the process of assuming himself, Milkman discovers that his dreams have become attainable.

Milkman acquires a sense of identity when he immerses himself in his extended past. He comes full circle from the individualism his father represents and advocates. Assuming identity is thus a communal gesture in this novel, as, indeed, Morrison suggests in her two earlier novels. Knowing oneself derives from learning to reach back into history and horizontally in sympathetic relationship to others. Milkman bursts the bonds of the Western, individualistic conception of self, accepting in its place the richness and complexity of a collective sense of identity.

Notes

1. Toni Morrison, *The Bluest Eye* (New York: Holt, Rinehart, and Winston, 1970), 3.

2. Toni Morrison, *Sula* (New York: Bantam, 1973), 118. Subsequent references are cited parenthetically in the text.

3. Toni Morrison, *Song of Solomon* (New York: New American Library, 1977), 55. Subsequent references are cited parenthetically in the text.

The South in Toni Morrison's
Song of Solomon
Initiation, Healing, and Home

CATHERINE CARR LEE

◆ ◆ ◆

S*ONG OF SOLOMON*, Toni Morrison's third novel in an increasingly varied and rich body of work, is a remarkable narrative. The novel's power lies not only in its recovery and representation of African American experience in the mid–twentieth century but also in Morrison's insistence on the necessity of healing her broken, alienated protagonist, Milkman Dead. Central to both his maturation and his healing is Milkman's recognition that the cultural past of the African-American South continues to create his twentieth-century present in ways that are not constraining but liberating. Critics have typically understood Milkman's growth and his healing in the context of the mythic quest or the classic initiation story.[1] To be sure, Morrison's novel reflects archetypal initiation patterns found throughout Western literature, as Milkman follows a quest, first for gold, then for knowledge about his ancestors. Like his predecessors in the *Bildungsroman*, Milkman moves from a selfish and juvenile immaturity to a complex knowledge of adulthood.[2] Yet, Morrison does not merely reinscribe the initiation motif. Rather, the novel subverts the dominant model of initiation found both in American fiction in general and in African-American literature in particular, as Morrison rewrites the classic American initiation story.

In stories as diverse as Nathaniel Hawthorne's "My Kinsman, Major Molineaux" and Ralph Ellison's *Invisible Man*, the American protagonist usually moves from a rural to an urban area, from the protection and identity of the nurturing family and friends to the isolation and alienation of Western individualism. Such a movement allows the youth to escape the confines of the past in order to create himself as an individual acting outside of time and convention. This freedom comes with a price, however: such an initiation typically brings separation, restriction, and a knowledge of evil.[3] This trope is problematized in many African-American works, such as Frederick Douglass's *Narrative* and Harriet Jacobs's *Incident in the Life of a Slave Girl*, in which the protagonist moves from an oppressive, enslaving, agrarian South to an enabling, industrial North. For the authors of these slave narratives, leaving behind family, friends, and even names was often essential for escape. For the African-American community in the twentieth century, however, Morrison suggests that the isolating individualism that erases the memory of the South destroys spiritual and moral identity.

Thus, the trip to the South is central to Morrison's subversion of the classic American initiation story. For the conventionally poor, naive, sensitive youth from the provinces, Morrison substitutes Macon Dead III, nicknamed Milkman, an emotionally isolated, alienated black man who has grown up in the industrial northern Midwest, in a Michigan city on the shores of Lake Superior.[4] As the protagonist, he is youthful only because he has "stretched his carefree boyhood out for thirty-one years" (Morrison 98). Still living in his parents' home, collecting rents for his father, Milkman has yet to reach emotional and social maturity. His poverty is spiritual, not material; his sensitivity is that of adolescent self-centeredness. His initiation takes him physically from the urban North through a progressively rural and southern landscape to the home of his ancestors in Shalimar, Virginia. What begins as a selfish quest for gold, for material success and escape,

becomes a quest for knowledge of his family history and an identity based on that history. *Song of Solomon* is, finally, the story not
just of one man's individualization but of the potential for healing
of a community.

Milkman is indeed naive about himself, his family, and his
community, but the very nature of the knowledge he acquires
marks *Song of Solomon* as a different kind of initiation story. The
initiate's knowledge is typically defined as a loss of innocence and
a recognition of restriction. Milkman begins, however, at the
point of restriction that comes from separation, from the hyper-
individualization that grows out of the American culture of competition, capitalism, and racism. Like the traditional American
initiate, he must recognize his own capacity for evil, but the
knowledge of his family's past and his place in a community that
evolved from that past enables Milkman to ascend rather than,
conventionally, to "fall through knowledge" (Fiedler 22). His journey into an African-American South strips him of superficial external moorings and submerges him in the communal and spiritual culture of his larger family. With his initiation, Milkman
moves from a passive, irresponsible ignorance to an active, authentic, and liberating participation in the corporate life of black
community.

The American South is crucial to this narrative of healing,
because the problem for Milkman and his family concerns not
just a relationship to the past, but to a past that is specifically
caught up with the history of slavery in the South. Morrison
signals the importance of the South with the very name of the
section of town where Milkman's aunt Pilate lives. Just as "Southside" serves as a reminder of the southern origins of the black
people who populate the novel, so Pilate offers Milkman an
emotional connection to his southern ancestors. Less directly,
the novel predicts the necessity of Milkman's journey to the
South with his strange, dreamlike walk down Not Doctor Street,
in the wake of a disturbing conversation with his father about
his mother. As he tries to make his way down the street, on his
way to Southside, he keeps running into people, "all going the
direction he was coming from" (78). Milkman will have to move

against the tide of black migration north in order to transcend his aimlessness, to live for something other than superficial satiation and pleasure.

Deeply connected to Milkman's aimlessness is his namelessness. Morrison uses knowing one's name as a metaphor for knowing one's past, and it is the South that holds the secret of Milkman's family name and family past. The novel's epigraph beckons to the power of the ancestral name: "The fathers may soar, and the children may know their names." It is a kind of blessing that Morrison bestows on her fictional black community, and, as Linda Krumholz has argued, it captures "the tension between black men's mobility . . . and familial and communal responsibilities" (555). Milkman's family has lost its ancestral name, achieving mobility at the cost of intimacy and identity. The original Macon Dead, Milkman's grandfather, received his name from a drunken Yankee at the Freedman's Bureau. According to Milkman's father, the first Macon kept the name because his wife insisted on it, because "it was new and would wipe out the past" (53). Yet losing the name of the ancestor causes the Dead family to lose history, community, and tradition as well; the past becomes "dead," and the loss of name damages the present understanding of that past.

Names in *Song of Solomon* are, of course, fraught with significance. The novel points, on the one hand, to the importance of names in traditional societies of West Africa—the origin of most Africans enslaved in North America—where names are identified with the individual's essence, with the core of one's being.[5] For American slaves, names provided a link with the African past; in the New World, slaves conducted secret naming ceremonies and used their African names when they could avoid the presence of whites. Yet the novel also points to the complicated status of surnames for African Americans in the United States. The denial of a family name, like the denial of marital legitimacy and the breaking apart of families, prevented stable family identities for enslaved Americans. As historian Leon Litwack points out, many slaveholders did not want blacks, be it before or after the Civil War, to take their own last names, and former slaves in turn rejected the surnames of their white owners as signs of illegitimate claims to ownership. But upon emancipation, when to be a citizen meant possessing both a first and a last name freedmen sometimes took their most recent master's name; more often, they claimed the name of the earliest master they could recall, in order to retain a sense of family and identity.[6] Others wanted to choose their own names, rejecting suggestions from Freedman's Bureau officials and choosing instead names that, although they were of European derivation, allowed them a sense of self-determination.

The healing of Milkman's brokenness—not only as an individual but as a representative of an entire black generation—requires Milkman's restoration to the community of his ancestors, and that requires, literally, the discovery of their names. Because Milkman has lost his name—and his heritage—he cannot establish meaningful connections with his family and his community. He grows up feeling excluded and alone. The first of several symbolic markers of Milkman's separation and his brokenness comes when he is the first black infant born in the all-white Mercy Hospital. His prolonged nursing also sets him apart. At the age of four, having discovered that he cannot fly, Milkman loses "all interest in himself" and likewise has no interest in those around him (9). His older sisters display only "casual malice" (10), while other children exclude him from neighborhood singing games—the kind of game, ironically, that will provide the answer to the mystery of his great-grandfather's life and identity.

As he grows older, Milkman's failures come from his sense of alienation. This alienation originates, in part, in his lack of awareness and insight and his inability to empathize with others. At the age of twenty-two, he is still trapped emotionally in the symbiotic state of the infant, for, as Morrison writes, he had never "thought of his mother as a person, a separate individual, with a life apart from allowing or interfering with his own" (75). Limited as they are, his efforts to connect with his family end only in failure. He tries to forge a bond with his mother, by hitting his father in her defense, but he realizes that "there was no one to thank him—or abuse him. His action was his alone" (68). In turn, he resists his father's invitation to a shared understanding. Macon tries to explain his abuse by telling Milkman about Ruth's incestuous love for her father. Milkman responds with a sense of dis-association: it was "as though a stranger that he'd sat next to on a park bench had turned toward him and begun to relate some intimacy . . . he himself was not involved or in any way threatened by the stranger's story" (74–75). He is blind to his selfishness in his relationship with his cousin Hagar, who is Pilate's granddaughter. Morrison conveys both Milkman's self-perception and the inaccuracy of that perception in four taut sentences that follow the assault on his father: "Sleeping with Hagar had made him generous. Or so he thought. Wide-spirited. Or so he imagined" (69). When he tires of Hagar, he contemplates writing a note that demonstrates his utter self-absorption: he will tell her that he is leaving her for her own good, in order not to be selfish.

Even Milkman's dreams and aspirations show his lack of imagination and engagement. Until his father offers him the prospect of finding Pilate's gold, Milkman has virtually no idea of what he wants to do with his adult life. He wants the gold to enable his escape from Not Doctor Street, yet he cannot "visualize a life that much different from the one he had," writes Morrison (180). "New people. New places. Command. That was what he wanted in his life" (180). This litany of desires is curiously without detail. Later in the paragraph, ironically juxtaposed to his dreams of escape, Milkman thinks that "he wanted to know as little as possible" (180).

Milkman's alienation stems as well from his refusal to take responsibility. He exploits Hagar for twelve years, long after she has become "the third beer . . . the one you drink because it's there" (91). His failure to accept commitment is evident in the "dream" he relates to Guitar, in which the plants in the garden grow rapidly over his mother, finally strangling her. Guitar wants to know why he did not try to help her, but Milkman insists that his mother enjoyed it; besides, it was a dream, he says, so he cannot be held accountable. Yet his own logic incriminates him, since he is not actually sure that it was only a dream. To his sister, "Magdalene called Lena," he insists that he has never interfered with the family, that "I live and let live," but that deliberate isolation is precisely his offense (216). He has never taken any notice of the conditions of their lives; he has lived with the members of his family as if they were strangers. As Lena tells him, he has been "peeing on" the family all of his life.

The news from Mississippi of Emmett Till's murder for whistling at a white girl illuminates the narrowness of Milkman's involvement with his community. The other men at Tommy's Barbershop react with "tales of atrocities, first stories they had heard, then those they'd witnessed, and finally the things that had happened to themselves," as they link the events of their own lives with those of the larger world (83). But Milkman's response is "Yeah, well, fuck Till. I'm the one in trouble" (88). Not only can he not engage with the larger world, Milkman cannot recognize that his alienation has its roots in the very white racism that allowed for the lynching of Emmett Till.

At the age of thirty-one, then, Milkman is still a narcissist; his life is stagnant and his growth suspended. Throughout, however, he has encountered a series of teachers who, in the tradition of the initiation story, push him forward to commitment even as they draw him inexorably to the South. He cannot respond immediately to their lessons, often feeling puzzled and confused, but he stores these experiences until the night of the Shalimar bobcat hunt, when he undergoes a metamorphosis. The lessons begin when Milkman is twelve, with his introduction to Pilate, the aunt who functions as a benevolent sorceress or a witch figure in his life. She helps his mother conceive him, then gives him a place where he can be "surrounded by women who seemed to enjoy him and who laughed out loud" (47). As "Mama" to her granddaughter, Hagar, as well as to her own daughter, Reba, Pilate is the primal earth mother, with her "berry-black lips," surrounded by oranges and peaches (37–38). She is united with nature, with which Milkman must reconcile in order to survive his initiation. Pilate begins by instructing Milkman in practical, everyday knowledge: to say what you mean, how to cook a perfect egg. Because she values nothing but human relationships, Pilate refers to Milkman as Hagar's brother, because, she says, "you treat them both the same" (44). She intersperses this instruction with information about the Dead family's past. Milkman learns that his father grew up on a farm and saw his own father shot from behind, blown five feet in the air by the white men who resented his success. The Macon Dead that Pilate tells him about is a different man than the father Milkman has known. Milkman would have liked the man his father once was, says Pilate: "he would have been a real good friend to you, too, like he was to me" (39).

Meeting Pilate makes Milkman feel for the first time that his name is important, that it joins him with someone to whom he wants to belong. When Pilate tells young Milkman that there "ain't but three Deads alive," Milkman screams that he, too, is a Dead. He misses, of course, Pilate's unintentional—or Morrison's deliberate—irony, for he is one of the Deads who is spiritually dead, and he will insist on his "deadness" for years to come. But Pilate is the only person to provide Milkman with what feels emotionally like a home, so he hesitates to steal the bag hanging in her house that he thinks contains her gold. Guitar tells him that "this ain't no burglary. This is Pilate . . . They're your people" (182). But Milkman has a vague understanding that Guitar misses: that in robbing his family, his community, he diminishes his own dignity and humanity. Milkman begins to make this connection when he and Guitar are arrested, and Pilate must do her "Aunt Jemima act" to get them released (211). What humiliates Milkman is not just her act, "but the fact that she was both adept at it and willing to do it—for him" (211). He recognizes, briefly, that his actions affect other people, and he also realizes that by hurting Pilate, he has hurt himself. Pilate is also Milkman's closest link with the sustaining power of the past. She has misunderstood the message from her father's ghost, that "you just can't fly on off and leave a body" (209). Pilate thinks he meant that "if you take a life, then you own it. You responsible for it. You can't rid of nobody by killing them. They still there and they yours now" (209). So she continues to carry what she thinks are the bones of the man whom Macon killed years before. As Milkman discovers later, the first Macon referred to his father, Solomon, who abandoned his wife and twenty-one children, but Pilate's interpretation points to the responsibility that Milkman must take.

Milkman's family members are his teachers too, although it takes years for him to realize it. Macon's knowledge is of a very different sort than Pilate's, as he erroneously tells Milkman: "Pilate can't teach you a thing you can use in this world. Maybe the next, but not this one" (55). Macon's world is the material one, but he provides additional links to the past. Macon tells his son about Circe, the black woman servant whose employer, Butler, killed his father; about the farm in Danville, Pennsylvania; and about the misnaming of the original Macon Dead. Macon also says that he "worked right alongside" his father, which Milkman later realizes is an expression of the love and respect his father shared with the first Macon Dead (51). Perhaps most important, though, Milkman understands the kind of man his father once was, as he hears his father's voice changing, becoming "less hard, and his speech was different. More southern and comfortable and soft" (52). For a moment Milkman glimpses what it is like to feel "close and confidential" with his father (54). Milkman's mother, Ruth, also provides information that he will understand only much later. She tells Milkman about his conception, about Pilate's early devotion to him, and about the sexual deprivation that Milkman eventually sees and how it "would affect her, hurt her in precisely the way it would affect and hurt him" (303). His sister, Lena, is another teacher, confronting him with his irresponsibility and selfishness, reminding him that he has been "using us, judging us: how we cook your food: how we keep your house" (216). Her final condemnation, that he is a "sad, pitiful, stupid, selfish, hateful man," will serve him later when he realizes that "hating his parents, his sisters, seemed silly" (218, 304).

As Milkman's best friend, Guitar plays a complex role. He functions as a teacher as well as an enemy.[7] As a teacher, Guitar pushes Milkman to recognize his weaknesses, his flawed priorities, and finally his identity. Guitar repeatedly reminds Milkman of his alienation and aimlessness, of his failure to commit himself to person or place, and he forces Milkman to acknowledge his boredom and inability to risk himself. Guitar knows that one must take chances, and when Milkman hesitates to steal the bag from Pilate's house, Guitar prods him on with "You got a life?

Live it! Live the motherfuckin life!" (184). In this case, Milkman's reluctance is well founded; he does not want to steal from the woman who first gave him a home. But Guitar aptly defines the problem of Milkman's emotionally unlived life.

With part II, Milkman begins his journey south ostensibly to retrieve the gold that his father and Pilate found years ago in a cave in Pennsylvania, gold which Macon believes Pilate stole from him. Critics tend to focus on the quest elements in part II, at the expense of the preparation for the quest in part I.[8] Still, Morrison introduces something of the magic of fairy tale when in the opening paragraph she compares Milkman with Hansel and Gretel and thereby signals that the usual limits of realistic representation no longer operate. Milkman's lust for the gold is also paired with Hansel and Gretel's hunger for candy, and in the world of *Song of Solomon*, the search for gold, as for candy, is corrupt.[9] It is the "shit that weighs you down" and is symbolized by the peacock that vainly spreads its tail just as Milkman and Guitar confirm their plans to steal the gold. For Milkman to fly, to transcend his alienation, he has to shed his inauthenticity.

The journey south introduces the first of Milkman's new set of teachers and helpers. Milkman perceives these teachers as instruments to bring him closer to the gold, but as the quest for gold becomes a quest for identity, their meanings change. In Danville, Pennsylvania, Milkman meets the Reverend Cooper, who provides important information about his ancestry and at the same time gives Milkman a sense that he is included in the larger Dead family. He greets Milkman with "I know your people!" and tells him the stories of his grandfather's murder and of Circe's caring for Pilate and Macon in the days to follow (231). During the next four days, the old survivors come to visit, the ones who knew his father and grandfather—a chorus of teachers reciting a litany of the earlier days—and Milkman learns something new about the relationship between the two men for whom he is named. Milkman cannot "recognize that stern, greedy, unloving man in the boy they talked about, but he loved the boy they described and loved that boy's father" (237). As the past becomes vivid in the words of the old men, Milkman sees the patterns of his father's life emerge, and he understands that the past he is hearing about shaped the present he knows. But the drive to own property that meant liberation to the first Macon Dead has been perverted into selfishness and endless acquisition by the second. It is a sign of Milkman's continuing corruption that the talk about his father's current financial success makes him long even more for Pilate's gold. To the other black men in Montour County, Macon Dead's farm symbolized the richness and possibility of the community. If Macon Dead could have a home, then "you got one too!" (237). And the message was "pass it on!" (238). This is what the second Macon Dead has forgotten; it is what Milkman must learn.

Circe, Milkman's second helper in part II, tells Milkman how to find the cave where Macon thinks the gold still lies, but she also provides information about Milkman's ancestors that he will later use in deciphering the Solomon song, chanted by the children in Shalimar. Circe tells him that his grandmother, an Indian named Sing, came with his grandfather, the first Macon, to Pennsylvania from Virginia, and she tells him the town's name, Charlemagne, a corruption of Shalimar. She also knows that old Macon's body was dumped in the very cave in which the gold was discovered, and later Milkman will realize that it was her father's bones that Pilate found when she returned to the cave. Finally, she reveals his grandfather's real name, Jake. But Circe serves as more than just a teacher; she is a living relic of the past that Milkman has previously only heard about. Circe mistakes Milkman for the Macon Dead she knew, Milkman's father. Although Morrison never indicates that Milkman and Macon resemble each other, Circe's mistake makes it clear that Milkman looks exactly like his father. With Circe, the past reaches out and intrudes on Milkman's present as surely as Circe reaches out to embrace him.

Milkman's trips through the woods to the Butler house and to the cave are part of his initiation as well, and they anticipate the bobcat hunt in Shalimar that will bring the shedding of his old, inauthentic self. Going into the Pennsylvania woods, Milkman is "oblivious to the universe of wood life," just as he has been oblivious to the emotions and experiences of the people around him (221). To find the house, he must make "a mile-long walk over moist leaves," dodging branches of overhead trees (240). To find the cave he has to go deeper into the woods, crossing and falling into a creek, then climbing the rocky hillside. His watch and cigarettes, those emblems of distraction and city life, are smashed and soaked; his thin-soled shoes are of little help. Once inside the cave, he has only his hands, feet, and instincts to guide him. His lighter sputters only long enough to show that the gold is gone. In this confrontation with a nature much wilder than the "tended woods" he knew back home, Milkman finds that some genuine feeling begins to emerge, experienced as a ravenous hunger unlike any he has known before (252). Afterward, Milkman sees the landscape with new eyes. As he travels to Virginia, the hills ahead of him are "no longer scenery.... They were real places that could split your thirty-dollar shoes" (259).

Milkman still has much to learn when he reaches Shalimar. He begins to take southern hospitality for granted, to feel at home in the South—especially so when his car breaks down in front of Solomon's Country Store. In Shalimar, Milkman hears the local children singing "a kind of ring-around-the-rosy or Little Sally Walker game" (266). This is the Solomon song, which Milkman later realizes holds the key to the mystery of his ancestry. At this point, this feeling of being at home is an extension of his sense of entitlement, and the mistakes he makes in Shalimar reflect his separateness. Milkman's first mistake underscores the power of naming and the importance of community. He calls the men in the store "them," and by failing to ask their names, Milkman denies their personhood and reveals his distrust. When he locks his car and then suggests that he would like one of their women, this serves only to isolate him further. In the ensuing fight, Milkman defends himself with a broken bottle before Mr. Solomon rescues him. Although Milkman is obviously marked as an outsider, he is beginning to lose the inadequate trappings of his old, superficial self. In Shalimar, his money cannot save him; his daddy cannot bail him out of trouble. All he has to fight with is what he finds immediately at hand.

In the community of Shalimar, the home of his ancestors, Milkman is still the ignorant, irresponsible, passive adolescent. To gain the knowledge of responsible adulthood, he must leave behind the fixed boundaries of his old, immature self and experience the chaotic, liminal, near-death experience of initiation. Like the quest hero, Milkman is, in the words of Vladimir Propp, "tested, interrogated, and attacked" (39), but the bobcat hunt that the older men invite him to join is more accurately a male initiation rite at the hands of the elders and wise men of African tribal cultures. As they usher the initiate into the ways and wisdom of the community, the men enact a ritual dressing of Milkman before the hunt; his city clothes are not adequate for the night ahead, just as his city self cannot serve him during the changes he will undergo.[10] Calvin Breakstone takes Milkman under his wing as a protégé, and Milkman's next step toward shedding his old self comes when he realizes that Calvin's lamp prevents his eyes from adjusting to the dark. In order to see what the night holds, he must "look at what it was possible to see" (276). Finally, Milkman's gaze now penetrates. At that moment he hears the wailing from Ryna's Gulch, and Calvin tells Milkman about the old legend that "a woman named Ryna is cryin' down there"—the Ryna who was abandoned by his great-grandfather, Solomon (277). By letting go of the secure but superficial mooring of artificial light, Milkman begins to gain access to the mysteries of his ancestry.

Milkman must still come to terms with a physical nature from which he has long stood apart, and he must do so without his teachers' help. In order to heal his spiritual brokenness, he must confront his physical limitations as he tries to keep up with the older men. After several hours of following the dogs, he gives up and reclines against a tree, only to find that he cannot avoid thinking about what has happened to him in Shalimar. He recognizes that he may have offended the men in Solomon's store, but he does not think he deserved their hostility. With all of its implications of privilege, "deserve" is the key word that triggers Milkman's recognition. The turning point in his journey of self comes when Milkman realizes:

He thought he deserved only to be loved—from a distance though—and given what he wanted. And in return he would be . . . what? Pleasant? Generous? Maybe all he was really saying was: I am not responsible for your pain; share your happiness with me but not your unhappiness. (280)

At this point, Milkman is still convinced that he has come to Shalimar either to find the gold or to be convinced that it has disappeared. As he sits in the silent darkness, he experiences a metaphorical death that releases him from an alienating self-centeredness and provides for the concomitant acceptance of his responsibility for sharing both the joys and the sorrows of his family and friends.[11]

In this state of separation—apart from all safety and security, all external makers and markers of identity—Milkman realizes that all he has is "what he was born with, or had learned to use. And endurance" (280). As he listens to the dogs and men signaling each other, he begins to draw upon the sixth sense he did not know he possessed: "an ability to separate out, of all the things there were to sense, the one that life itself might depend on" (280–81). He learns that the men and dogs can talk to each other, and Milkman himself realizes that these are the tribal elders with all the wisdom of the world, "because if they could talk to animals, and the animals could talk to them, what didn't they know about human beings? Or the earth itself, for that matter" (281). Milkman is an initiate to the community of hunters. He tries to "listen with his fingertips," and that sixth sense warns him of Guitar's approach (282).

Like the hero of the archetypal folktale, Milkman must engage in combat with the villain—who in this novel is his best friend—and receive a brand or wound.[12] His throat and fingers are cut, and as he succumbs to the sorrow he feels at dying, he relaxes his throat muscles. The last vestiges of his former self perish. With Milkman's spiritual rebirth into the community of the hunters, he can locate the baying dogs. His sixth sense is with him now: "He didn't miss; his sense of direction was accurate" (283). The men give Milkman a good-natured ribbing about tripping over his gun, but they offer no meanness this time, as they ask, "Was you scared?" (284). Milkman's response reflects his new sense of confidence and belonging, as well as an almost literal truth: he was "scared to death" (284). When he leaves the woods with the hunters the next morning, Milkman is no longer alienated from the earth nor from his fellow human beings; he is "walking the earth like he belonged on it" (284). The men reward him with the heart of the bobcat, then send him to Sweet, "a nice lady up the road a ways. She'd be proud to take you in" (288). The encounter with Sweet is a healing experience for Milkman and signals Milkman's integration. In the course of the novel, Milkman has never volunteered to do anything for another person, but his lovemaking with Sweet is mutual and redemptive.

Milkman cannot uncover the mystery of his great-grandfather, however, nor can he enter the community that will complete his new identity until he admits just how much he wants to "find" his "people" (295). And he cannot make that admission until he realizes that "his people" include the very ones he was so eager to escape. Vernell, the wife of one of the hunters, sends Milkman to a local Indian woman, Susan Byrd, but she suggests that this is not his family after all. Ready to abandon the search for both gold and ancestors, he makes the connection of past and present when he realizes that "there was something he felt now—here in Shalimar, and earlier in Danville—that reminded him of how he used to feel in Pilate's house" (296). Pilate is the link, for having first experienced "home" with Pilate, Milkman can recognize it again. It is Pilate he misses most; he becomes "homesick . . . for the very people he had been hell-bent to leave" (303). Paradoxically, the closer Milkman comes to discovering the legend of Solomon and the key to his ancestry, the better he can understand the lives of his mother and father. He does not yet know about Hagar's death, but as he admits his responsibility for degrading her, he again hears the children sing the Solomon song. This time he recognizes it as a version of "Sugarman done fly away" (5), a song he has heard Pilate sing all of his life. The names of Solomon, Jake, Ryna, and the others now make sense. He realizes Susan Byrd is his grandmother's niece. She confirms this and tells him the secret of Solomon: he was a flying African, and he tried to carry his youngest child, Jake, with him but had to let him fall. Jake was Milkman's grandfather, the man who changed his name to Macon Dead. By learning his ancestors' names, Milkman has learned who he is. As he says to Sweet about the Solomon song and the circle game played by the children in Shalimar, "I can play it now. It's my game now" (331).

Milkman's trip south to Shalimar, to the liberating discovery of family and past, parallels Solomon's return to Africa, to origins, and to freedom.[13] Even so, Solomon abandoned his community, and though he tried to carry his youngest child, he flew to Africa and freedom fully intending to leave his wife and twenty other children behind. With recognition of his responsibility for Hagar's death, Milkman carries the knowledge of his family's southern past back to his community in Michigan, along with a new understanding of his parents, his sisters, and Pilate. He has learned that, in the words of his grandfather's ghost, "you just can't fly on off and leave a body" (336). He understands, too, that "names had meaning. . . . When you know your name, you should hang on to it, for unless it is noted down and remembered, it will die when you do" (333). Gone is his failure to attach to place. Now he has roots in every place that Pilate, his father, and his grandparents have lived. He shares that heritage.

In a conclusion that is problematic for many readers, Milkman and Pilate return to the cave in Pennsylvania so that Pilate can properly bury what she now knows are her father's bones. They are tracked down by Guitar, who believes Milkman has found the gold and betrayed him by cutting him out of his share. As Milkman and Pilate stand on a plateau at the mouth of the cave, Guitar fells Pilate with a bullet meant for Milkman. With the final realization of his love for Pilate, who could fly "without ever leaving the ground," Milkman prepares to make the ultimate sacrifice of love for Guitar (340). He stands up, fully expecting to be killed instantly, and calls to Guitar, "Over here, brother man! Can you see me? . . . Here I am!" (341). Guitar is still his "brother," and if Guitar needs his life, Milkman can give it:

Without wiping away the tears, taking a deep breath, or even bending his knees—he leaped. As fleet and bright as a lodestar he wheeled toward Guitar and it did not matter which one of them would give up his ghost in the killing arms of his brother. For now he knew what Shalimar knew: If you surrendered to the air, you could ride it. (341)

This conclusion raises the question of whether Milkman really flies in the triumph of individual will, or if he plummets to his death in a statement of existential despair, by what Susan Blake calls a "solitary leap into the void" (79). Both possibilities, however, invite mistakenly individualistic readings. Milkman does offer his life to Guitar, but Morrison writes that "it did not matter which one of them would give up his ghost in the killing arms of his brother" (341) Milkman's flight, the final parallel with Solomon, is not away from something but to his "brother" Guitar, a member of his present community. Milkman, who by his initiation into community now embodies that community, leaps not into the void but into the "arms of his brother."[14] Such a death would be a healing sacrifice of love for Guitar.

Yet this leap may not bring Milkman's death at all. Many critics have failed to note that just before Milkman leaps off the plateau, Guitar sets his rifle aside. Perhaps, then, Guitar no longer wants to kill Milkman, and the "arms of his brother" may not be killing at all (341).[15] In this conclusion, Morrison continues to overturn the conventional initiation story that previous generations of literary scholars have described. Frye, for example, claims that the "central form of romance is dialectical: everything is focused on a conflict between the hero and his enemy, and all the reader's values are bound up with the hero" (81). Morrison, however, transcends this dialectic. It does "not matter," she writes, "which one of them would give up his ghost in the killing arms of his brother" (341). Significantly, the pronoun "his" refers not to Milkman or Guitar alone, but to both.

Thus, where the classic American initiation story takes the youthful initiate from the bosom of hearth and family, leaving him isolated and alone, Morrison begins with a twentieth-century modern man, alienated and fragmented, and ends with that man's successful connection with a people. Through his initiation into the southern community of his ancestors, Milkman gains not the typical knowledge of limitations nor the knowledge that comes through the fall into evil, but rather the understanding that the past continues to constitute the present in ways that are not constraining but liberating. He discovers both the fact and the meaning of his African-American heritage. Morrison reverses not only the structural pattern found in the typical American initiation story but the ontological pattern as well. *Song of Solomon* addresses the need for the contemporary African-American psyche to embrace community, the community that comes from a shared culture and history, and so she denies historical discontinuity and transcends the postmodernist impulse toward despair.[16] The novel ends with the triumphant hope of continuation for an interconnected African-American culture and heritage.

Notes

1. For discussions of *Song of Solomon* as a quest or initiation story, see Barthold, Blake, Bruck, Campbell, Fabre, Harris, Lee, Royster, and Smith. Classic descriptions of the archetypal initiation theme and the heroic quest motif appear in Eliade, Frye, and Propp.

2. For a discussion of the *Bildungsroman*, see Holman, *Windows on the World*.

3. West writes that initiation brings "a knowledge of the limitations of existence—the limitations of both nature (the present) and the myth (the past)." To come to terms with the "problem of existence," he suggests, the protagonist has "to recognize that there is a problem" and then "understand that the problem is capable of only a limited solution" (96–97). Fiedler argues that the initiate, like Adam and Eve in the Christian originary myth, must "fall through knowledge" (22).

4. On the classic story of the "Young Man from the Provinces," see Trilling, *The Liberal Imagination: Essays on Literature and Society*.

5. According to Byerman in *Fingering the Jagged Grain: Tradition and Form*

in Recent Black Fiction, Milkman's discovery of his family name carries connotations of "certain magical qualities connected with black folklore." Byerman suggests that naming for Morrison "has associations with African cultures in which the name is the expression of the soul" (201). For a discussion of names in African culture, see Janheinz Jahn, *Muntu: An Outline of Neo-African Culture,* and Sterling Stuckey, *Slave Culture.* As Jahn explains, child naming in some areas has been ritualized for years: "the new-born child becomes a *muntu,* a person, only when the father or the sorcerer gives him a name and pronounces it. Before this the little body is a *kintu,* a thing; if it dies, it is not even mourned" (125). Stuckey points out that, in Africa, "a man's name is often identified with his very soul, and often with the souls of ancestors" (195).

6. Litwack, *Been in the Storm So Long,* suggests that such a choice was made from "a sense of historical identity, continuity, and family pride. . . . not to honor a previous master but to sustain some identification with the freedman's family of origin" (250).

7. Dorothy Lee and Peter Bruck discuss Guitar in their considerations of the novel as quest. According to Lee, "Guitar operates in the tradition of the trickster and other ambivalent archetypal figures who, by challenging the hero, push him to his destination" (*"Song of Solomon:* To Ride the Air" 66). Bruck calls Guitar an "alter ego" and suggests that "Milkman and Guitar represent two sides of one aspect: the alienation of the black man from himself and his people." As Bruck puts it, the philosophies of both individuals "turn out to be inadequate within the context of the action" (300).

8. See Bruck, "Returning to One's Roots," and Krumholz, "Dead Teachers." Bruck notes that Milkman's departure "introduces several elements which clearly place *Song of Solomon* in the tradition of the novel of initiation" (14), while Krumholz points out that the events in chapter 11 (the second chapter of part II, beginning with Milkman's arrival in Shalimar and ending with his lovemaking with Sweet) "enact most clearly the form and function of an initiation ritual" (558).

9. See Barthold, *Black Time,* for her comments on "the association of sweetness with death" in the novel (176).

10. See Byerman, *Fingering the Jagged Grain;* Bruck, "Returning to One's Roots"; and Lee, "*Song of Solomon:* To Ride the Air." Byerman calls the hunt "the male initiation rite that Milkman has never had" (205); Bruck describes it as "a traditional action in which man unites himself through shared activities and a reverence for the wilderness with both his an-

cestors and his fellow men" (295–96). Lee suggests that with names like Omar, King Walker, Calvin, Luther, and Small Boy, the old men on the hunt are "the circle of village elders, of poets, kings, and men of God" (69).

11. Krumholz turns to anthropologist Victor Turner to explain the separation and reincorporation that Milkman as quest hero must undergo. Turner, she says, "divides the ritual process into three stages: rites of separation, rites of limen or margin, and rites of reaggregation. . . . Turner theorizes 'marginality' or 'liminality' as a space and time within ritual in which social classifications break down and social relations are transformed. . . . Within the limen all participants, having temporarily put off their status, will see the world differently" (558).

12. See Propp, *Morphology of the Folktale*, 51–52.

13. Susan Blake points out that Morrison uses a highly individualistic variant of the folktale about flying Africans. She suggests that "in making Milkman's flying ancestor a single individual and focusing his story on the wife and children he left behind, Morrison refers not to a community united by its political experience, but to a conflict of identification between political and personal communities" (80). This folktale was collected from a number of people by the Georgia Writers' Project in *Drums and Shadows* and by Langston Hughes and Arna Bontemps in *The Book of Negro Folklore* (62, 64).

14. Samuels notes that, in traditional African societies, the initiate must be "carefully tutored in the art of communal living" (63). The individual then exists "only as a representative of the whole" (63).

15. Lubiano, "The Postmodern Rag," notes "that Guitar places his rifle on the ground does not make him any less deadly" (111). Lubiano overlooks, however, the fact that Milkman has already provided Guitar with another chance to kill him. Morrison writes that Milkman "knew there wouldn't be another mistake; that the minute he stood up Guitar would try to blow his head off. He stood up." Milkman proceeds to shout: "Guitar! . . . Over here, brother man! Can you see me?" He waves his hand over his head, then continues to call out: "Here I am! . . . You want me? Huh? You want my life?" (340–41). Guitar has ample opportunity to shoot Milkman before he finally sets aside the rifle.

16. See Lubiano, "The Postmodern Rag." Lubiano describes *Song of Solomon* as "a postmodernist text" and argues that the novel "dramatizes the deconstruction of narrative convention, the complications of race, and the struggles over identification in ways that bring to narrative life the nexus of the personal and the political" (93, 95). While her discussion

of the novel's postmodernist use of "black American vernacular signifying" is illuminating (93), I disagree with her conclusion that the novel's ending is not unifying and transcendent.

Works Cited

Barthold, Bonnie J. *Black Time: Fiction of Africa, the Caribbean, and the United States*. New Haven, Conn.: Yale University Press, 1981.

Blake, Susan L. "Folklore and Community in Song of Solomon." *MELUS* 7, no. 3 (1980): 77–82.

Bruck, Peter. "Returning to One's Roots: The Motif of Searching and Flying in Toni Morrison's *Song of Solomon*." In *The Afro-American Novel since 1960*, edited by Peter Bruck and Wolfgang Karrer, 289–305. Amsterdam: Gruner, 1982.

Byerman, Keith. *Fingering the Jagged Grain: Tradition and Form in Recent Black Fiction*. Athens: University of Georgia Press, 1985.

Campbell, Jane. *Mythic Black Fiction: The Transformation of History*. Knoxville: University of Tennessee Press, 1986.

Douglass, Frederick. *Narrative of the Life of Frederick Douglass, an American Slave, Written by Himself*. 1845. Reprint, New York: New American Library, 1968.

Eliade, Mircea. *Rites and Symbols of Initiation*. Trans. Willard R. Trask. New York: Harper Torchbooks, 1965.

Fabre, Genevieve. "Genealogical Archaeology; or, The Quest for Legacy in Toni Morrison's *Song of Solomon*." In *Critical Essays on Toni Morrison*, edited by Nellie Y. McKay, 105–14. Boston: Hall, 1988.

Fiedler, Leslie. "From Redemption to Initiation." *New Leader*, 26 May 1958, 20–23.

Frye, Northrup. *Anatomy of Criticism*. Princeton, N.J.: Princeton University Press, 1957.

Georgia Writers Project. *Drums and Shadows*. 1940. Reprint, Westport, Conn.: Greenwood Press, 1973.

Harris, A. Leslie. "Myth as Structure in Toni Morrison's *Song of Solomon*." *MELUS* 7, no. 3 (1980): 69–76.

Holman, C. Hugh. *Windows on the World*. Knoxville: University of Tennessee Press, 1979.

Hughes, Langston, and Arna Bontemps, eds. *The Book of Negro Folklore*. New York: Dodd, Mead, 1958.

Jacobs, Harriet. *Incidents in the Life of a Slave Girl*, edited by Lydia

Marie Child. 1861. Reprint, New York: Harcourt Brace Jovanovich, 1973.

Jahn, Janheinz. *Muntu: An Outline of Neo-African Culture.* Trans. Marjorie Grene. London: Faber and Faber, 1961.

Krumholz, Linda. "Dead Teachers: Rituals of Manhood and Rituals of Reading in *Song of Solomon.*" *Modern Fiction Studies* 39 (1993): 551–74.

Lee, Dorothy. "The Quest for Self: Triumph and Failure in the Works of Toni Morrison." In *Black Women Writers (1950–1980): A Critical Evaluation,* edited by Mari Evans, 337–70. New York, Doubleday, 1984.

———. "*Song of Solomon*: To Ride the Air." *Black American Literature Forum* 16 (1982): 66.

Litwack, Leon. *Been in the Storm So Long: The Aftermath of Slavery.* New York: Knopf, 1979.

Lubiano, Wahneema. "The Postmodern Rag: Political Identity and the Vernacular in *Song of Solomon.*" In *New Essays on Song of Solomon,* edited by Valerie Smith, 93–116. New York: Cambridge University Press, 1995.

Morrison, Toni. *Song of Solomon.* New York: New American Library, 1977.

Propp, Vladimir. *Morphology of the Folktale.* Trans. Laurence Scott. 2d ed. Austin: University of Texas Press, 1968.

Royster, Philip M. "Milkman's Flying: The Scapegoat Transcended in Toni Morrison's *Song of Solomon.*" *CLA Journal* 24 (1981): 419–40.

Samuels, Wilfred. "Liminality and the Search for Self in Toni Morrison's *Song of Solomon.*" *Minority Voices* 5, nos. 1–2 (1981): 59–68.

Smith, Valerie. "The Quest for and Discovery of Identity in Toni Morrison's *Song of Solomon.*" *Southern Review* 21 (1985): 721–32.

Stuckey, Sterling. *Slave Culture: Nationalistic Theory and the Foundations of Black America.* New York: Oxford University Press, 1987.

Trilling, Lionel. *The Liberal Imagination: Essays on Literature and Society.* New York: Viking, 1950.

Part II

♦ ♦ ♦

MYTH AND FOLKLORE

"Unruly and Let Loose"

Myth, Ideology, and Gender in Song of Solomon

MICHAEL AWKWARD

◆　◆　◆

I write without gender focus. . . . It happens that
what provokes my imagination as a writer has
to do with the culture of black people. I regard
the whole world as my canvas and I write out of
that sensibility of what I find provocative *and* the
sensibility of being a woman. But I don't write
women's literature as such. I think it would confine me. I am valuable as a writer because I am
a woman, because women, it seems to me, have
some special knowledge about certain things. [It
comes from] the ways in which they view the
world, and from women's imagination. Once it is
unruly and let loose, it can bring things to the
surface that men—trained to be men in a certain
way—have difficulty getting access to.
　　　—Toni Morrison, "An Interview with
　　　Toni Morrison, Hessian Radio Network,
　　　Frankfurt, West Germany" (conducted by
　　　Rosemarie K. Lester)

I

I N   S E V E R A L   R E S P E C T S , *Song of Solomon* is perhaps the most
challenging text that Toni Morrison has yet produced. The
interpretive challenges presented by the novel have as their primary source the nature of the author's appropriation of the myth

around which she structures what has been called a tale of Afro-American "genealogical archaeology" (Fabre 105). As Dorothy Lee asserts in her discussion of the epic qualities of Morrison's text, the author "draws on specific Afro-American legends of Africans who could fly and who used this marvelous ability to escape from slavery in America; that is, literally to transcend bondage" (64). However, Morrison does not simply "draw on" this myth; rather, what she offers in the narrative of Solomon's mythic flight is a radically transformed version of this legend which suggests the immense, and in many respects injurious, changes that have occurred over the course of the history of blacks in America. Indeed, a careful analysis of the subtle, appropriative nature of Morrison's mythic figurations (including what is apparently a traditional heroic male act of archaeology—its protagonist Milkman Dead's "archetypal search for self and for transcendence," Lee 64) reveals her complex inscription of ideology or, more accurately, *ideologies*: the Afrocentric and feminist politics that inform *Song of Solomon*.

Comments offered by Morrison in "Rootedness: The Ancestor as Foundation" appear to corroborate the general critical emphasis on the epic qualities of *Song of Solomon*. In a discussion of what she views as the Afro-American novel's destiny to replace the celebrated forms of black expressivity (blues, jazz, spirituals, and folktales) as a primary locus for Afro-American cultural wisdom's preservation and transmission, Morrison argues:

> The novel is needed by African-Americans now in a way that it was not needed before—and it is following along the lines of the function of novels everywhere. We don't live in places where we can hear those stories anymore; parents don't sit around and tell their children those *classical, mythological, archetypal stories* that we heard years ago. But *new information* has got to get out, and there are several ways to do it. One is the novel. (340; my emphases)

Despite its apparent support of an unproblematized reading of her third novel as black male odyssey par excellence, Morrison's statement strongly suggests a dual—and, in some respects, potentially conflictive—function for the novel and, particularly, for a purposefully "classical, mythological, archetypal" text such as *Song of Solomon*. These dual functions are: (1) to preserve the traditional Afro-American folktales, folk wisdom, and general cultural beliefs, and (2) to adapt to contemporary times and needs such traditional beliefs by infusing them with "new information" and to transmit the resultant amalgam of traditional and "new" to succeeding generations. While both of these functions are ideologically charged—they are informed by the desire to convey to Afro-American readers "how to behave in this new world" (340)—it is quite easy to see that certain profound conflicts might arise between the old (the archetypal tales) and the new.

What the criticism devoted to *Song of Solomon* has failed to respond to in an adequate manner where Morrison's employment of myth and epic is concerned is the author's inscription of the "new." For Morrison's version of the myth of the flying African is in several crucial respects strategically altered in the form of an updated version of the traditional narrative, which is "revitalized by a new grounding in the concrete particularities of a specific time and place" (Lee 64). That new grounding is represented by the apparent absence on the part of Solomon, the figure in the Morrisonian version who possesses the secrets of flight, of an accompanying sense of social responsibility. The nameless black slaves in versions of the flying African myth such as Julius Lester's "People Who Could Fly," invested with the transcendent power of the word by a young witch doctor, literally rise en masse in response to the plight of blacks weakened as a consequence of working in heat that made "the very air seem . . . to be on fire" (149). This young witch doctor, who "carried with him the secrets and powers of the generations of Africa" (149), employs these black powers to lead a stirring mass exodus from Deep South fields. When the young witch doctor is himself struck by an overseer who recognizes his role in aiding the infirm to "surrender to the air" (*Song of Solomon* 341), he instructs "everyone" to escape: "He uttered the strange word, and all of the Africans dropped their hoes, stretched out their arms, and flew away, back to their home, back to Africa" (Lester 152).

What is striking about this traditional version of the myth,[1] particularly in comparison to its updating in *Song of Solomon*, is the communally beneficial nature of the witch doctor's employment of the (liberating, black) word. In Lester's version of the myth, tribal wisdom is employed to make possible a group transcendence of the debilitating conditions of American oppression. The young African witch doctor, possessed of the power of flight, employs his knowledge at the appropriate moment—when the representative of white power punishes the weakened and defenseless and seeks to destroy the bearer of African cultural wisdom—to effect a communal escape from the site of mistreatment and oppression.

Morrison's appropriation of the myth, while it preserves a clear connection to mythology concerning black flight's possibilities, divests the narrative of its essential communal impulses. In *Song of Solomon*, the empowered Afro-American's flight, celebrated in a blues song whose decoding catapults Milkman into self-conscious maturity, is a solitary one; in other words, his discovery of the means of transcendence—the liberating black word—is not shared with the tribe. He leaves his loved ones, including his infant son, Jake, whom he tries unsuccessfully to carry with him, with the task of attempting to learn for themselves the secrets of transcendence. The failure of Solomon's efforts to transport Jake along with him, in fact, serves to emphasize the ultimately individualistic nature of the mythic figure's flight.[2] And while the narrative suggests that the offspring of the legendary Solomon do not perceive themselves as negatively affected by his act—they, in fact, construct praise songs in recognition of his accomplishments—his mate, Ryna, who has borne his twenty-one children, is so aggrieved at her loss that she goes mad. (Her grief, like Solomon's transcendent act, assumes legendary proportions in the history of Milkman's people.)

The conflict between the archetypal and the new in *Song of Solomon*, then, is of particular significance where gender is concerned because, as is generally the case in Western mythic systems, including the genre of the epic, Morrison's updated version suggests that masculinity has become a virtual prerequisite for participation in transcendent action. In this respect, Morrison's appropriation differs significantly from Lester's version of the traditional myth, where flight is delineated not as an individual but as a communal act, an act not limited to the biologically male.

An analysis which suggests, either implicitly or explicitly, that the novel's inscription of an ideology of race is privileged over its figurations of a politics of gender cannot capture the complexities of Morrison's mythic narrative. For, despite Morrison's ambiguous claim, recorded in this essay's epigraph, that she writes "without gender focus," her attraction to the "unruly" features of "women's imagination," which "can bring things to the surface that men—trained to be men in a certain way—have difficulty getting access to" (Lester 54), inspires her demonstration of certain masculinist features of mythic narrative specifically and of cultural practice generally. The text of *Song of Solomon* serves as a wonderfully appropriate site for a black feminist criticism—for a discourse attuned to intersections between Afrocentric and feminist ideologies.

Such an analysis needs to be preceded, however, by a discussion of the relationship between myth and ideology, which might inform our comprehension of their intersections in Morrison, and by a brief exploration of the largely androcentric epic tradition, whose masculinist biases the "unruly" black and female author critically revises.

II

The folklorist Alan Dundes has suggested that "myth is a sacred narrative explaining how the world and man came to be in their present form" (1). But if myth, as Dundes argues, possesses an origin-clarifying function, its articulation also provides a means of explaining how man and woman can cope, in a culturally approved fashion, with difficulties wrought in the present by natural and supernatural forces. The mythic/epic hero's merits, and the quality of his achievements, are measured in terms of what

George deForest Lord calls "the success of the hero in search of himself and his success in restoring or preserving his culture" (1). Consequently, myth's function is to contribute to the maintenance of the norms and values of the culture out of which "sacred narrative" emerges.

Richard Stotkin's work illuminates the ideological underpinnings of myth. He defines myth as a "body of traditional stories that have . . . been used to summarize the course of our collective history and to assign ideological meanings to that history" (70), and he analyzes the essentially ideological function of myth in the following way:

> The terms "myth" and "ideology" describe essential attributes of every human culture. Ideology is an abstraction of the system of beliefs, values, and institutional relationships that characterize a particular culture or society; mythology is the body of traditional narratives that exemplifies and historicizes ideology. Myths are stories, drawn from history, that have acquired through usage over many generations a symbolizing function central to the culture of the society that produces them. Through the processes of traditionalization historical narratives are conventionalized and abstracted, and their range of reference is extended so that they become structural metaphors containing all the essential elements of a culture's world view. . . . [M]yths suggest that by understanding and imaginatively reenacting the conflict resolutions of the past, we can interpret and control the unresolved conflicts of the present. (70)

Myths, then, are implicitly ideological in their conveyance and advocacy of their culture's belief systems in symbolic forms that are both historically significant and immediately relevant. To use Morrison's phrase, they inform their culture's inhabitants "how to behave" in a time-tested, culturally approved manner.

Stotkin's sense of myth's implicitly ideological function of "defining and defending [the society's] pattern of values" (78) accords with Morrison's own formulations concerning mythic narratives.

Arguing that fiction "must be political" ("Rootedness" 344) in order to be of value to society, Morrison insists that novels have always "provided social rules and explained behavior, identified outlaws, identified the people, habits, and customs that one should approve of" (340). Apparently, her interest in myth derives, at least in part, from an awareness of myth's usefulness in the transmission of ideology and in the preservation of cultural wisdom, values, and world views.

Morrison's position as black and female, however, problematizes her relation to myth because traditional myths, like most other cultural forms preserved from an androcentric past, tend to inscribe as part of their truth a subordinate and inferior status for women. While a close examination of Morrison's corpus discourages a reading of her work as radically feminist, clearly the author's novels are infused with a consistently female-centered perspective. Such an ideological stance leads Morrison to confront the sometimes virulently phallocentric nature of traditional Western myths, including Afro-American ones.[3] Indeed, Gerry Brenner's essay on *Song of Solomon* asserts that Morrison ironically applies, and forcefully rejects, the (masculinist) monomythic principles delineated by Otto Rank (115). Brenner's astute perceptions concerning Morrison's comprehension of the sexism implicit in the epic suggest the appropriateness of an analysis of the ways in which the novelist's woman-centered ideology complicates her use of (Afrocentric) myth.

Such an analysis is facilitated by the formulations of feminist critic Rachel DuPlessis, particularly her discussion of contemporary women writers' manipulation of traditional myth. DuPlessis, who has argued that twentieth-century women's literature is characterized by manifestly ideological efforts to create narrative strategies "that express the critical dissent from dominant [androcentric] narrative" (5), says of the female confrontation of traditional mythological forms:

> When a woman writer chooses myth as her subject, she is faced
> with material that is indifferent or, more often, actively hostile
> to historical considerations of gender, claiming as it does uni-

versal, humanistic, natural, or even archetypal status. To face myth as a woman writer is, putting things at their most extreme, to stand at the impact point of a strong system of interpretation masked as representation, and to rehearse one's own colonization or "iconization" through the materials one's culture considers powerful and primary. (106)

Joseph Campbell's discussion in the classic study *The Hero with a Thousand Faces* of women's roles within the male monomyth confirms DuPlessis's assertions concerning female exclusion as subject from sacred narrative. Campbell suggests (although without the sense of censure that informs DuPlessis's formulations):

> Woman, in the picture language of mythology, represents the totality of what can be known. The hero is the one who comes to know. . . . Woman is the guide to the sublime acme of sensuous adventure. By deficient eyes she is reduced to inferior states; by the evil eye of ignorance she is spellbound to banality and ugliness. But she is redeemed by the eye of understanding. The hero who can take her as she is, without undue commotion but with the kindness and assurance she requires, is potentially the king, the incarnate god, of her created world. (116)

According to Campbell, the informing principles of myth inscribe woman as supplement and object, as a lesser being "redeemed" by the heroic male "eye of understanding," as one who requires male "kindness and assurance" to escape pejorative evaluations of her character and being.

Clearly, Campbell's influential formulations demonstrate the virtual impossibility of an uncritical contemporary female author's employment of traditional myth. For, in his discussion and apparent advocacy, for instance, of the Adamic myth of woman's origins inside man, Campbell validates the phallocentric belief that women's role is to complete—to make whole—the heretofore psychologically fragmented and defeminized male hero. The mythic (and historical) role of the female as supplement, then, reflects androcentric ideology in ways which suggest the utter difficulty and manifest dangers for female writers of employing traditional myths in uncritical ways. To do so is, in DuPlessis's words, "to rehearse one's own colonization or 'iconization.'"

White female writers who feel altogether excluded from and subjugated by traditional Western sacred narratives view these myths' radical subversion as a means of "delegitimating the specific narrative and cultural orders of [the past]" (DuPlessis 34). For such writers, among whom DuPlessis counts Adrienne Rich, Sylvia Plath, and Margaret Atwood, the goal of myth's appropriation is both a critique of the phallocentric nature of traditional myth and the creation of the possibilities for female-centered myths with woman as hero and subject.

However, for an Afrocentric female writer like Morrison who, despite its frequent phallocentrism, sees great value in Afro-American sacred narrative, the employment of traditional myth is problematic because of the necessity of affirming the ideological perspectives of these narratives where they involve the nature of black survival, while at the same time critiquing their frequent androcentricism. In other words, the author must produce narratives which clearly demonstrate her advocacy of Afrocentric ideology, while simultaneously condemning myth's general failure to inscribe the possibilities of a full female participation as subject in the story of black American self-actualization and cultural preservation.[4]

Its success at navigating between these ideological terrains suggests that *Song of Solomon* neither falls outside of the womanist and Afrocentric concerns of Morrison's other 1970s novels nor does it, as Susan Willis has asserted in a provocative analysis of Morrison's corpus, serve to "reinvent the notion of patrimony that emerges even as [Milkman] puts together his genealogy" (59–60). To read *Song of Solomon* in terms of its informing ideologies facilitates the reader's discernment of the ways in which the novel offers a disruption of the androcentric sequence both of Western sacred narrative in general and, specifically, of (appropriated) Afro-American myth.

III

Morrison's appropriation of the monomyth is, indeed, quite subtle, a subtlety suggested by the relative lack of extended critical comment about her choice of a male protagonist. Despite the clearly female-centered nature of her earlier novels, *The Bluest Eye* and *Sula*, critics generally have been remarkably untroubled by Morrison's creation of an apparently androcentric narrative. Such an untroubled response is manifest even in Genevieve Fabre's essay on the novel, despite the fact that this essay begins by situating Morrison in a continuum of black female writers who attempt "to achieve literacy . . . [and] freedom" and argues that "black women writers call attention to the distinctness of their experiences and vision" by composing works "deliberately disruptive and disturbing in their bold investigations [that] are part of a struggle against all forms of authority" (106). Although the essay demonstrates an acute understanding of Morrison's Afrocentric and feminist concerns, Fabre proceeds to offer a reading of *Song of Solomon* which concentrates almost exclusively on Milkman's "genealogical archaeology" and virtually ignores the problematics of gender as a major consideration. Fabre's curious reticence about gender in her analysis of Morrison's novel, however, does encourage a crucial question: how does what she calls Morrison's "dramatiz[ation of] an archetypal journey across ancestral territory" (107) really reflect, where it pertains to the insights Fabre offers in her introductory contextualization of the novelist's ideological aims, "the essential significance of [black female] *difference*"?[5]

An answer to this question is not quickly forthcoming, for in addition to what critics have generally read as Morrison's inscription of a privileged maleness in *Song of Solomon*, several of her own comments seem intended to discourage analyses of her work whose orientation is primarily—and limitedly—feminist. In "Rootedness," for example, she says, in response to a question concerning "the necessity to develop a specific black feminist model of critical inquiry": "I think there is more danger in it than fruit, because any model of criticism or evaluation that excludes males from it is as hampered as any model of criticism of Black literature that excludes women from it" (344). Perhaps even more inhibiting to a limitedly feminist reading of *Song of Solomon* are comments she offers to explain the roots of Hagar's ultimately debilitating problems, despite her possession of a wondrously self-actualized mentor—her grandmother Pilate. Morrison says of Hagar:

> The difficulty that Hagar . . . has is how far removed she is from the experience of her ancestor. Pilate had a dozen years of close, nurturing relationships with two males—her father and her brother. And that intimacy and support was in her and made her fierce and loving because she had that experience. Her daughter Reba had less of that and related to men in a very shallow way. Her daughter [Hagar] had even less of an association with men as a child, so that the progression is really a diminishing of their abilities because of the absence of men in a nourishing way in their lives. Pilate is the apogee of all that: of the best of that which is female and the best of that which is male, and that balance is disturbed if it is not nurtured, and if it is not counted on and if it is not reproduced. That is the disability we must be on guard against for the future—the female who reproduces the female who reproduces the female. (344)

Morrison rejects the feminist idea(l) of exclusively female communities as the best means of maximizing possibilities of black female psychic and emotional health. Indeed, the question of (gender-specific) exclusion is profoundly important to Morrison's formulations here, for it serves as her motivation both for assertions about the potential dangers of a narrowly focused black feminist criticism and, in her reading of incidents in *Song of Solomon*, for the ultimate demise of Hagar. Clearly, for Morrison, black female psychic health cannot be achieved without the cooperative participation of both females and males in its creation and nurturance. Indeed, male participation helps to provide the novice female with a sense of "balance" between "the best of that which is female and the best of that which is male" without which gendered and tribal health is, for Morrison, quite unlikely.

Such comments might be read as confirmation of Willis's afore-mentioned assertion that *Song of Solomon* "tends to reinvent the notion of patrimony" (60). However, the novel's complex employment of Afrocentric and feminist ideologies can be more fruitfully read in terms of DuPlessis's formulations with respect to contemporary women writers' efforts to disrupt traditional androcentric narrative sequences and strategies. According to DuPlessis, contemporary women writers' work is committed to "rupturing language and tradition sufficiently to invite a female slant, emphasis, or approach" and to "delegitimating specific narrative and cultural orders of [the past]" (32). I want to argue here that Morrison's appropriations of the monomyth and of Afro-American sacred narrative are motivated by such rupturing, delegitimating impulses.

I will further explore the sense of narrative rupture and breakage implicit in Morrison's appropriations of the male monomyth, focusing on two crucial aspects of the novel: (1) Morrison's literal breaking of Milkman's male heroic quest with the specifically antithetical story of Hagar's demise, and (2) the particular implications of the narrative of Solomon's flight.

IV

In order to fully discuss Morrison's manipulation of the privileged text of mythic (male) transcendence, I must begin with a brief delineation of the particulars of Milkman's journey. Milkman's quest is undertaken initially to provide him access to gold he believes Pilate has left behind as a means of securing a lasting economic and emotional self-sufficiency. In other words, his quest is inspired by an urge to avoid emotional commitment and familial responsibility:

> He just wanted to beat a path away from his parents' past, which was also their present and which was threatening to

become his present as well. He hated the acridness in his mother's and father's relationship, the conviction of right-eousness they each held on to with both hands. And his efforts to ignore it, transcend it, seemed to work only when he spent his days looking for whatever was light-hearted and without grave consequences. He avoided commitment and strong feel-ings, and shied away from decisions. He wanted to know as little as possible to feel only enough to warrant the curiosity of other people—but not their all-consuming devotion. Hagar had given him this last and more drama than he could ever want again. (*Song of Solomon* 180–81)

Milkman's journey begins, then, as an effort to gain freedom from obligation to others by taking possession of a familial trea-sure. Instead of gold, however, what he finds, after a series of episodes which conform to traditional monomythic paradigms for the male hero who has been called to adventure (Lee 67), is a mature sense of his familial obligations, an informed knowledge of familial (and tribal) history, and a profound comprehension of tribal wisdom. His newly achieved knowledge of self and culture is manifested dramatically during the course of an initiatory trial-by-fire in Shalimar in which black male elders invite the bourgeois urbanite on a long, arduous hunting trek and then leave the novice hunter behind to fend for himself. Forced to use his wits to navigate a forest filled with wild animals, Milkman considers the treatment he has received since his arrival and, more impor-tant, the ways he has (mis)treated others. Asking himself, "What kind of savages were these people," and believing momentarily that "he had done nothing to deserve their contempt" (279), a significantly more introspective Milkman recognizes the necessity of abandoning such immature perspectives:

It sounded old. Deserve. Old and tired and beaten to death. Deserve. Now it seemed to him that he was always saying or thinking that he didn't deserve some bad luck, or some bad treatment from others. He'd told Guitar that he didn't even "deserve" his family's dependence, hatred, or whatever. That he didn't even "deserve" to hear all the misery and mutual accusations his parents unloaded on him. Nor did he "deserve" Hagar's vengeance. But why shouldn't his parents tell him their personal problems? If not him, then who? And if a stranger could try to kill him, surely Hagar, who knew him and whom he'd thrown away like a wad of chewing gum after the flavor was gone—she had a right to try to kill him too. (279–80)

His achievement of a radically reconceptualized view of self and family and of his responsibilities thereto occurs when, near the end of his ancestral quest, he is overcome by a feeling of homesickness as he listens to a group of Shalimar children singing "that old blues song Pilate sang all the time: 'O Sugarman don't leave me here' " (303). This homesickness is accompanied by and is, indeed, a function of a more mature and complete awareness of the factors which motivated his family's behavior. He comprehends, for example, that his mother's eccentricities—including the fact that she nursed him well past an age that such a practice was necessary for his nourishment—are in part the result of "sexual deprivation": "now it seemed to him that such sexual deprivation would affect her, hurt her in precisely the way it would affect and hurt him" (303). Subsequently, he wonders, "What might she have been like had her husband loved her?" (304). Further, he begins to understand the source of his father's perversely acquisitive nature:

> As the son of Macon Dead the first, [his father] paid homage to his own father's life and death by loving what that father had loved: property, good solid property, the bountifulness of life. He loved these things to excess. Owning, building, acquiring—that was his life, his future, his present, and all the history he knew. That he distorted life, bent it, for the sake of gain, was a measure of his loss at his father's death. (304)

In addition to comprehending the ridiculousness of hating his parents and sisters and being overcome with a "thick" "skin of shame" for "having stolen from Pilate" (304), he turns his thoughts to Hagar, the person whose life his selfishness has most seriously affected. Wondering why he had not exercised more sensitivity in ending their relationship, he sees that his egotistical masculinist treatment of Hagar had extended even to his response to her hysterical attempts to end his life:

> He had used her—her love, her craziness—and most of all he had used her skulking, bitter vengeance. It made him a star, a celebrity in the Blood Bank; it told men and other women that he was one bad dude, that he had the power to drive a woman out of her mind, to destroy her, and not because she hated him, or because he had done some unforgivable thing to her, but because he had fucked her and she was driven wild by the absence of his magnificent joint. (305)

A thoughtful and less self-protective appraisal of his personal history, motivated by the trials and tribulations that constitute his heroic ordeal and which include his rejection of an injuriously materialistic perspective, forces Milkman to comprehend the serious errors of his self-centered ways. Like the traditional mono-mythic hero, he achieves a sense of his identity which is firmly rooted in his relationship to his family and community. For he has learned, in short, that he can achieve a sense of self only when he is able to embrace his unavoidable responsibilities to family and humanity, when he can recognize and relish a sense of membership with his people. Liberated from the shallow and selfish perspectives which had previously characterized him, Milkman has, in short, ended his division from self and tribe and become whole, has achieved a "coming together . . . into a total self" (70).

Ultimately, Milkman, whose gender permits Morrison to construct the narrative of his ancestral quest in general compliance with the parameters of the classical monomyth, is able to perform the culture-preserving service necessary for the maintenance of his community. In accordance with the requirements for the successful monomythic hero, he returns to his Michigan community to share what he has decoded of the sacred narrative's cryptic lyrics with a family hopelessly divided by decades of mistrust and perverse mistreatment of one another. Milkman's odyssey confirms the accuracy of his father's previous conflation of selfhood and knowledge. Earlier, when Milkman intervenes in a psychologically and physically violent dispute between his mother and father by striking Macon Dead II, his father says to him: "You a big man now, but big ain't nearly enough. You have to be a whole man. And if you want to be a whole man, you have to deal with the whole truth" (70). Having investigated, in a seemingly thorough manner, his ancestral heritage, Milkman learns a good deal of "the whole truth," which provides him access to what Joseph Campbell calls "the unquenched source through which society *is* reborn" (20). An achieved sense of wholeness and access to the "unquenched source"—in particular, the history of the Dead clan; more generally, Afro-American culture and its timeless truths—allows Milkman to embark on the monomythic hero's "second task and deed": "to return then to [his 'disintegrating society'] transfigured, and teach the lesson he has learned of life renewed" (20).

Those lessons, however informative and powerful, cannot alter the most chilling consequence of his former "disintegrat[ed] psyche" (Joseph Campbell 20): his mistreatment of Hagar and her ultimate death. Concurrent with Milkman's achievement of indispensable awareness of self and culture is Hagar's painful quest to achieve bourgeois American society's standards of female beauty. Indeed, Milkman's and Hagar's gendered situations in a patriarchal capitalist system ultimately delimit their journeys' very nature and success.

V

Chapter 13 of *Song of Solomon*, which records the circumstances surrounding Hagar's death, offers a literal—and strategic—breaking of the male monomythic sequence. The structure of Morrison's novel encourages a contrast between Milkman's (male) monomythic quest for self and community and his cousin Hagar's

deathward march toward what Susan Willis has identified as reification (89). This juxtaposition is quite striking. For example, the
journeys of both characters are embarked upon as a consequence
of their attitudes about bourgeois capitalist values. Milkman,
whom Morrison is able to write into the traditional (male) epic
quest plot, seeks to escape his environment not because its bourgeois values are oppressive, but because they demand a psychic
involvement and sense of empathy for which he is clearly un-
prepared. On the other hand, Hagar's journey to reification and,
ultimately, physical death has its source in her adoption of a
patriarchal society's almost timeless figuration of woman as object, in her futile attempt to achieve the bourgeois society's notions of female beauty. Having apparently inherited from her female forebear Ryna the capacity for immeasurable grief as a
consequence of male abandonment, Hagar concludes, after gazing
in a mirror at her own image, that Milkman's failure to love her
is a function of her unglamorous, un-*Cosmopolitan* appearance.

Hagar's female status denies her entry as actor and subject to
paradigmatic epic means of transcendence. Consequently, she is
denied access to the transformative possibilities of a regenerative
necessary distance from a corruptive mainstream American bourgeois value system. Because the mythic black narrative of communal transcendence is no longer extant—and has, in fact, been
replaced by an individualistic and androcentric (familial) text—
Hagar has no means of achieving a nurturing knowledge of self
and culture that would make it possible for her to reject the
debilitating tenets of what George deForest Lord calls "a destroyed
city, a ruined culture" (221). Hence, she can see possibilities for
self-improvement only in the terms that a "ruined" bourgeois
American society suggests are proper for her gender. In other
words, in a society where female self-actualization is, by and large,
impossible outside of the context of an interactive relationship
with a man, Hagar's concentration on Milkman's unwillingness
to love her is, however injurious, utterly logical. While Milkman
comes to a marvelously useful comprehension of history, myth,
and nature, Hagar's status as bound, in both the spatial and the
narrative senses of the phrase, to oppressive domestic plots—a

virtual requirement for the abandoned female lover in the Western epic—precipitates a virtual dissociation of sensibility and an acceptance of the bourgeois society's views of women. This acceptance is reflected particularly in her whole hearted adoption of its ideas of female beauty.

It is specifically in terms of the image of female mirror gazing that Morrison figures the conclusion of Hagar's grief-inspired aphasia and her discovery of what she believes is a means by which to rekindle Milkman's interest. When an almost catatonic Hagar sees herself in a compact mirror Pilate holds before her, she is convinced that she has found the source of Milkman's antipathy—her appearance:

> "No wonder," she said at last. "Look at that. No wonder. No wonder . . ."
>
> "Look at how I look. I look awful. No wonder he didn't want me. I look terrible." Her voice was calm and reasonable, as though the last few days hadn't been lived through at all. "I need to get up from here and fix myself up. No *wonder!*" Hagar threw back the bedcover and stood up. "Ohhh. I smell too. Mama, heat me some water. I need a bath. . . . Oh Lord, my head. Look at that." She peered into the compact mirror again. "I look like a ground hog. Where's the comb?" (312)

Hagar sets out enthusiastically to achieve the bourgeois society's ideal of beauty. Believing "I need everything" to transform her black difference—what she refers to as her "ground hog" appearance—into the bourgeois society's glamorous feminine ideal, she spends an entire business day "shopp[ing] for everything a woman could wear from the skin out" (314). She purchases, among other things, "a Playtex garter belt, I. Miller No Color hose, Fruit of the Loom panties, . . . two nylon slips" (314), an expensive Evan Picone outfit, and cosmetics. Hers is a shameless act of commodity consumption, a desperate attempt to make herself into an incontestable example of feminine beauty in order to be worthy of Milkman's love. Her instruments of transformation are soaked and soiled, however, in a downpour of rain, and her efforts to employ these ripped clothes and rain-soaked cosmetics to remake herself proves far from successful. Hagar understands this when she sees Pilate's and Reba's reaction to her appearance:

> It was in their eyes that she saw what she had not seen before in the mirror: the wet ripped hose, the soiled white dress, the sticky, lumpy face powder, the streaked rouge, and the wild wet shouls of hair. All this she saw in their eyes, and the sight filled her own with water warmer and much older than the rain. (318)

Hagar comes to the bitter realization that her efforts to achieve American society's ideal of female beauty are utterly fruitless. Her brief, painful attempt to compensate for lacking the physical qualities of which she knows Milkman approves—"silky, [penny-colored] hair," "lemon-colored skin," "gray-blue eyes," and a "thin nose" (319–20)—ends, not with transcendent knowledge of the world as does the male protagonist's epic journey but, rather, with an awareness that her (ruined) society will never provide her opportunities for the types of transformations necessary to win the love of the man with whom she feels she belongs. Exhausted and feeling the full hopelessness of her dilemma, she tells Pilate: "He's never going to like my hair" (320).

Morrison interrupts Milkman's monomythic quest or, in DuPlessis's phrase, breaks the (sacred) narrative sequence, in order to expose phallocentric myth's failure to inscribe usefully transcendent possibilities for the female. This interruption serves to problematize a strictly celebratory Afrocentric analysis of Milkman's achievements. Such an analysis fails to permit focus on the clear presence of (female) pain that permeates *Song of Solomon*'s final chapters. Male culpability in the instigation of such pain is evident, for example, in Milkman's revelations about the motivations for his treatment of Hagar. He comes to understand that he "had used her—her love, her craziness—and most of all . . . her skulking, bitter vengeance" (304) to achieve heroic—or what the narrative refers to as "star"—status.[6]

Analyses of Morrison's novel must be attentive both to the transcendent joy of knowledge-informed male flight and to the immeasurable pain of desertion felt by females like Hagar and Ryna, whose agony at the loss of Solomon "like to killed the woman" (326) and was so profound at its intensity that "she screamed and screamed, lost her mind completely" (327). Future readings must, in other words, acknowledge that the blues lyrics and the novel encode *both* an Afrocentric appreciation of the power and importance of transcendence and a convincing critique of the fact that, in the updated version of the myth, that power is essentially denied to Afro-American women. Morrison's appropriation of the myth approximates the narrative structures of phallocentric Western myths to the extent that males are figured as actors, while females are aggrieved, deserted, and—because of the culture's and, hence, the narrative form's, masculinist perspectives—permanently grounded objects. The ideological complexity of Morrison's representation of her woman-centered and Afrocentric politics is suggested in the lyrics' inscription of transcendence and abandonment: "Solomon done fly, Solomon done gone" (307).

VI

Morrison's delineation in her novel of feminist concerns is perhaps most clearly evident in the (predominantly) female voices of descent that operate a censurous chorus in the last chapters of *Song of Solomon*. Shalimar females such as Susan Byrd and Sweet are, by and large, remarkably unimpressed by Solomon and by his transcendent act. Susan Byrd, in fact, openly criticizes him for his desertion of Ryna and his offspring. While Byrd recounts to Milkman the provocative aspects of Solomon's mythic flight— she tells Milkman, "according to the story, he . . . flew, like a bird. Just stood up in the fields one day, ran up some hill, spun around a couple of times, and was lifted up in the air. Went right on back to wherever it was he came from" (326)—her narrative focuses primarily on the pain felt by others as a consequence of his desertion. Indeed, it is Susan Byrd who informs Milkman of the derivation of the name Ryna's Gulch: "sometimes you can hear this funny sound by [the gulch] that the wind makes. People say it's the wife. Solomon's wife, crying. Her name was Ryna" (326–27). In addition to censurous assertions such as "he disappeared and left everybody" (326), she comments further on the ramifications of his leave-taking flight:

They say she screamed and screamed, lost her mind completely. You don't hear about women like that anymore, but there used to be more—the kind of woman who couldn't live without a particular man. And when the man left, they lost their minds, or died or something. Love, I guess. But I always thought it was trying to take care of children by themselves, you know what I mean? (326).

While we might rightly question here the reliability of Susan Byrd's "speculations" (327)—for instance, the song of Solomon is no mere, negligible "old folks' lie"; further, Hagar's response to Milkman's desertion is of a kind with Ryna's, and her grief clearly has nothing to do with the difficulty of single parenthood—certainly the reader can trust her recollections of the particulars of the mythic narrative. That the reader should trust her view of the magnitude of the deserted female's pain is confirmed by the reactions of Sweet and, ultimately, of Milkman, to male acts of abandonment and transcendence.

Milkman's archaeological act fills him with an "incredible high" (330) under whose influence he relates to his Shalimar lover, Sweet, the fact that he is a descendant of Solomon. Having taken possession of his familial history—he asserts proudly of the ring shout that accompanies the recitation of the song of Solomon, "It's my game now" (331)—he says of his forebear: "The son of a bitch could fly! You hear me, Sweet? That motherfucker could fly! Could fly! He didn't need no airplane. Didn't need no fuckin tee double you ay. He could fly his own self!" (332) Unimpressed by the knowledge of Milkman's royal heritage—after all, as Susan Byrd tells him, "everybody around here claims kin to him" (326)—Sweet tries to force her lover to consider the consequences of Jake's transcendent act by asking, "Who'd he leave behind?" (332). Still mesmerized by his status as descendant of such a magical figure, Milkman giddily responds: "Everybody! He left everybody down on the ground and he sailed on off like a black eagle" (332). It is only when he is forced to confront the consequences of his desertion of Hagar that he is capable of sensitivity to the socially irresponsible nature of his ancestor's actions and, further, of his own.

Such confrontation occurs when, upon his return to Michigan, Milkman is exposed to male flight's significant, sometimes deadly, consequences. Recovering in Pilate's cellar from a blow by his justifiably angered aunt, which had rendered him unconscious, Milkman comes to understand the tragic ironies of a phallocentric social (and narrative) structure which fails to permit female access to the culture's sources of knowledge and power. The narrative informs us of Milkman's revelations: "He had left her. While he dreamt of flying, Hagar was dying" (336). Milkman, who, despite his infinite leap in knowledge, clearly still has much to learn, then recalls Sweet's question about the victims of Solomon's departure, a question which he had not seriously pondered previously. He begins to see a clear connection between his act and that of his mythic forebear, the full impact of whose flight he can now understand:

> Sweet's silvery voice came back to him: "Who'd he leave behind?" He left Ryna behind and twenty children. Twenty-one, since he dropped the one he tried to take with him. And Ryna had thrown herself all over the ground, lost her mind, and was still crying in a ditch. Who looked after those twenty children? Jesus Christ, he left twenty-one children! . . . Shalimar left his, but it was the children who sang about it and kept the story of his leaving alive. (336)

It is only at this point, when he learns of the painful consequences of the celebrated male act of flight, that Milkman's comprehension of his familial heritage and the song of Solomon can be said to move toward satisfying completion. Such understanding requires coming to terms with his familial song's complex, sometimes unflattering meaning and acknowledging both its prideful flight and the lack of a sense of social responsibility in the mythic hero Solomon's leave-taking act.

Song of Solomon, then, is a record both of transcendent (male) flight and of the immeasurable pain that results for the female who, because of her lack of access to knowledge, cannot participate in this flight. In breaking the monomythic sequence, Morrison provides the possibilities for a resistant feminist reading, which suggests the consequences of male epic journeys: the death-in-life, or actual death, of the female whose only permissible role is that of an aggrieved, abandoned lover.

Thus, an analysis that foregrounds not only Milkman's archaeological question, but also Hagar's disintegration—in other words, an Afrocentric feminist reading of *Song of Solomon*—allows for an interpretation that most closely suggests the complexity of Morrison's appropriation of the epic form and the Afro-American folktale. Such an analysis is necessary if we are to comprehend the black and feminist poetics which inform not only *Song of Solomon* but the author's entire corpus. Rather than reinventing patrimony, Morrison's novel affirms the timeless relevance of the folktale's cultural truths, while exposing contemporary perversions of the myth's insistence on the importance of transcendent flight as implicitly phallocentric in their inscription of a perpetually inferior—non-"heroic"—status for the female.

Morrison's male epic does not represent a break with the female-centered concerns of works such as *The Bluest Eye* and *Sula* but is a bold extension of these concerns in a confrontation with the tenets of Western literature's most "sacred narrative" form. Like Guitar, who insists that he has earned the right to censorous analyses of the actions of Afro-Americans, Morrison's text asks, in effect, "Can't I criticize what I love?" While she dearly wishes to preserve the wonder and wisdom of black culture, Morrison perceives the need to invest the preserved forms of culture with "new information." If cultures generally are not static but are in the process of continual and dynamic development, clearly Afro-American culture, if it is to be valuable in the present as a means of explaining a rapidly changing world in which women are increasingly important and influential actors, cannot continue to produce perspectives which lead to the further creation of narratives that trivialize or marginalize the female. Such recognition does not mean a replacement of Afrocentric ideology with feminism but the creation of spaces that will allow for their necessary and potentially fruitful interaction. In that sense, *Song of Solomon* not only reflects the perspectives of Afro-American culture but seeks to contribute in significant ways to its transformation.

Notes

1. I term Lester's version of the flying Afro-American myth "traditional" because, in its setting (black slaves working southern plantation fields) and theme (the possibility for physical or psychic escape from white racist dehumanization of the black body), "People Who Could Fly" echoes other recorded versions of the myth. For other versions, see "All God's Chillen Had Wings," in Hughes and Bontemps (62–65); J. D. Suggs's "The Flying Man," in Dorson (279); and "Flying People," in Brewer (309). Hughes and Bontemps's version is in many striking ways similar to Lester's tale; one significant difference between the two, however, is the fact that the male figure empowered with the word in the Hughes-Bontemps text is old, while in the Lester version, he is young.

2. Morrison's appropriative, transformative intent is signaled clearly by her emphasis on Solomon's failure to bring Jake along with him on his flight to (African) origins. Solomon's failure to include his offspring is in dramatic contrast to Hughes and Bontemps's version, which begins by introducing a crying child whose birth had weakened the black young mother who represents the tale's initial transcendent figure (63).

3. For examples of traditional masculinistic Afro-American folklore, see Julius Lester, especially "The Girl with the Large Eyes" (57–61) and "Jack and the Devil's Daughter" (73–90).

4. What complicates such a reading of Morrison's feminist encounter with myth, however, is the fact that the traditional Afro-American folktale upon which she bases the song of Solomon cannot accurately be

termed phallocentric. Indeed, as I have demonstrated, the sacred narrative of the flying Africans portrays communal—male and female—flight from a corrupt (American) society. Thus, it is in Morrison's appropriation that the myth can be said to represent an androcentric narrative. This fact suggests, it would appear, that in her "new grounding" of the myth, Morrison wishes to demonstrate the extent to which the Afro-American value system has suffered, at its deepest structure—as recorded in the mythological narratives black people create to define themselves—from corruption by an individualistic and phallocentric Western belief system. Thus, it is not in Morrison's reading of the traditional folktale itself but, rather, in her transformation of it in the blues lyrics that constitute the song of Solomon, that DuPlessis's formulations concerning a resistant female mythological writer seem appropriate. It is in her response to a version of the myth that she herself constructs that we can locate in *Song of Solomon* a tension between critique and affirmation, her apparently bifurcated perspective.

5. Fabre is not alone in her neglect of the full implications of gender in *Song of Solomon*. To cite, briefly, two other examples: Royster notes in passing that *Song of Solomon* "is the first of her novels that employs a male protagonist" (419), but he fails to allow this obviously important matter to inform his reading; similarly Jane Campbell, who argues that Morrison has "invested *Song of Solomon* with an epic quality" (137), does not consider the significance of gender to the novelist's figuration of what she calls "ancestral quests." However, in a recent English Institute session, "Toni Morrison in Perspective," which I attended after the present essay had been completed, Kimberly Benston provocatively focused attention, among other matters, on the implications of Morrison's choice of a male protagonist.

6. Clearly, Hagar's tragic plight is accelerated by her status as woman in a masculinist plot which insists that a female is nothing without a man. Hagar is unable to find and, indeed, is not even permitted to search for in any potentially fruitful locale the type of significant and sustaining personal and tribal meaning in history and myth, a fact which signals her place outside of the myth's transcendent action. Morrison employs song to contrast the disparate successes of Milkman's and Hagar's quests. The male protagonist finds new life, as it were, in the cryptic blues lyrics of the song of Solomon. In contrast, the use of song in the concluding scene of chapter 13—Pilate's and Reba's mournful pleas at Hagar's funeral for "Mercy" and Pilate's reenactment of a lullaby ("Who's been

botherin my sweet sugar lumpkin? / Who's been botherin my baby?" [322]) she'd sung to her granddaughter "when she was a little girl"— signals the anguish of the female characters at their inability to protect Hagar from the deadly effects of her rejection by Milkman, who had "been botherin my baby girl."

Works Cited

Benston, Kimberly. "Re-Weaving the 'Ulysses Scene': Enchantment, Post-Oedipal Identity and the Buried Text of Blackness in *Song of Solomon*." Paper presented at the English Institute, 48th Session. Harvard University, 25 Aug. 1989.

Brenner, Gerry. "*Song of Solomon*: Rejecting Rank's Monomyth and Feminism." In *Critical Essays on Toni Morrison*, edited by Nellie Y. McKay, 114–24. Boston: Hall, 1988.

Brewer, J. Mason. *American Negro Folklore*. Chicago: Quadrangle, 1968.

Campbell, Jane. *Mythic Black Fiction: The Transformation of History*. Knoxville: University of Tennessee Press, 1986.

Campbell, Joseph. *The Hero with a Thousand Faces*. New York: Pantheon, 1949.

Dorson, Richard. *American Negro Folktales*. Greenwich, Conn.: Fawcett, 1956.

Dundes, Alan, ed. *Sacred Narrative: Readings in the Theory of Myth*. Berkeley: University of California Press, 1984.

DuPlessis, Rachel Blau. *Writing beyond the Ending: Narrative Strategies of Twentieth-Century Women Writers*. Bloomington: Indiana University Press, 1985.

Fabre, Genevieve. "Genealogical Archaeology; or, The Quest for Legacy in *Song of Solomon*." In *Critical Essays on Toni Morrison*; edited by Nellie Y. McKay, 105–14. Boston: Hall, 1988.

Hughes, Langston, and Arna Bontemps, eds. *The Book of Negro Folklore*. New York: Dodd, Mead, 1958.

Lee, Dorothy H. "*Song of Solomon*: To Ride the Air." *Black American Literature Forum* 16 (1982): 64–70.

Lester, Julius. *Black Folktales*. New York: Grove, 1969.

Lester, Rosemarie K. "An Interview with Toni Morrison; Hessian Radio Network, Frankfurt, West Germany." In *Critical Essays on Toni Morrison*, edited by Nellie Y. McKay. 47–56. Boston: Hall, 1988.

Lord, George deForest. *Trials of the Self: Heroic Ordeals in the Epic Tradition.* Hamden, Conn.: Archon, 1983.

McKay, Nellie Y., ed. *Critical Essays on Toni Morrison.* Boston: Hall, 1988.

Morrison, Toni. "Rootedness: The Ancestor as Foundation." In *Black Women Writers 1950–1980: A Critical Evaluation,* edited by Mari Evans, 339–45. New York: Doubleday, 1984.

———. *Song of Solomon.* New York: Signet, 1977.

Royster, Phillip. "Milkman Flying: The Scapegoat Transcended in Toni Morrison's *Song of Solomon." College Language Association Journal* 24 (1982): 419–40.

Stotkin, Richard. "Myth and the Production of History." In *Ideology and Classic American Literature,* edited by Sacvan Bercovitch and Myra Jehlen, 70–90. New York: Cambridge University Press, 1986.

Willis, Susan. *Specifying: Black Women Writing the American Experience.* Madison: University of Wisconsin Press, 1987.

Song of Solomon

Rejecting Rank's Monomyth and Feminism

GERRY BRENNER

◆　　◆　　◆

A ROUND MILKMAN, the hero of her much-admired *Song of Solomon*, Toni Morrison wraps various collective fictions: a riddling nursery rhyme that presages his birth and, later chanted by children, leads him to discover his heritage; fables, like the one his father, Macon Dead, tells of the man who rescues a baby snake only to be poisoned to death by its bite; fairy tales, like "Rumpelstiltskin," "Jack and the Beanstalk," and "Hansel and Gretel"; a common black folktale, like "People Who Could Fly" (as collected by Julius Lester);[1] and family legends, like that of Milkman's great-grandfather's ability to fly. Even through family names and nicknames Morrison underscores a preoccupation of all four of her novels: for better and worse, humans use and make fictions to give their lives meaning and significance. Underlying these commoner fictions, however, is Otto Rank's powerful monomyth: the myth of the birth of the hero. Its features—with only minor glossing—attach to Milkman and categorically lay claim to his place among the heroes from whose stories Rank extrapolates his monomyth: Moses, Oedipus, Perseus, Gilgamesh,

Tristan, Romulus, Jesus, and Lohengrin—to name but half.[2] Despite Morrison's shrewd use of the monomyth on Milkman's behalf, she skillfully mocks him and the novel's other men. Offsetting his and their deflation is a subtle spectrum of praiseworthy women, prime among whom is the novel's only character of a heroic stature, Pilate.[3] "Marvelous" details circle her with a mythic nimbus that—combined with the humane values by which she conducts her life—rejects the sexism of Rank's monomyth and the expectations of feminists.

The nine parts of Rank's monomyth map the standard saga of the hero.[4]

The hero is the child of distinguished parents, usually the son of a king. Milkman's father, the city's most affluent black property owner, stands as virtual king. His "lemon-yellow" mother, Ruth, is the sole daughter of the wealthy, "most respected," and "the most important Negro in the city" (22).[5] Dr. Foster has equally regal stature. To this pair, Morrison adds Milkman's even more distinguished forefathers. Grandfather Macon Dead (aka Jake Solomon), was an extraordinary man who, in sixteen years, made "one of the best farms in Montour County." In his fellow blacks' eyes, he stood for "the farmer they wanted to be, the clever irrigator, the peach-tree grower, the hog slaughterer, the wild-turkey roaster, the man who could plow forty in no time flat and sang like an angel while he did it"; his farm "colored their lives like a paintbrush and spoke to them like a sermon" (237). And great-grandfather Solomon/Sugarman—virile progenitor of twenty-one sons and renowned for his ability to fly—is commemorated in nursery rhyme and at his launching site, Solomon's Leap. (Milkman's nocturnal hunt with the elders of Shalimar begins and ends, not by happenstance, at a defunct gas station still presided over by a man who is no one less than King Walker.)

His origin is preceded by difficulties, such as continence, or prolonged barrenness, or secret intercourse of the parents due to external prohibition or obstacles. After finding his wife lying naked on the bed—and sucking the fingers—of her dying father (which he interprets as perverse, if not incestuous), Macon Dead abandons conjugal relations with her. A decade later, his sister Pilate dissolves his abstinence with herbs whose powers bring him, puzzled, back to Ruth's bed for four days, effecting Milkman's conception. His attempts at aborting the fetus are thwarted by Pilate and Ruth, ensuring that Ruth's "aggressive act [is] brought to royal completion" (133).

During or before the pregnancy, there is a prophecy, in the form of a dream or oracle, cautioning against his birth and usually threatening danger to the father (or his representative). Milkman's birth is heralded by the suicidal leap from the top of Mercy Hospital by an insurance salesman wearing blue wings who lands on a velvet rose-petal-strewn and snow-blanketed pavement; his "flight" is accompanied by Pilate's song of Sugarman/Solomon: "*O Sugarman done fly away/Sugarman done gone/ Sugarman cut across the sky/Sugarman gone home.*" Born the next day, Milkman becomes the first black child born in Mercy.

As a rule, he is surrendered to the water, in a box. Modernizing the monomyth, Morrison changes the element from water to air, thereby sustaining both the folktale's belief in a group of blacks who could fly and her hero's lineage; for in addition to the belief that Solomon could fly, even Milkman's grandfather, when shot to death, "was blown off a fence five feet into the air." The suicide's oracular leap from Mercy (his note declaring that he would "fly away on my own wings") signals the birth of Milkman, as though he, like his grandfather, drops from the sky. Because of the hero's potential threat, the father traditionally maims the infant before abandoning him; the result, the limping hero, is mirrored in the uneven length of Milkman's legs: "he acquired movements and habits to disguise what to him was a burning defect" (62).

He is then saved by animals, or by lowly people (shepherds). Milkman is repeatedly saved by lowly women: Pilate, Ruth, Circe, Sweet, and Susan Byrd—of whom more anon.

He is suckled by a female animal or by a humble woman. Macon's rejection of Ruth's affection demotes her from "queen" to humble woman, for which loss she compensates by suckling her son into his fourth year, the discovery of which yields his nickname of Milkman.

After he has grown up, he finds his distinguished parents, in a highly versatile fashion. Milkman's quest to Danville, Pennsylvania, and to Shalimar ("pronounced *Shalleemone*"), Virginia, results not in the gold his father led him to expect he would find, but in the treasure of discovering his lineage, of unraveling the knotted mysteries that hid from him the legendary lineaments and mythic prowess of his ancestors. "Versatile fashion" generously allows for Milkman's episodes with Sweet, Circe, and Susan Byrd, as well as his nocturnal hunt with the four elders of Shalimar.

He takes revenge on his father, on the one hand, and is acknowledged on the other. Milkman's journey and discoveries further free him from his father's grasping anality and fixation on respectability; this implies his revenge in the forms of his total repudiation of Macon Dead's obsessive capitalism, his esteem of Pilate's regard and values (eschewed by his father), and his scorn for the hate-steeped, vindictive racism of a surrogate father, Guitar. Acknowledgment comes with the special favors of Circe, Sweet, and Susan Byrd; with Hagar's death, symbolically lamenting the permanent loss of her lover; with Guitar's fanatic resolve to slay him as a scapegoat; and with Pilate's journeying with him to bury the bones of her father atop Solomon's Leap.

Finally, he achieves rank and honors. Milkman accepts the heritage of his ancestors and lays claim to rank among them with his novel-ending plunge from Solomon's Leap, having earned such rank by solving the mystery of the bones Pilate long carried with her and hung from the ceiling of her home for three decades.

Although Morrison follows each of the road signs along the map of Rank's monomyth, she obscures that map by blurring the dates of the novel's events and, more important, undercuts its conventional celebration of the role of the hero in our culture.[6] Shrewdly, she mocks the novel's men, especially its alleged hero. She finds little value in Ruth's father, Dr. Foster, the image-proud black professional. Despite his stature as "the most important Negro in the city" (22) and his reputation among some whites as a "miracle-doctor" (65), he does little to better the plight of his fellow blacks, regarding himself as having risen above them. The wealth he accumulates goes into four different banks, into a "great big house," into expensive clothing in which to dress his only daughter, and into the two-horse carriage that makes him the "second man in the city" (71) to own one. His son-in-law, Macon Dead, vilifies him as incestuous toward his daughter, contemptuous toward his granddaughters (because born without their mother's lemon-yellow skin), and hypocritical toward the "Negroes in the town [who] worshipped him": "He didn't give a damn about them, though. Called them cannibals" (71). Biased though Macon's view is, even Ruth owns her father's arrogance and destructiveness (124).

Morrison more savagely mocks Macon Dead, the acquisitive black. Property owner and land developer, his ruthlessness with delinquent tenants, his fixation on caste and respectability, his intractable notion of Ruth's relationship with her father, and his greed in encouraging Milkman and Guitar to steal what he assumes is gold in his sister's suspended green tarp—all tally to label him Freud's classic anal-retentive personality: parsimonious, obstinate, and compulsively orderly. Guitar, the vindictive racist whose membership in the brotherhood of the Seven Days feeds racial hatred, gets Morrison's scorn, too. Self-denying though he is, ready to sacrifice personal pleasure for the cause of the secret society, Morrison aligns him with Macon and Dr. Foster as one more pathetic—if not neurotically hollow—man, no model of manhood for white or black.

Nor is Milkman. Titular hero though his fit with Rank's criteria makes him, he too is an intolerable egotist.[7] True, he strikes out at his father, presumably in defense of his mother. But more typically, he "almost never thought about her" (69). And after a fourteen-year relationship with Hagar, he naively believes—at thirty-one years of age!—that he can decently end it by sending her money in a thank-you note. Indeed, as Guitar tells him, he is not a "serious person" (104), and as Pilate tells both Ruth and Hagar, Milkman "wouldn't give a pile of swan shit for either of you" (138).

But what of his heroic quest? On the face of it, Milkman's adventures in Danville and Shalimar, which make up the bulk of the novel's second half, surely heed the rule that the hero's discovery of "his distinguished parent[age]" be in "a highly versatile

fashion." It is with rich invention that Morrison unfolds the ordeals of Milkman's journeys. He withstands the stench of the dog-
befouled, decaying Butler home where the supposedly dead,
supra-100-year-old Circe embraces him and plays gothic cicerone
to his ancestry. He overcomes the mortifyingly minor mishaps of
his trek to the cave where he expects to find gold. He survives
the knife-and-broken-bottle fight in Shalimar. He aborts Guitar's
homicidal attempt on his life during the coon-become-bobcat
hunt with King Walker's elders. And be wrestles with the nursery
rhyme, whose meaning his visits with Susan Byrd help him finally
to decipher.

Material though this all is for a hero's adventures—and for
the epiphanies and knowledge expected of such a hero—its subtext is satiric.[8] Beneath all of these episodes resonates a malice-
tinged chuckle, delight in humbling the hero. Watch his face twist
as he tries not to inhale the fetid dog stench during his interview
with Circe. See his composure go slack when she scolds him:
"You don't listen to people. Your ear is on your head, but it's not
connected to your brain. . . . If you think I stay on here because
I loved [Mrs. Butler], then you have about as much sense as a
fart!" (249). Look at his mouth, pulling wide with fastidious disgust during his search for the gold. After removing his shoes and
socks and rolling up his cuffs to ford the shallow stream between
him and the cave in the distance, he gets a complete dunking,
and then, in the cave, he soils himself on the bat shit on its walls
and the dirt of its floor—on which he must crawl in darkness,
groping to find and feel all around the wide hole in which the
gold allegedly waits. The aftermath to this cloacal interlude re-
stores little dignity, for he returns to Danville like some vaudeville
character, his flopping sole tied to his shoe. Milkman survives the
knife-and-broken-bottle skirmish in Shalimar, but the episode
documents less his combative prowess than his stupidity, insensitive to the blacks upon whose culture he has intruded. And his
nocturnal hunt with the elders who gather at King Walker's finds
him as unfit for a test of physical endurance as Susan Byrd's
crosstalk and the schoolchildren's nursery rhyme find him slow
at feats of intellectual penetration.

Should the satiric subtext slip past her readers, Morrison repeatedly invites a fundamental question of her hero: does he do anything to warrant that honorific? Alas, little. Like Dr. Foster, Macon Dead, and Guitar, Milkman has the potential to become a hero—though perhaps not a Rankian one. But just as their self-centered, goal-dominated ambitions reflect warped forms of self-aggrandizement so, too, do Milkman's journey and discovery of his parentage end in attempts at self-glorification. Indeed he learns some truth about his past. And he shares that truth with Pilate, to whose credit it is that her father's bones, which she has unwittingly honored for threescore years, will be given fit burial on Solomon's Leap. But Milkman's discovery of his lineage is little more than an intoxicant to gratify his wish for some grandiose illusion—that in his gene pool lies the birdlike ability to soar. Upon that illusion he acts in his novel-ending leap into the arms of his assailant, the psychopathic Guitar.[9]

Morrison's prose seems to celebrate that illusion, enough so that most readers mistake her irony for endorsement.[10] But beneath the positive thrust of her imaginative prose and the seemingly upbeat ending of her novel lies Morrison's disdain for Milkman because of what he fails to learn on his journey—that in his gene pool also swims the congenital habit of desertion. The nursery rhyme changed by the Shalimar schoolchildren indicts Solomon as a feckless father for abandoning the woman from whose womb he has fathered twenty-one children, Ryna: "*O Solomon don't leave me here / Cotton balls to choke me / Solomon don't leave me here / Bukra's arms to yoke me*" (307). Likewise did Jake Solomon desert his adoptive mother, Heddy Byrd, whom he left to go north with Sing, as did Macon Dead desert both his sister in the cave and his wife to her own bed; Milkman's desertion of Hagar, then, honors the tradition of the man's prerogative—to escape domestication, to fly from responsibilities, in the name of self-fulfillment or self-discovery or self-indulgence. Waking to find himself tied up on Pilate's cellar floor, Milkman realizes that Hagar's death must account for Pilate's act of knocking him senseless with a wet bottle when he returned from Shalimar: "Sweet's silvery voice came back to him: 'Who'd he leave behind?' " He even recalls Jake

Solomon's commandment to Pilate, "You just can't fly on off and leave a body." But Milkman assigns himself no culpability: "What difference did [Hagar's death] make? He had hurt her, left her, and now she was dead—He was certain of it. He had left her" (336). So when Milkman leaps at the novel's end into Guitar's arms and certain death, his act is but one more gesture of irresponsibility; he flies, indeed, from the burdens of doing something meaningful in life, preferring the sumptuous illusion that he will ride the air.

By appropriating Rank's monomyth, tailoring her hero to fit its criteria, and then bringing us close to see the incongruity of her thirty-two-year-old wearing a suit leagues larger than he, Morrison continues the ambiguous and ambivalent analysis of myths on which all of her novels pivot. But if she holds her hero up to a set of criteria only to ridicule him—albeit subtly—she also resists the temptation to use her novel as a feminist platform for celebrating wholesale its women. Rather, she alternates the current of her attitude toward them, portraying a spectrum from pathetic to praiseworthy. Most pathetic is Hagar. As if it were not enough to carry the biblical burden of her name—concubine to patriarchal Abraham, mother to outcast Ishmael, and handmaiden to jealous Sarah—she is utterly resourceless in a crisis. Forsaken by Milkman, she becomes obsessively jealous, impotently vindictive, and, most pathetic of all, deluded with the notion that the acquisition of allegedly beautifying commodities will magically repossess Milkman.[11] Less pathetic is Magdalene called Lena, doomed to spinster-hood by her father's pretensions and her own resignation to her role as her mother's guardian: "I didn't go to college because of [father]. Because I was afraid of what he might do to Mama" (217). In Morrison's spectrum Lena's ascendancy over her niece Hagar is due to her refusal to accept her role meekly. Discovering that Milkman has told their father of First Corinthians' affair with a man far beneath the caste of the Deads—a delinquent tenant, to boot—she confronts Milkman in the scene that ends the first part of the novel. Forceful and partially gratuitous (certainly signaling some personal anger in Morrison's own life), Lena's speech gathers women's deepest domestic resentments against men, heroes or not, berating Milkman for his pampered arrogance, his notions of domestic noblesse oblige, his obtuse chauvinism, and his utter insensitivity to his sisters' suppressed lives:

> Our girlhood was spent like a found nickel on you. When you slept we were quiet; when you were hungry, we cooked; when you wanted to play, we entertained you; and when you got grown enough to know the difference between a woman and a two-toned Ford, everything in this house stopped for you. You have yet to wash your underwear, spread a bed, wipe the ring from your tub, or move a fleck of your dirt from one place to another. And to this day, you have never asked one of us if we were tired, or sad, or wanted a cup of coffee. You've never picked up anything heavier than your own feet, or solved a problem harder than fourth-grade arithmetic. Where do you get the *right* to decide our lives? (216–217)

Like Hagar's overreaction to the loss of Milkman, Lena's deep-seated resentment against men underscores Morrison's disdain of heroes and hero worship.

Ruth Foster Dead seems little more than a weak replica of her biblical namesake, exemplar of dutiful, self-abnegating obedience, certainly no candidate for praise. Yet Ruth's small-scale concerns show her carving some minimal means of sustenance and significance for her life: "content to do tiny things," she nurtures "small life that would not hurt her if it died: rhododendron, goldfish, dahlias, geraniums, imperial tulips" (64). More, she knows how to avenge herself on her husband: "it may have been that suspicion of personal failure and rejection (plus a smidgen of revenge against Macon) that made her lead her husband down paths from which there was no exit save violence. . . . but of helplessness" (64). Ruth's minor, domestic triumphs over her pigheaded, repressive husband encourage First Corinthians' rebellion against the ingrained snobbery of her father's expectations. Secretly she gets a job as a maid and, at forty-five, begins an affair that leads to a marriage that emancipates her from domestic bondage, even though it might enslave her to another.[12] Deserving greater praise is Circe. Overcoming the infamy of her classical namesake and her identity as lifelong slave to ruthless gentry, her sedentary, cloistered passivity has led neighbors to assume her dead. Among them she is legendary, both for her midwifery (she "Delivered everybody," her only loss in childbirth being Sing) and for her role as avenger: "any evening up left to do, Circe took care of" (235). But little do her neighbors know how committed she is to "evening up." Milkman's visit discovers that she survives in the old Butler mansion, breeding Weimaraners to bring on the home the ruination and rot that characterized its owners, moral swine, in Circe's eyes.

But it is on Pilate that Morrison devotes her celebratory prose. Despite the stigma of her name and her own reputation and appearance as a "raggedy bootlegger," Morrison assigns her uncanny powers. Miraculously born, she springs to life from the womb of her already-dead mother, Sing, and has no navel to show for her birth, spooking all who later discover her scarlessness. Bereft of father, abandoned by brother, and routinely ostracized by blacks who learn of her lack of navel, her odyssey of twenty-three years before arriving in Michigan with daughter and granddaughter makes child's play of Milkman's journeys. Intuitively sensing the harm to Ruth of Macon's decade-long abstinence, Pilate concocts an aphrodisiac that brings him to Ruth's bed. Her voodoo doll halts his attempts to abort Ruth's pregnancy, and her song to the rhyme of Sugarman/Solomon outside Mercy Hospital accompanies the blue-winged angel's descent to a snow-blanketed pavement strewn with red-velvet rose petals, the event that presages Milkman's birth. She rescues not only her daughter, Reba, from a beating by a casual lover (93–94), but also Milkman and Guitar from arrest by "her Aunt Jermima act" (211), vouching that their theft of her green tarp of bones was but a joke on an old lady, quoting chapter and verse from the Bible, and virtually shrinking to make her act credible. Around her have gathered fabulous beliefs: that she has "the power to step out of her skin, set a bush afire from fifty yards, and turn a man into a ripe rutabaga" (94). And as though by some preternatural sense, she had returned to Danville three years after the murder of her father and unwittingly gathered up his bones, bones which she properly buries, just before she is slain. Despite the comic tilt to the nimbus that hovers over her (sometimes her mind arrived "at the revelations of a three-year-old" [149]), undeniable is her nurturant power, the quality shared by several of the novel's women—Circe, Sweet, Susan Byrd, and Mary, the barmaid/part-owner of "the bar/lounge that did the best business in the Blood Bank" (84).

For feminists expecting Morrison to fashion some outsized heroine of Wagnerian stature, Pilate is as much a disappointment as Milkman should be for critics who find heroic lineaments in him. As one feminist articulates the case against Pilate, she "originates" nothing, lacks "conscious knowledge," and has an "oddly garbled" "sense of mission."[13] Yet Pilate is a "culture bearer," someone whose primary function is to sustain the durable human values of the past, not to be a trend-setter who innovates newfangled values or models or standards.[14] No rural throwback who lives on the margins of modern society, Pilate inherits our celebrated American tradition of individualism, and she challenges and rejects her society's values by living in its very midst, refusing to retreat from it. Indeed, her actions repeatedly show that she chooses to reject the idea of "originating" something, a masculine goal that leads to such dehumanizing gods as exploitative capitalism (Macon Dead), racist vindictiveness (the Seven Days), commercial enslavement (Hagar), and escapist fantasy (Milkman). Abandoned by brother and lovers, shunned by neighbors, she overcomes adversity and rejection without recrimination or self-pity. Resourceful and independent, she scorns civilized creature comforts, ekes out a satisfying life for herself, Reba, and Hagar, and protects herself and those she cares for in times of crisis— as when she rescues Reba from the abusing lover. No passive woman, she intercedes when occasion warrants, helping the desperate Ruth to conceive and deliver Milkman. But unlike her predecessor—the meddling, managerial, and matriarchal Eva Peace of *Sula*—after Milkman's birth it only takes her brother's signal for Pilate to walk away from his house bearing no resentment, jealousy, or wish for sibling harmony: she had "respect for other people's privacy" (150).

"Wide-spirited," she lays no guilt trip on Milkman, never telling him of her role in his birth, never insinuating any debt he owes her. Nor does Pilate meddle in her granddaughter's life, despite the consequences and the criticism she has received for not guiding Hagar more than she does.[15] But Pilate knows well the hazard of trying to teach others her values, shows by the example of how she lives what it is that she values, letting the results be what they will; besides, the responsibility to raise Hagar is primarily Reba's, not Pilate's. Finally, since no amount of parental guidance guarantees the values one's offspring will acquire, to fault Pilate for Hagar's death exposes the judgmental attitude of someone looking for a scapegoat. Despite Pilate's refusal to be her homonym, a pilot, her lack of meddlesomeness in how Hagar lives her life reflects no indifference on her part, as her behavior at Hagar's funeral shows. To Reba's spontaneous obbligato, she chants, "Mercy," sings "the very same reassurance she had promised her when she was a little girl," speaks to each person at the funeral, calling Hagar "my baby girl," and then, "suddenly, like an elephant who has just found his anger and lifts his trunk over the heads of the little men who want his teeth or his hide or his flesh or his amazing strength, Pilate trumpeted for the sky itself to hear, 'And she was loved!' " (323).

Lack of "conscious knowledge," presumably a major flaw in Pilate's character, also seems to ask that she fit some masculine, rational model. But it matters not whether the bones she has carried to Michigan are those of a husband (as she tells the policemen), of a murdered white man (as she believes), or of a father (as Milkman informs her). What matters is her regard of the bones as symbols of an obligation to a past event and a human relationship. She misunderstands her father's "posthumous communication," "Sing. Sing." For she hears it as his injunction for her to sing, rather than as his crying out his wife's name. But singing, "which she did beautifully, relieved her gloom immediately" (148), showing that her ignorance of one meaning of her father's words did not render worthless another meaning. More, it is arguable whether she lacks "conscious knowledge," for whether by intuition, induction, or deduction, she knows of Hagar's hunger, of Macon's attempts to abort Milkman, of the imminence of Ruth's delivery, and of Milkman's and Guitar's need of her false testimony at the police station. Finally, Pilate repeatedly addresses the rudimentary problems that face her existence, solving them with intelligence and "a deep concern for and about human relationships" (150): "she tackled the problem of trying to decide how she wanted to live and what was valuable to her. When am I happy and when am I sad and what is the difference? What do I need to know to stay alive? What is true in the world? Her mind traveled crooked streets and aimless goat paths, arriving sometimes at profundity, other times at the revelations of a three-year-old" (149).

Her mission, far from "oddly garbled," can be dealt with briefly. Her mission is exemplary, because it is nothing less than to live her life in manifest repudiation of the grasping ambitiousness and obsessive desires of those around her, who end up as grotesques, fanatics, neurotics, or fantasists. Pilate hungers not for family dynasty, for domestic respectability, for the authority of some Big House Mammy, or even for others' regard. Her heroism resides in her self-acceptance and self-content, the heroism of performing routine responsibilities without fretting about whether she is "macon" something of her life. Add to that her old-fashioned, simple ethic of love: "Watch Reba for me," she tells Milkman with her last breath. "I wish I'd a knowed more people. I would of loved 'em all. If I'd a knowed more, I would a loved more" (340).

History, literature, and life ask us to bestow adulation upon heroes elevated by fictions that burnish their images and airbrush their defects. Morrison understands our human need to augment our lives with heroes capable of expressing the deeper wishes and ambitions and possibilities of our kind. But she also mocks the bizarre caricatures that humans become in imitating such heroes, pities the warped behavior in which emulation of them results. While for some it may not be enough to model oneself after Pilate, better that than after someone silly enough to thrill to the notion that the capacity to fly is important.

Notes

1. Julius Lester, *Black Folktales* (New York: Grove, 1970), 147–52.

2. Most studies of *Song of Solomon* remark on Morrison's use of myth, the majority using the term loosely or citing such general features as those of Jung's or Campbell's departure-initiation-return cycle: Jacqueline de Weever, "Toni Morrison's Use of Fairy Tale, Folk Tale, and Myth in *Song of Solomon,*" *Southern Folklore Quarterly* 44 (1980): 131–44; A. Leslie Harris, "Myth as Structure in Toni Morrison's *Song of Solomon,*" *MELUS* 7 (1980): 69–76; Norris Clark, "Flying Black: Toni Morrison's *The Bluest Eye, Sula* and *Song of Solomon,*" *Minority Voices* 4 (1980): 51–63; Jane S. Bakerman, "Failures of Love: Female Initiation in the Novels of Toni Morrison," *American Literature* 52 (1981): 541–63; Charles Scruggs. "The Nature of Desire in Toni Morrison's *Song of Solomon,*" *Arizona Quarterly* 38 (1982): 311–335; Dorothy H. Lee, "*Song of Solomon*: To Ride the Air," *Black American Literature Forum* 16 (1982): 64–70; and Cynthia A. Davis, "Self, Society, and Myth in Toni Morrison's Fiction," *Contemporary Literature* 23 (1982): 323–42. The exception to such general use of the term is Wilfred D. Samuels, "Liminality and the Search for Self in *Toni Morrison's Song of Solomon,*" *Minority Voices* 5 (1981): 59–68, but Samuels's, discussion, which details the particulars of the rites of passage identified by Lord Raglan's *The Hero* and two more recent books on the matter, loses Morrison's novel in a forest of scholarly—if not pedantic—apparatus.

3. Both Bakerman, in "Failures of Love," and Davis, "Self, Society, and Myth," find Pilate too flawed for such a role, pp. 554–58 and pp. 337–41, respectively. And Scruggs, "Nature of Desire," finds her pathetic, p. 321. But see Nellie McKay, "An Interview with Toni Morrison," *Contemporary Literature* 24 (1983): 418–22, for Morrison's own valuation of Pilate.

4. For Rank's essay, first published in 1914, see *The Myth of the Birth of the Hero and Other Writings,* ed. Philip Freund (New York: Random House, 1959), 14–96. The summary of traits appears on p. 65.

5. All quotations in my text are from the Signet 1978 paperback edition of *Song of Solomon*, page numbers parenthesized.

6. In her interview with Nellie McKay, Morrison makes a statement which may make readers duly skeptical of my argument that she appropriates Rank's monomyth: "Other kinds of structures are imposed on my works, and therefore they are either praised or dismissed on the basis of something that I have no interest in whatever, which is writing a novel according to some structure that comes out of a different culture" (425). Perhaps this statement is in response to Samuels's essay and the "twenty-two elements" of Lord Raglan's heroic pattern or rites of

passage which guide his discussion. Whether she has any interest in Rank's monomyth, of course, is for my readers to decide.

7. Samuels, Scruggs, Lee, and Davis (see note 2) argue the authenticity of Milkman's heroic stature, although Davis, pp. 333–37, chafes at doing so.

8. Scruggs, "Nature of Desire," argues differently, attributing to Milkman two epiphanies and the completion of his "moral education," pp. 331–32. Also acknowledging his pair of epiphanies is Elizabeth B. House, " 'The Sweet Life' in Toni Morrison's Fiction," *American Literature* 56 (1984): 196.

9. In her interview with Nellie McKay, Morrison maintains that Milkman's novel-ending act does "something important" with what he has learned (428): "Milkman's hope, almost a conviction, has to be that he can be like [Pilate]" (421), for he "is willing to die at the end, and the person he is willing to die for is a woman [Pilate]" (419). With all due respect to the author's interpretation of her character, it seems that her intention to convey her idea of Milkman's motives either failed to be achieved by her prose or came aground upon the counterintention of her possibly unconscious hostility toward him. More than she herself may realize, her statement in McKay's interview may apply to this discrepancy: "In all the history of black women . . . we have been both the ship and the harbor. . . . We can do things one at a time, or four things at a time if we have to" (413; second ellipsis McKay's).

10. Bakerman, "Failures of Love," also notes that "Milkman's quest is ironically successful" (554).

11. See Susan Willis, "Eruptions of Funk: Historicizing Toni Morrison." *Black American Literature Forum* 16 (1982): 34–42, for Hagar's "bourgeois reification and commodity consumption."

12. Bakerman, "Failures of Love," regards First Corinthians as the only woman in the novel who achieves a slim "chance for even modified happiness" (563).

13. These criteria are from Davis, "Self, Society, and Myth," 339. Bakerman, "Failure of Love," also finds against Pilate, claiming that she's ill-equipped for success, a failure (556), but her discussion of the shortcomings of Pilate, Hagar, and First Corinthians are not overtly feminist.

14. The term "culture bearer," like that of "wide-spirited," is Morrison's even though she does not use the first to describe Pilate; see McKay, "Interview," pp. 415, 418.

15. To Bakerman, "The failure of Pilate's life foreshadows Hagar's tragedy" ("Failures of Love," 556).

Part III

♦ ♦ ♦

NARRATIVE INFLUENCE

Doe Hunting and Masculinity

Song of Solomon *and* Go Down, Moses

JOHN N. DUVALL

◆　◆　◆

> ... not *Lucius Quintus* @c @c @c, but *Lucas Quintus*, not refusing to be called Lucius, because he simply eliminated that word from the name, not denying, declining the name itself, because he used three quarters of it; but simply taking the name and changing, altering it, making no longer the white man's but his own, by himself composed, himself self-progenitive and nominate, by himself ancestored.
>
> —William Faulkner, *Go Down, Moses*

> Surely, he thought, he and his sister had some ancestor, some lithe young man with onyx skin and legs as straight as cane stalks, who had a name that was real. A name given to him at birth with love and seriousness.
>
> —Toni Morrison, *Song of Solomon*

W E A R E N O T S U R P R I S E D when we discover traces of classical mythology, slave narratives, or biblical poetry in *Song of Solomon*.[1] Yet to speak of the way a text of Toni Morrison and one of William Faulkner enter into dialogue is to run a decided risk of a racism that conjures up vivid images of domination in our American past. Are you not, after all, implying that without this white, southern male's seminal text, that of the African-American woman would never have come to fruition?

But in positing an intertextual relation between *Song of Solomon* and *Go Down, Moses*, I am not granting the latter any privilege as master text.[2] The critical dialogue in which *Song of Solomon* engages *Go Down, Moses* suggests rather that Morrison's novel reclaims Faulkner's in ways that question the male-centered world of the hunt and that refuse the gambit of tragedy.

In 1955, as a master's student at Cornell, Toni Morrison completed her thesis, "Virginia Woolf's and William Faulkner's Treatment of the Alienated." The thesis stands as a piece of intellectual autobiography that provides a glimpse into the development of her novelistic imagination. Morrison's sixteen-page Faulker chapter focuses on Thomas Sutpen and Quentin Compson.[3] In *Absalom, Absalom!* and *The Sound and the Fury*, Morrison sees "elements of Greek tragedy," such as "the fall of a once great house" and "old family guilts inherited by an heir"; moreover, "the fact that incest plays such an important part . . . is evidence that Faulkner patterns these histories after the Greeks."[4]

Morrison's characterization of *Absalom* and *The Sound and the Fury* also accurately describes Isaac McCaslin's alienation from his past as he comes of age in a defeated South and discovers in the ledgers the horror of his grandfather's incest and miscegenation. Her own character, Milkman Dead in *Song of Solomon*, similarly comes of age alienated from his family history, almost as a result, one might say, of patriarchs such as Lucius Quintus Carothers McCaslin, whose forced mixture of the races in Mississippi results in the lighter-skinned African Americans accorded special status in Milkman Dead's Michigan. In other words, Ike's family problem, as he confronts the racism of the white community, is too much history; Milkman's difficulty in seeing the racism within the African-American community (at least in part I) is not enough. But while *Go Down, Moses* is another tragedy (inasmuch as Roth Edmonds repeats his great-great-great-grandfather's incestuous miscegenation, the act that motivated Isaac's repudiation in the first place), *Song of Solomon*, although similarly structured by intergenerational repetitions, finds Milkman ultimately breaking free of certain destructive cycles of the Dead family and patriarchal social organization.

A number of other parallels invites a consideration of these two narratives together. In both novels, the male protagonists apparently come to some transcendent moment while hunting, for hunting is something more than the literal stalking of animals; the hunted animals in both are totemic substitutes for characters. Both novels blur boundaries between the natural and supernatural worlds. But perhaps most important, the creation of the adult subjectivity of Isaac McCaslin in *Go Down, Moses* and Milkman Dead in *Song of Solomon* serves as the site of conflict and competition. Certainly those who struggle to create Isaac's and Milkman's subjectivities bear certain parallels. Macon Dead, for example, approximates McCaslin Edmonds, while Guitar and Pilate split the function of Sam Fathers.[5]

In *Go Down, Moses*, McCaslin Edmonds speaks with the paternal voice of the Old South, inviting Isaac to take his rightful place in L.Q.C., McCaslin's patriarchal design. Similarly, Macon hopes to create in Milkman a son who will approve of the middle-class values Macon has adopted. Undoubtedly, Macon's perspective on life is best summarized in his words to his twelve-year-old son upon finding that Milkman has disobeyed him by visiting Pilate:

> After school come to my office; work a couple of hours there and learn what's real. Pilate can't teach you a thing you can use in this world. Maybe the next, but not this one. Let me tell you right now the one important thing you'll ever need to know: Own things. And let the things you own own other things. Then you'll own yourself and other people too.[6]

Macon's teachings are subverted, however, from two directions— by his sister Pilate and by Milkman's friend Guitar—and their presence together seems to constitute a play on Sam Fathers. Both act as Milkman's guides to ostensibly different world pictures— Pilate, the part-Indian advocate of the rights of ghosts, and Guitar, the materialist who wishes to awaken Milkman to African Americans' real conditions of existence. Although Macon, the bourgeois fetishizer of material, seems to recognize the threat Pilate poses to his desire to shape his son, the unacknowledged threat that resides in Guitar's friendship with Milkman forms the basis of much of the novel's plot.

Guitar Baines, removed from the well-heeled world of Not Doctor Street, acts as Milkman's guide to the wilderness of Southside, where the African-American underclass lives. The novel's opening underscores the importance Guitar will have as Milkman's guide and mentor. When Milkman's mother, Ruth, goes into labor, Guitar is sent around to the emergency room to fetch help (*Song* 7). Later, at age seventeen, Guitar befriends the twelve-year-old Milkman, and from that time on, Guitar is always there for his young friend. That the older boy befriends a younger one is unusual, but the friendship is odder still when we recall that approximately seven years earlier Macon turned Guitar's family out on the street for not paying the rent.

Why, then, does Guitar want to claim Milkman? As a member of the Seven Days, a secret society that hunts down and kills whites for the murders of African Americans that go unnoticed by white justice, Guitar is forbidden to marry and will never have a son. Milkman represents the possibility of creating an ideological heir, just as the Indian Sam Fathers sees Ike as the hope for a spiritual heir. The childless and dispossessed Fathers effects a refiliation by subverting the teachings of McCaslin, offering instead both practical and mystical knowledge of the wilderness. In effect, Sam has managed to make an heir of a member of the dominant class that dispossessed the Chickasaws; as a consequence of Ike's appropriating the Indian world picture, he repudiates his white past and patrimony. Guitar's coup would be just as great as Sam's were he to succeed. Milkman's status as a member of the African-American middle class makes him an attractive conquest to Guitar. What finer ideological offspring could Guitar wish for than the son of the man who dispossessed the Baines family? What's at stake, then, in Macon's and Guitar's struggle to claim Milkman is whether Milkman will grow up to be "white" or "black"; that is, will Milkman accept the values of the African-American middle class, which sees a possible assimilation into middle-class American culture, or will he cast his lot with the African-American community?

One particular moment in which Guitar tries to comfort his friend occurs after Milkman strikes Macon for hitting Ruth, Milkman's mother. Guitar's sympathy takes the form of a brief narrative based on his hunting experience:

> Anyway I stayed on the trail until I saw some bushes. The light was good and all of a sudden I saw a rump between the branches. I dropped it with the first shot and finished it with the second. Now, I want to tell you I was feeling good. I saw myself showing my uncles what I'd caught. But when I got up to it—and I was going real slow because I thought I might have to shoot it again—I saw it was a doe. I felt . . . bad. You know what I mean? I killed a doe. A doe, man. . . .
>
> So I know how you felt when you saw your father hit your mother. It's like that doe. A man shouldn't do that. You couldn't help what you felt. (86)

Guitar's story would certainly be understood by Ike McCaslin, who knows that one does not kill does because they, more than bucks, ensure that there will be deer to kill in the future. But in "Delta Autumn," doe hunting takes on a number of meanings. For one of the men, it's a way to tease Roth Edmonds about the young African-American woman with whom Edmonds has had an affair. Does, however, take on a different significance for Ike in the context of America's involvement in World War II: "It's a good time to mention does. . . . Does and fawns both. The only fighting anywhere that ever had anything of God's blessing on it has been when men fought to protect does and fawns."[7] But from the protection of women and children, the metaphor returns by the story's end to the specificity of the young African-American woman. After learning that his kinsman Roth Edmonds has repeated the very act—incestuous miscegenation—that caused him, Ike, to repudiate his patrimony, the old man intuits that the deer Roth has killed is a doe.

In both *Go Down, Moses* and *Song of Solomon*, then, killing a doe also means hurting an African-American woman. Yet in Guitar's realization that Milkman does not grasp the metaphor ("Chances were Milkman didn't even know what a doe was" [86]), there seems a kind of wry intertextual gloss that calls into question the efficacy of the metaphor, a metaphor that suggests that the female's safety depends upon the honor of the good male hunters. In particular, Guitar's metaphor sheds a different light on his membership in the Seven Days.

I would like to approach an understanding of Guitar's involvement in the Seven Days somewhat obliquely, holding in suspension the doe-hunting metaphor and drawing temporarily on a different metaphor—that of urinating. On one of the Dead family's weekly Sunday drives when Milkman is a little boy, he asks his father to stop so that he can relieve himself. Milkman's sister Lena accompanies the boy. She returns in tears because Milkman has peed on her (34–35). By itself the moment is not significant. After all, sometimes a cigar is just a cigar and sometimes even a penis is just a penis. But at the end of part I, Lena, more than twenty-five years later, recalls the moment for Milkman and turns it into a metaphor for the thoughtless way he has treated the women of the family, since "there are all kinds of ways to pee on people" (215):

> You've been laughing at us all your life. Corinthians. Mama. Me. Using us, ordering us, and judging us. . . . You don't know a single thing about either one of us—we made roses; that's all you knew—but now you know what's best for the very woman who wiped the dribble from your chin because you were too young to know how to spit. Our girlhood was spent like a found nickel on you. When you slept, we were quiet; when you were hungry, we cooked; when you wanted to play, we entertained you; and when you got grown enough to know the difference between a woman and a two-toned Ford, everything in this house stopped for you. You have yet to wash your underwear, spread a bed, wipe the ring from your tub, or move a fleck of your dirt from one place to another. And to this day, you have never asked one of us if we were tired, or sad, or wanted a cup of coffee. You've never picked up anything heavier than your own feet, or solved a problem

harder than fourth-grade arithmetic. Where do you get the *right* to decide our lives? (217)

When Milkman fails to answer the question, Lena continues: "I'll tell you where. From that little hog's gut that hangs between your legs" (217). Something more than Milkman's literal phallus, however, grants him authority within the family, and Lena recognizes this too. Again we are pointed back to the moment when Milkman strikes his father. Lena concludes: "You are exactly like him. . . . You think because you hit him once that we all believe you were protecting [our mother]. Taking her side. It's a lie. You were taking over, letting us know you had the right to tell her and all of us what to do" (217). The reproduction of the father function and the preservation of patriarchal privilege reside in Milkman's striking Macon. By hitting his father, Milkman claims his privilege as an adult male to control and select the sexuality of "his" women.[8] Lena's anger boils over in this moment, after all, because Milkman has determined that it is inappropriate for his sister Corinthians to see Porter. Although Milkman might have a legitimate reason for his objection to Porter (namely, his involvement with the Seven Days), Milkman goes about breaking off his sister's relationship in a heavy-handed way, telling Macon, and thus, once again, aligning himself with the father's authority.

Milkman is not the only male in Morrison's novel who pees on women. In fact we see all three men in conflict over Corinthians—Milkman, Macon, and Porter—in moments of urination. When Macon discovers the gold of the old white man he presumably has killed in the cave, he, "like a burglar out on his first job, stood up to pee" (171). Here too Macon is linked to the peacock ("luxury fanned out before him like the tail-spread of a peacock" [171]), a recurring figure that in this context suggests a pun lurking in the bird's name.[9] Macon's urinating signals the shift about to take place in his relationship with his sister Pilate. His insistence that the gold will allow them to recoup the loss of their farm in the aftermath of their father's murder meets her equally strong belief that it would be wrong to take the gold of the man Macon has just killed. This moment, in which brother and sister come to blows, creates a permanent break between the two.

Porter's act of urinating is by far the most spectacular of the three. Standing in the window of his attic apartment (an apartment Macon owns), the drunken Porter threatens suicide. His drunken shouts turn from a demand that the crowd of women "send me up somebody to fuck!" (25) to his assertion that "I love ya! I love ya all" (26). Between the former and the latter, Porter "leaned his shotgun on the window sill, pulled out his penis and in a high arc, peed over the heads of the women, making them scream and run in a panic that the shotgun had not been able to create" (25–26). Porter's mixed messages—one of self-interest, the other suggesting altruism—take on special significance when we recall that his attempted suicide results from his work as a member of the Seven Days. His ambivalent utterances, spoken in drunkenness, reveal an ideological fraternity among Porter, Macon, Milkman, and Guitar, a fraternity founded on the belief in male privilege, particularly the possession of women. Moreover, Porter's assertion to the women below that "I love ya" casts an odd light on Guitar's insistence that his killing of whites is motivated purely by love of African-American people. To link Milkman and Guitar in ideological brotherhood might seem particularly objectionable given Milkman's lack of social or race consciousness and Guitar's deep awareness of the injustices suffered by the African-American underclass. Nevertheless, the way these males position themselves in relation to the female points to a profoundly similar world picture.

In order to elucidate my meaning, we need to ask, What precisely is the Seven Days, and can we take the group at the evaluation of its members? The Seven Days began as a particular response to a particular kind of violence: "It got started in 1920, when that private from Georgia was killed after his balls were cut off and after that a veteran was blinded when he came home from France in World War I" (156). What Guitar leaves unsaid is crucial. The one man was castrated and the other blinded because white American males perceived a threat to their possession of white women. The returning veterans had experienced a radically less segregated world in France, a world in which white women would have been available to them sexually. (Indeed, Empire State, a member of the Seven Days, married a white woman while in France.) The violence against the African-American man conveyed a particular message: in the United States, one form of miscegenation, African-American men and white women, will not be tolerated. Tellingly, the kinds of crimes the Days often avenge are typically the rape of an African-American woman by a white man or the lynching of an African-American man for his interest in a white woman. At one point, the historical figure Emmett Till becomes a focal point for the men of the Days. Their discussion at Tommy's Barbershop, one might note, turns on the plight of African-American men: "Ain't no law for no colored man except the one sends him to the chair" (82).

In the Seven Days' focus on African-American men, African-American women (and hence the African-American people as a whole) tend to get lost. One of the more extended passages where we hear the teachings of Guitar Baines occurs in chapter 10. Milkman has complained that everyone in his family wants something from him, and Guitar responds:

> Look. It's the condition our condition is in. Everybody wants the life of a black man. Everybody. White men want us dead or quiet—which is the same thing as dead. White women, same thing. They want us, you know, "universal," human, no "race consciousness." Tame, except in bed. But outside the bed they want us to be individuals. You tell them, "But they lynched my papa," and they say, "Yeah, but you're better than the lynchers are, so forget it." And black women, they want your whole self. Love they call it, and understanding. "Why don't you *understand* me?" What they mean is, Don't love anything on earth except me. (224)

In Guitar's view, the African-American man is the supreme marginal figure, silenced not only by whites, but undermined and unmanned even by African-American women.[10] At this point Milkman objects to Guitar's major premise—that his violence is motivated by the love of African-American people—pointing out that "except for skin color, I can't tell the difference between what white women want from us and what the colored women want. You say they all want our life, our living life. So if a colored woman is raped and killed, why do the Days rape and kill a white woman? Why worry about the colored woman at all?" (225).

Guitar's angry response to this question cuts to the heart of the matter in much the same way as Porter's drunken shouts do, revealing a level of meaning not apparent to him: Guitar's "nostrils flared a little: 'Because she's *mine*' " (225). As the chief spokesman for the Seven Days, Guitar here makes it abundantly clear that all of the Days, not just Porter, pee on women, particularly African-American women. In his response, we see the issue of race bracketed momentarily and instead discover what is really at issue—male possession of women. Thus the Seven Days' "heroic" stance on saving the African-American race parallels Milkman's "defense" of his mother. Both are about males staking claim to woman-as-property, so that we might say that the rule of Milkman in the family or of the Days in society is one and the same—perpetuation of patriarchal authority, pea/e-cock power.

The Seven Days epitomizes patriarchal organization. The group is all male and does not permit its members to marry or to form permanent attachments with women. The very name suggests the originating authority of the monotheistic God the Father of the West, who created the heavens and earth in six days and rested on the seventh.[11] But there is no rest for the Seven Days (Guitar's day is the Christian sabbath) in its unarticulated effort to establish masculinity as violent mastery and manhood as the right to say what one's women do. African-American male violence does not simply imitate white male violence; the former *self-consciously* imitates the latter, as Guitar's explanation of the Days' eye-for-an-eye numbers game illustrates (115). Thus, the unrecognized mission of the Seven Days seems to be the following: if white male violence works to keep African-American men from white women, then African-American men need to organize to ensure continued property rights in African-American women.

Guitar's emphatic reason for "protecting" African-American women ("Because she's *mine*") resonates with another moment in *Go Down, Moses*. In part 5 of "The Bear," a year and a half after the deaths of Sam Fathers, Lion, and Ben, Ike goes one last time to the hunting camp before the timber company to which Major DeSpain has sold the timber rights begins to denude the area. On his way to meet Boon under a sweetgum tree in a clearing, Ike encounters a huge rattlesnake, over six feet long, that he addresses as Sam in "The Old People" had addressed the spirit of the big buck six years earlier: " 'Chief,' he said: 'Grandfather' " (330). This address prepares us for what we suppose will be another transcendent moment where Ike communes with his ideological parent, Sam Fathers. However, the part-Chickasaw he next sees is the inept hunter Boon, sitting under the gum tree with his disassembled rifle, while in the tree, forty or fifty squirrels are trapped with no chance of escape. Boon shouts at the approaching figure that he does not recognize as Ike: "Get out of here! Dont touch them! Dont touch a one of them! They're mine!" (331). Boon, speaking a message antithetical to the wisdom of Sam Fathers, has been co-opted by the values of the timber company to which he owes his job as town marshal and can see in the absurd plenty in the gum tree only something to be hoarded.

In turn, then, the sweetgum tree under which Boon sits in *Go Down, Moses* takes us to the sweetgum in chapter 11 of *Song of Solomon* where Milkman sits, exhausted from hunting with the men of Shalimar, Virginia. As Milkman rests, he begins to question the self-centered attitude he carries with him. In this moment, Milkman very nearly becomes the ideological heir to Guitar in much the same way that Ike becomes the spiritual heir to Sam Fathers—via the male communion of the hunt. Listening to the hunters signal their dogs, Milkman feels that he understands hunting and, by knowing what hunting is, that he understands Guitar:

> Down either side of his thighs he felt the sweet gum's surface roots cradling him like the rough but maternal hands of

a grandfather. Feeling both tense and relaxed, he sank his fingertips into the grass. He tried to listen with his fingertips, to
hear what, if anything, the earth had to say, and it told him
quickly that someone was standing behind him and he had
just enough time to raise one hand to his neck and catch the
wire that fastened around his throat. (282)

Milkman's epiphany shatters with Guitar's attempt on his life.
But something larger ruptures in this moment and its aftermath.
On the verge of accepting Guitar's world view in which he does
need the protection of good male hunters, Milkman is nearly
killed by his mentor. Milkman escapes to find that the hunters
have treed a bobcat with its "glistening night eyes" (283). From
the outset, Guitar is described as "a cat-eyed boy" (7), so the
bobcat's death and subsequent butchering at King Walker's gas
station take on a special significance.

As the hunters butcher the bobcat, the scene alternates between the graphic details of the way the cat is dismembered and
Milkman's memories, which are italicized, of pieces of the teachings of Guitar Baines.[12] Each cut rends another hole in the fabric
of Guitar's patriarchal world picture:

> Luther reached into the paunch and lifted the entrails. He
> dug under the rib cage to the diaphragm and carefully cut
> around it until it was free.
> *"It is about love. What else but love? Can't I love what I criticize?"*
> Then he grabbed the windpipe and the gullet, eased them
> back, and severed them with one stroke of his little knife.
> *"It is about love. What else?"*
> They turned to Milkman. "You want the heart?" they asked
> him. Quickly, before any thought could paralyze him, Milk-
> man plunged both hands into the rib cage. "Don't get the
> lungs, now. Get the heart."
> *"What else?"*
> He found it and pulled. The heart fell away from the chest
> as easily as yolk slips out of its shell.
> *"What else? What else? What else?"* (285–86)

As the hunters finish their work, Milkman asks them what they plan to do with the bobcat. The hunters' two-word response ("Eat him") returns us to an earlier key moment in Milkman and Guitar's friendship, when they prepare to steal Pilate's "gold," the bag that actually contains the remains of Jake, Milkman's paternal grandfather. Milkman and Guitar, passing a Buick dealership, see a white peacock, which Milkman notes for its strutting and inept flying. Guitar suggests catching it and to his friend's puzzled question ("What we gonna do if we catch him?"), he replies: "Eat him!" (179). Here Milkman asks Guitar why the peacock "can't fly no better than a chicken," and Guitar responds:

> "Too much tail. All that jewelry weighs it down. Like vanity. Can't nobody fly with all that shit. Wanna fly, you got to give up the shit that weighs you down."
>
> The peacock jumped onto the hood of the Buick and once more spread its tail, sending the flashy Buick into oblivion. (180)

Macon, as I noted earlier, is linked to the peacock, but in this passage we begin to see Milkman as the peacock, for Milkman from the time he is fourteen also struts (62). That the bird stands on the Buick seems suggestive, since Macon purchases a new Buick every two years; thus, the peacock on the car indicates the way Macon's wealth props up Milkman. Guitar's evaluation of the peacock's failure to fly well certainly is apropos of the Milkman who flies off to Danville, Pennsylvania, to find the gold, since Milkman carries with him all the markers of comfortable middle-class life, notably, his Cutty Sark, a gold Longines watch, and his Florsheim shoes. And, after offending the men at Solomon's store in Shalimar by his showy display of wealth and inquiries about their women, Milkman is linked both metonymically and metaphorically to another cock, "a black rooster [that] strutted by, its blood-red comb draped forward like a wicked brow" (268).

Song of Solomon's drama of the peacock and the bobcat raises questions about the nature of the male world of the hunt—a world *Go Down, Moses* celebrates—through a complex series of self-reflexive turns: while hunting for gold, which only slowly reveals itself as a hunt for his heritage, Milkman goes on a coon hunt during which he becomes the "coon" who is hunted. Milkman's hunt is play and sport. He does not really need the gold. But Guitar and the men of Shalimar play for keeps; their hunting is deadly serious. The poor men of Shalimar need the meat they kill, and Guitar kills, he believes, for a higher cause. In King Walker's gas station, Milkman finally sees through the falseness of Guitar's teachings, a new state objectified by the final image of the dead bobcat's head: "The tongue lay in its mouth as harmless as a sandwich" (286). No more will Guitar's words and language on race influence Milkman's thinking. Guitar's claim to kill for love ("It is about love. What else?") stands exposed; it is not about love but something else indeed—male power and possession. Milkman does not jettison entirely his relationship with Guitar, for he takes up the hunters' offer to get the heart—that which was nurturing and sustaining in his friendship with Guitar. Both the racism and the nostalgia about hunting, the entrails of that cat Guitar, are part of the shit that weighs Milkman down and will not let him fly. Milkman, in short, after the attack of his cat-eyed friend and the subsequent death and dismemberment of the bobcat, loses the limp that looks like a strut and ceases to be both the vain peacock and the cock who pees on women.

Milkman's encounter with the prostitute Sweet neatly objectifies his transformation, since her occupation would normally position her as a commodity, her sexuality bought, not shared; she is the kind of woman men routinely treat with no consideration. Yet Milkman interacts with her in a way that directly addresses the catalog of shortcomings Lena had pointed out to him at the end of part I and serves almost as reparation for the thoughtless way he had used his cousin Hagar:

> He soaped and rubbed her until her skin squeaked and glistened like onyx. She put salve on his face. He washed her hair. She sprinkled talcum on his feet. He straddled her behind and massaged her back. She put witch hazel on his swollen neck.

He made up the bed. She gave him gumbo to eat. He washed
the dishes. She washed his clothes and hung them out to dry.
He scoured her tub. She ironed his shirt and pants. He gave
her fifty dollars. She kissed him on the mouth. He touched
her face. She said please come back. He said I'll see you tonight.
(288–89)

But what exactly allows Milkman now to engage in reciprocal
relations with women, and if he can achieve some distance on
the male hunt metaphor, why can't Ike? Neither his mother nor
his wife provide Ike an alternative to the metaphor of the hunt.
Yet almost simultaneously with Milkman's rejecting the excesses
of Guitar's thinking, we see Milkman's unconscious movement
toward the other mentor of his youth, Pilate, inasmuch as he
imagines the bobcat's heart pulling out of his chest cavity "as
easily as yolk slips out of its shell" (286). This image takes us back
to the first meeting between Milkman and Pilate during which
she makes for him the perfect soft-boiled egg.[13] And so over his
breakfast eggs the next morning, he specifically asks his new
friends in Shalimar if they ever have heard of Pilate Dead.

In moving toward the perspective of Pilate, Milkman aligns
himself with the one character in the novel who has achieved a
special purchase on patriarchal forms of social organization. Because she has no navel, she is prevented from joining a community in the prescribed fashion, as a woman claimed in marriage
by a man; to have sex with a man is to reveal she has no navel
and thus to be shunned for her difference. After her split with
Macon, she is taken in by a preacher's family and begins her new
life as a female Huck Finn. (The preacher's house, she tells Ruth,
was "a nice place except they made me wear shoes" [142].) She
quickly discovers the problems associated with her sexuality. Pilate
becomes the object of the preacher's advances, which causes the
preacher's wife to send her packing. Twice cast out from groups
of migrant farm workers, Pilate finds things no better in towns:
"All her encounters with Negroes who had established themselves
in business or trades in those small midwestern towns had been
unpleasant. Their wives did not like the trembling unhampered

breasts under her dress, and told her so" (145). And in town, the only job options open to African-American women are laundress or prostitute.

Continually rejected, Pilate reevaluates life in a new way that places her in the tradition of Emersonian self-reliance, making her a kind of cross between Thoreau and Hester Prynne:

> She threw off every assumption she had learned and began at zero. First off, she cut her hair. That was one thing she didn't have to think about anymore. Then she tackled the problem of trying to decide how she wanted to live and what was valuable to her. When am I happy and when am I sad and what is the difference? What do I need to know to stay alive? What is true in the world? (149)

Like Hester, who places her hair under her cap, Pilate cuts her hair to signal a repression of her sexuality, since that is what has caused her the most trouble. Again like Hester, Pilate sets up housekeeping on the margins of the community. While Hester only dreams of a time when women's and men's roles will be reformulated, Pilate establishes a woman-centered alternative community that consistently operates without regard for middle class conventions or the expectations of men.[14]

Moreover, a ghostly visitor to Pilate's wine house, had the people of South Side but known, would have been deemed a far surer sign of Pilate's unnaturalness than that stigmatized by the missing navel. For Pilate communes with her dead father, Jake/Macon, who comes to her wearing "a white shirt, a blue collar, and a brown peaked cap" (150). Throughout part I and most of part II, Milkman consistently fails to recognize the possibility of ghosts. Freddie's claim that his mother died of ghosts only elicits Milkman's laughter. Later he will not credit his own senses when the ghost of his paternal grandfather witnesses Milkman's and Guitar's attempt to steal Pilate's "gold"—actually the bones of the grandfather. Indeed, even when face to face with a possible ghost, Milkman does not believe. Having arrived in Danville, Pennsylvania, and trying to discover where Circe lives, Milkman asks directions of a man whose description matches Jake's above: "One of them was a Negro. A tall man, elderly, with a brown peaked cap and an old-fashioned collar" (229)—Oleh, Chief, Grandfather, indeed![15]

Milkman's encounter with Circe is even more decidedly ghostly, marked by a particular recurring smell that announces the onset of possible supernatural moments in *Song of Solomon*: "A sweet spicy perfume. Like ginger root—pleasant, clean, seductive" (241).[16] The odor of ginger masks what had seconds earlier been an overwhelming stench of decay. From this dreamlike encounter with a woman who, as Milkman notes, "*had* to be dead" (243), he gets decisive clues both to the reality of ghosts and to uncovering his family's history—the names of his paternal grandfather and grandmother, Jake and Sing. (Milkman knows that Pilate claims her father appears to her speaking a single word—sing—which she takes as a command to sing.)

Like Ike McCaslin, who as a youth is granted his desired glimpse of the bear, Old Ben, after relinquishing his watch and compass, Milkman solves the riddle of his family's past in the song the children of Shalimar sing only after losing his watch, the final marker of his allegiance to his father's middle-class world. The Milkman, then, who returns to Michigan is a changed man. He believes in ghosts.[17] More important, he acknowledges his implication in Hagar's death.[18] Like Pilate, who keeps the bones she believes are the remains of the white man Macon may have killed because she maintains that one is responsible for one's dead, Milkman will now possess a box of Hagar's hair.

In almost a mirror reflection to the way Milkman becomes the spiritual heir to Pilate, Pilate's granddaughter, Hagar, is seduced by the world view of Macon Dead. Chapter 13, which interrupts and delays Milkman's triumphant return, chronicles what happens to Hagar after Milkman leaves her still standing in Guitar's apartment after her failure to kill Milkman. While Milkman moves slowly away from his father's and Guitar's teachings, Hagar loses her hold on the alternative formation represented by Pilate's house. Indirectly, one might argue, Hagar's death may be traced to Macon Dead inasmuch as she becomes crazy as a result of loving Macon's son, who is raised to reproduce Macon's middle-class values. (Milkman in name is, of course, quite literally another Macon Dead.) Milkman's rejection of Hagar precisely because she does not fit his middle-class design causes her to desire to be like the women Milkman desires—light-skinned and possessing all the totemic markers of middle-class feminine beauty. So at the very time that Milkman on his journey through Pennsylvania and Virginia progressively loses all the signs of middle-class gentility (his Cutty Sark, Florsheim shoes, and Longines watch), Hagar gathers to herself its feminine counterparts (an Evan Picone shirt, Con Brios, and Van Raalte gloves). It would, however, be inappropriate to label Macon as the sole or final author of Hagar's desire, for he merely embodies the larger metaphysical system that informs men that they have priority over women and that tells African Americans that white is good and black is bad.

IF ALL HE LEARNED were that his great-grandfather reputedly could fly, then Milkman's joy at the novel's end would be silly. Morrison's first novel to foreground the activity of men, however, raises a tough question—one that cannot be answered fully in a text marked as literary: is it possible for African-American men to reconceive their masculinity in a nonpatriarchal fashion, that is, in a way that does not reduce African-American women to objects to be possessed? The example of Milkman Dead suggests that the possibility is open for such a reconception. Ike McCaslin fails to provide the key to a nonpatriarchal society because his renunciation—his refusal to profit from a system of male power that perpetuates racial injustice—is just that, simple negation and refusal, a withdrawal from life. He generates no alternative vision of how to live in the world, and the transmission of patriarchal authority is in no way disrupted by Ike's refusal to be its embodiment; his passivity leads to Roth Edmonds's tragic reenactment of the incestuous miscegenation that so horrified him.

But Milkman has his Pilate/pilot, a woman who opens paths more sustaining than Sam Fathers's hunting trails. She teaches him how to treat women as fully human and that flying is a state of being rather than a physical act: "Now he knew why he loved her so. Without ever leaving the ground, she could fly" (340). As she lies dying in Milkman's arms, she tells him: "I wish I'd a knowed more people. I would of loved 'em all. If I'd a knowed more, I would a loved more" (340). The kind of flying Milkman ultimately understands and values is Pilate's flying, the ability to transcend self and self-love. What weighed Milkman down for so much of *Song of Solomon* is male ego (much as Hagar is destroyed by her desire to be the desire of male ego), forged in the structures of a patriarchal society.

Finally, then, it does not matter whether Milkman survives his encounter with Guitar at the end of the novel.[19] Milkman has achieved the very connectedness to an African-American community that Guitar all along has criticized his friend for lacking. Guitar may believe himself to be the one acting from higher principles, yet Milkman, who even in this moment sees Guitar as his brother, now achieves the transcendence he wrongly felt he had won under the sweetgum tree. Guitar's adherence to the vision of masculinity as violent mastery may win the day, but Milkman's transformation suggests that masculinity can be conceived in terms other than deadly possession.

Notes

I wish to thank two librarians at Memphis State [now the University of Memphis] for their assistance. Deborah Brackstone in interlibrary loan was instrumental in securing a copy of Morrison's master's thesis, and Harriet Alexander in reference generously opened her files of photocopied articles from her work on an annotated bibliography of Morrison.

1. William K. Freiert ("Classical Themes in Toni Morrison's *Song of Solomon*," *Helios* 10, no. 2 [1983]: 161–72) finds that "five classical mythological themes . . . permeate *Song of Solomon*: those of Ulysses, Oedipus, Mother-Earth, Daedalus, and Orpheus" (161). Susan L. Blake ("Folklore and Community in *Song of Solomon, MELUS* 7, no. 3 [1980]: 77–82) discovers that Solomon's song "is a variant of a well-known Gullah folktale about

a group of African-born slaves who rose up one day from the field where they were working and flew back to Africa" (77). Any number of critics have touched on the novel's relation to the biblical Solomon.

2. Harue Minakawa ("The Motif of Sweetness in Toni Morrison's *Song of Solomon*," *Kyushu American Literature* 26 [1985]: 47–56) briefly notes a connection between *Song of Solomon* and *Go Down, Moses*: "Milkman goes through a process similar to what Ike McCaslin goes through in 'The Bear.' Hunting strips one to the essentials" (52–53). More recently, David Cowart has explored stylistic and thematic similarities between Morrison and Faulkner in his "Faulkner and Joyce in Morrison's *Song of Solomon*," *American Literature* 62 (1990): 87–100. Cowart's object is to determine whether Morrison's fiction measures up on the yardstick of Faulkner and Joyce; Cowart judges her to succeed inasmuch as she performs "meaningful variations on the themes—freedom, identity, history" (89) to create "a fiction of universal humanity and moral authority" (100). My concern here is not to identify whether Morrison's prose is Faulknerian or her themes are universal; rather, I hope to show that Morrison's articulating the specificity of African-American experience calls into question our ability to define universal archetypes, such as masculinity. My study takes as its jumping-off point two essays by Craig Werner. Both his "Tell Old Pharoah: The Afro-American Response to Faulkner," *Southern Review* 19 (1983): 711–35, and "Minstrel Nightmares: Black Dreams of Faulkner's Dreams of Blacks" in *Faulkner and Race*, ed. Doreen Fowler and Ann J. Abadie (Jackson: University Press of Mississippi, 1987), 35–57, trace the specific responses in both fiction and essays of a number of black writers in the twentieth century to Faulkner. Werner, unlike Cowart, realizes that "the dialog between Faulkner and Afro-American culture involves several levels of distortion and reification grounded as much in the wider cultural context as in the content of a particular work or works" ("Minstrel" 39). I hope in this essay to have resisted any urge to construe a minstrel fiction that takes Morrison's concern for the African-American community only as a surface masking an underlying universal since universality is a category that has been defined and controlled by the white patriarchal hegemony.

3. Although not specifically addressed in Morrison's thesis, *Go Down, Moses* is in her bibliography, as are all of Faulkner's novels published prior to 1955. For Morrison's own ambivalent account of her study of Faulkner, see "Faulkner and Women" (in *Faulkner and Women*, ed. Doreen Fowler and Ann J. Abadie [Jackson: University Press of Mississippi, 1986], particularly 295–97).

4. Morrison [Chloe Ardellia Wofford], "Virginia Woolf's and William Faulkner's Treatment of the Alienated," master's thesis, Cornell University, 1955, p. 24.

5. Two thoughtful articles note the subversion of Macon's teachings. In "Open Movement and Self-hood in Toni Morrison's *Song of Solomon*" (*Centennial Review* 28, no. 1 [1984–1985]: 58–75) Robert James Butler, who sees the novel growing "out of this dialectic between the possibilities of space and the securities of place" (63), focuses on Guitar's influence on Milkman. In "The Quest for Discovery of Identity in Toni Morrison's *Song of Solomon*" (*Southern Review* 21 [1985]: 721–32), Valerie Smith, arguing that the novel opposes linear time, exemplified by Macon Dead, and cyclical time, as Pilate lives it (726), foregrounds Pilate's shaping hand.

6. Toni Morrison, *Song of Solomon* (New York: New American Library, 1978); hereafter, citations given parenthetically in the text.

7. William Faulkner, *Go Down, Moses* (New York: Random House, 1942), 339.

8. Juliet Mitchell's *Feminism and Psychoanalysis* (New York: Random House, 1975) summarizes the Freudian/Lacanian view: "The phallus is not identical with the actual penis, for it is what it signifies that is important.... The phallus ... indicates the desire of the mother (the desire for the phallus) into which the child is born.... The primary dyadic relationship between mother and child ... enters immediately into the possibility of a dialectical relationship between three terms: mother, child, and phallus. So already, even so to speak *before*, [the child] wants to be the phallus for the mother.... In submitting to the completely unreal possibility of castration the little boy acknowledges the situation and learns that one day he, too, will accede to the father's function. He pays thereby his symbolic debt to the father he has murdered in his rivalous thoughts. So the phallus is intimately connected both with the symbolic father and the law" (396–97).

9. Earlier, Macon's walk is described as a strut, again linking him to the peacock (17).

10. Because *Song of Solomon* envisions the possibility of the transformation of the African-American male, Milkman serves a similar purpose as Mr.—— in Alice Walker's *The Color Purple* (New York: Harcourt, Brace Jovanovich, 1982). Although Morrison has not received as harsh a censure from African-American male critics as Walker, Morrison's novel serves as another site in the ongoing debate about whether African-American women have the right to speak about sexism in the African-American community until the problems of racism have been eradi-

cated. Ishmael Reed particularly has been vitriolic in his attack on feminism, which he sees exclusively as the thinking of white women designed to divide the African-American community. For Reed, in "Stephen Spielberg Plays Howard Beach" (part of "The Black Person in Art: How Should S/he Be Portrayed?" ed. Henry Louis Gates, Jr., *Black American Literature Forum* 21 [1987]: 3–25), men who see value in the feminist perspective are "wimps" (8). One might note that Guitar Baines encodes Reed's position into *Song of Solomon*. Guitar's insistence that the African-American male is the supreme marginal figure is Reed's exactly. Answering his own question, "Why you so mean and hard?" Reed responds: "Because I am an Afro-American male, the most exploited and feared class in this country. All of the gentlemen, all of the ones who tried to be nice, are in the cemetery or sitting on a stoop humiliated and degraded and waiting for someone to hand them a bar of soap or waiting for the law some woman has called on them" (*Shrovetide in Old New Orleans* [Garden City, N.Y.: Doubleday, 19781], 114). Reed's insistence that African-American women can challenge oppression only on one front seems at best counterproductive. While African-American women do succeed more readily than African-American men—perhaps because women are perceived as less of a threat to the white establishment (see Andrew Hacker's "Affirmative Action: The New Look," *New York Review of Books*, 12 October 1989, p. 68)—the uneducated African-American woman still labors under a double alienation of race and gender.

Another reason, perhaps, that Morrison has not been as controversial as Walker is that Morrison's last two novels have moved away from a critique of African-American masculinity. *Tar Baby* is highly critical of Jardine, the black woman who forgets her cultural origins. *Beloved* at times seems to serve as reparation for any ill will generated by *Song of Solomon. Beloved* portrays the Sweet Home slave men as paragons of virtue and chastity who master their sexual desires to allow the new slave, Sethe, time to choose which of them she will have as a husband; white men exclusively are rapists in this fictional world.

11. That the members of the Seven Days invoke the authority of monotheistic Christianity to name their organization recalls Julia Kristeva's point in *About Chinese Women*, trans. Anita Barrows (London: Marion Boyars, 1977) that "monotheistic unity is sustained by a radical separation of the sexes: indeed, this separation is its prerequisite. For without this gap between the sexes . . . it would be impossible, in the symbolic sphere, to isolate the principle of One Law—One, Purifying, Transcendent Guarantor of the ideal interests of the community" (19). The Seven Days, by passing judgment and telling its victims, "Your day has come,"

aligns itself with transcendent authority and attempts to be the guarantor of the ideal interests of the African-American community, all the
while despising African-American women.

12. Charles Scruggs ("The Nature of Desire in Toni Morrison's *Song
of Solomon*," Arizona Quarterly 38 [1982]: 311–35) also briefly comments
on this scene, suggesting that when Milkman removes the bobcat's
heart, he "realizes that Guitar was trying to tell him how he could save
his own life, that he could save it only if he bridged the gap between
himself and others, between himself and the past" (322). Far from teaching Milkman how to save himself, Guitar's teachings reinscribe a significant aspect of the Dead father's ideology of possession.

13. Perhaps another marker of the influence that Pilate comes to
have on Milkman is his repetition of one of her particular phrases. After
his fight with Saul at Solomon's store, Milkman thinks (through the narrator's indirect discourse) of the men of Shalimar as "some of the meanest
unhung niggers in the world" (273). At Milkman's first encounter with
Pilate, she makes them self-conscious about his and Guitar's use of language and calls them "the dumbest unhung Negroes on the earth" (37).

14. I agree with Susan Willis's claim in "Eruptions of Funk: Historicizing Toni Morrison" (*Black American Literature Forum* 10, no. 1 [1982]: 34–
42) that Morrison's "three-woman utopian households" (41) contrast
with Faulkner's failure to conceive of female bonding as alternative community in *Absalom, Absalom!* though I have argued elsewhere (Duvall,
Murder and the Communities: Invisible, Outlaw, and Unspeakable Communities [Austin:
University of Texas Press, 1990]) that Faulkner does more than simply
provide "a retrenched espousal of the male-dominated social model"
(Willis 41).

15. That Milkman comes to a belief in ghosts as a result of his
movement toward Pilate reminds us that Isaac McCaslin is similarly
introduced to a world beyond the material by his mentor in "The Old
People," when Sam Fathers shows the boy the spirit of the dead buck.

16. See, for example, the description of the ginger-smelling air prior
to Guitar's and Milkman's unacknowledged encounter with the ghost
of Jake (186–87).

17. Milkman's belief in ghosts is a sign that he has moved beyond
his father's middle-class values, values which derive from the white rul-
ing class. Morrison (see Mel Watkins, "Talk with Toni Morrison," *New
York Times Book Review*, 11 September 1977, pp. 48, 50) tells a pointed story:
"Once a woman asked me 'Do you believe in ghosts? I said, 'Yes. Do
you believe in germs?' It's part of our cultural heritage" (50).

18. In "*Song of Solomon*: Morrison's Rejection of Rank's Monomyth and

Feminism" (*Studies in American Fiction* 15 [1987]: 13–24), Gerry Brenner's claim that the Milkman who returns to Pilate "assigns himself no culpability" (18) for Hagar's death depends on a perversely decontextualized interpolation of the word "it" in the line "What difference did it make?" (336). Let's look at what precedes this sentence:

> Hagar was dead. The cords of his neck tightened. How? In Guitar's room, did she . . . ?
>
>   What difference did it make? He had hurt her, left her, and now she was dead—he was certain of it. (336)

Brenner reads the sentence as follows: "What difference did [Hagar's death] make?" The context however, suggests a much more plausible reading. Milkman starts to ask himself if Hagar killed herself as he had suggested she do in Guitar's room, but then he realizes that how she died is irrelevant: "What difference did it make [how Hagar died]?" Milkman recognizes that his treatment of her implicates him in her death no matter what the particular circumstances surrounding that death are. Brenner's negative view of Milkman results from a strained argument that Toni Morrison intended an ironic use of Otto Rank's monomyth to dupe unsuspecting readers into accepting Milkman as the novel's hero.

19. The moment is hardly the suicidal gesture that some critics have made it out to be (Brenner, "Morrison's Rejection," 18; Butler, "Open Movement," 72). Guitar's rifle has Milkman pinned down. There are not many options for life-affirming action open to Milkman, but he does act with a knowledge of his lifelong friend and stands up. Guitar's sense of fair play—there are rules good hunters follow, after all—and his love for his friend lead him to lay aside his rifle.

Although I do not wish to grant special privilege to the author's reconstruction of this scene, Morrison's comment on the novel's ending seems germane. In an interview with Pepsi Charles (*NIMROD* 21–22 [1977]: 43–51) Morrison calls *Song of Solomon* an "absolute triumph" since "a man learns the only important lesson there is to learn. And he wins himself, he wins himself. And the quality of his life improves immeasurably. Whether its length improves or lengthens is irrelevant" (50).

Civilizations Underneath

African Heritage as Cultural Discourse in
Toni Morrison's Song of Solomon

GAY WILENTZ

◆ ◆ ◆

IN EACH OF HER ACCLAIMED NOVELS, Toni Morrison writes what she calls "village literature, fiction that is really for the village, for the tribe" (LeClair 26). Yet Morrison has been hailed as one of the greatest writers (I will do away with any of the qualifiers) of the twentieth century. She has been compared to Faulkner and Márquez in her use of stream of consciousness and magic realism, but we need to look a little closer at Morrison's own comments and her historical roots to explore the rich complexity of her written work. Although she wrote her master's thesis on Faulkner and has acknowledged influence by Márquez and other Latin American writers, Morrison's writings are deeply entrenched in her own black folk roots and the community in which she grew up. Moreover, her text is informed by her mother's stories, her tribe, and her ancestors—African and African American. In "Rootedness: The Ancestor as Foundation," Morrison yearns for a closer identification of the black American artist with her community:

> There must have been a time when an artist could be genu-
> inely representative of the tribe and in it; when an artist could
> have a tribal or racial sensibility and an individual expression
> of it. There were spaces and places in which a single person
> could enter and behave as an individual within the context of
> the community. (339)

The relationship between the artist and the community that Morrison describes is an Afrocentric one, the discourse based in an
African orature whose artists are both participants in and repre-
sentatives of the community.[1] Morrison hopes to recreate this
participatory experience in her fiction.

Although she does not discuss Morrison, Catherine Belsey, in
Critical Practice, might call a work like *Song of Solomon* an "interrogative" text which "literally invites the reader to produce answers
to the questions it implicitly or explicitly raises" (91). Within the
context of Afrocentric cultural discourse, the questions raised in
the novel are interrogative in the manner of a dilemma tale
(Abrahams 16–17). Certainly, the finale of the novel reflects the
openendedness of this West African form of orature. Morrison's
use of African modes of storytelling and orature is a way of bridg-
ing gaps between the black community's folk roots and the black
American literary tradition. Furthermore, through this dilemma
tale, Morrison compels us to question Western concepts of reality
and uncover perceptions of reality and ways of interpretation
other than those imposed by the dominant culture. By examining
Song of Solomon as literature beyond the limitations of Euro-
American discourse, I focus on Morrison's use of African values,
characteristics, and community as an alternative to mainstream
assimilation or radical separatism. Furthermore, I center on Morrison's attempt to transform Eurocentric cultural discourse
through the acceptance of African heritage, told by generations
of women storytellers. In the weaving of this tale, Morrison can
be seen as an Afrocentric tale teller who overturns Western biblical and cultural notions by revealing the legends and folkways
of her community. From the double entendre of the title to the
mythical, contradictory ending, Morrison bears witness to "that

civilization that existed underneath the white civilization" (Le-Clair 26), a society in which the fathers soared and the mothers told stories so that the children would know their names.

It may be useful before I examine the novel to define my use of *Afrocentric discourse* and the importance of African cultural traditions to contemporary African-American life. My use of the term *Afrocentric* comes from *Toward the Decolonization of African Literature*. Afrocentric discourse refers to the connections among those of African descent, and particularly the literary "achievements of the African peoples, in the homeland and in the diaspora" (Chinweizu and Maduibuike 3). Molefi Kete Asante further defines Afrocentricity as a critical perspective "which means, literally, placing African ideals at the center of any analysis that involves African culture and behavior" (*Afrocentric* 6). To examine literature in the African diaspora, an Afrocentric approach exposes what has been hidden by the dominant discourse. For even in the African-American community, attitudes about African heritage have differed. Dialogue on Africa and African heritage has been prominent in the course of African-American history. Depending on the historical moment, one side of the conflicting dialectics—the desire to assimilate or to assert one's own ethnic identity—has been stronger. But within communities, African cultural practices have remained even when the historicity of an age has reflected an assimilationist stance. At our historical moment, serious attention has been paid to documenting continuing African cultural practices.[2] Recent studies like *Africanisms in American Culture* examine not only West African but also Central African "cultural carryovers" (Holloway xiii). According to Asante, Afrocentricity pervades every aspect of African-American culture (as well as much of the dominant Euro-American society). Moreover, he states, "Black Americans retained basic components of the African experience rather than specific artifacts" ("African" 21). So, when Morrison recreates African cultural traditions in *Song of Solomon*, she is formulating her discourse within an Afrocentric world view.

Song of Solomon is a complex novel with an unresolved ending which has been seen as a biblical allegory, a detective novel, and a young man's search for his roots. Some male critics, like Mel

Watkins of the *New York Times*, have more closely identified with this novel than with *The Bluest Eye* or *Sula* since it is not about "the insulated, parochial world of black women," but about black men (50). Indeed, the novel includes a prominent male character, Milkman; however, the work is equally concerned with the world of black women, disparaged by Watkins, and the focal character of the novel is Milkman's aunt, Pilate. In a similar manner, Eurocentric literary critics—more versed in Faulkner than black folk culture, in New Criticism than cultural criticism—initially privileged the influence of written discourse on Morrison's writings rather than her oral antecedents, no matter how many times she explained her sources.[3] A cursory reading of the novel does not expose its oral antecedents as clearly as a first reading of Walker's *The Color Purple*, for example. *Song of Solomon* is dense, filled with visual description and literary devices.[4] Yet Morrison's role as an Afrocentric storyteller is unmistakable, and the orature of her foremothers as well as the oral traditions of the black community is evident in both the language and the structure of the novel. Morrison comments on her own process of recreating the richness of black speech in her writings. "I have to rewrite, discard, and remove the print quality of the language to put back the oral quality, where intonation, volume, gesture are all there" (Tate 126). The voicings of the stories that were told to her when young and the unique resonances of family and community filter through her characters: "When I think of things my mother or father or aunts used to say, it seems the most absolutely striking thing in the world. That is what I try to get into my fiction" (Watkins 48).

Morrison's attention to her writings' oral antecedents extends further than her precise recreation of the voicings of her community; her works incorporate the use of African-American folktales, folk songs, and legends.[5] *Song of Solomon*, based on a story she learned from her maternal grandparents, is imbued with folk myths and legends from the African diaspora. Most important is the tale of the flying Africans—who escaped slavery by flying back to Africa. Legends abound throughout the New World about Africans who either flew or jumped off slave ships as well as those who saw the horrors of slavery when they landed in the Americas and, "in their anguish, sought to fly back to Africa."[6] For Morrison, as for Paule Marshall (whose slave walk back) and Ishmael Reed (whose slave Quickskill flies Air Canada), the notion of using the supernatural, especially this most exalted form of freedom, to overcome a catastrophe captivated her: "I wanted to use black folklore, the magic and superstitious part of it. Black people believe in magic. . . . It's part of our heritage. That's why flying is the central metaphor in *Song*" (Watkins 50). Although I explore this issue in more detail in relation to the novel's conclusion, clearly one's perception regarding whether the slaves killed themselves or flew back to Africa is culture bound.

From the opening of the novel, when insurance agent/Seven Days member Robert Smith either commits suicide or flies away on his own wings, Morrison questions the imposed values and perceptions of the dominant culture and begins to offer alternative cultural knowledge and belief based on black Americans' African traditions and heritage. Also revealing is the folksong of Sugarman/Solomon's flying away, sung by Pilate at Milkman's birth. The song is the key to Milkman's quest and illustrates the function of the African-American woman in passing on stories to future generations. The novel, structured in the manner of a surreal detective story, has a multifaceted plot, but it is Milkman's relationship with Pilate, his female "ancestor," which transforms his search for gold into an acknowledgement of his heritage. It is Pilate's role as an African woman to be the "custodian of the culture" (Arhin 92–94). In a quest to learn the complete family history partially related by Pilate, Milkman repeats Pilate's journey to Virginia to find her mother's family and ends up uncovering the legend of his ancestors—that of the flying Africans.

In *Black Feminist Criticism*, Barbara Christian comments, "In dramatizing the traditions of her community, Morrison's novels resemble the oral technique of the storyteller" (57). Equally pertinent to this study is the importance of storytelling within the context of the novel itself. In the manner of an African woman storyteller, Morrison tells the tale of the flying Africans to keep her traditions and culture alive on paper. Within the discourse of the novel, her characters voice the stories of family and ancestral life, although some "informants" are more reliable than others. Joseph Skerrett, in "Recitations to the Griot," points out the importance of Morrison's transformation of the orature: "Milkman's parents, Macon and Ruth, are not effective informants for Milkman. Their narration of their own parts of the mystery of his heritage is partial, egocentric, defensive. . . . It is only Pilate for whom storytelling is not self-dramatization, self-justification, or ego-action" (194–95). Although Pilate is unmistakably Morrison's preferred storyteller, the other stories and the differing voices further emphasize the oral quality of the novel. For it is the sum of the stories, told by this community of voices in the Midwest, Northeast, and South, and Milkman's ability to select among them, which gives us a greater sense of the workings of the oral tradition. With that sense comes the realization that, when a tale is "not actually being told, all that exists of it is the potential in certain human beings to tell it" (Ong 11). It is this apprehension of the possible loss of the orature and cultural history which informs this novel and most of Morrison's works. Milkman Dead, the recipient of these stories, has an overachieving, dominant, "Black white man" for a father and a beaten-down, faded rose for a mother, and is—at thirty years old—bored. Only his rapport with Pilate, whose scent is of African ginger, has kept Milkman alive (both literally and metaphorically). Not only does she save him (as a fetus) from his father's aggression, but it is her sensory world of African smells, tastes, and visions which both engages his curiosity and enlivens his recursive memory. Moreover, Milkman's unraveling of his family history hinges on the decoding of the folksong Pilate sings at his birth.

In the dedication of *Song of Solomon*, Morrison writes, "The fathers may soar/And the children may know their names." But there is a group missing from the dedication whose presence is overpowering in the novel itself—the mothers (grandmother, aunt, older sibling, female ancestor). When the father soars off, there must be someone left to teach the children their names. Although I discuss the importance of naming and the woman's blues of "you can't fly off and leave a body" later, it is evident

that the tales of the flying Africans and the stories of endurance
and strength in the face of slavery and oppression, as well as the
values of the African communities from whence they came, have
been encapsulated in the orature of the women—left behind not
only to sing the blues but to sing of home. Within an African
context, the role of the woman has been that of educator of the
children into the culture. Ada Mere, Igbo sociologist, comments
on the role of women as tale tellers and instructors. Women, she
writes, "are the most primary and constant agents of child socialization" (3); furthermore, as agents of this education, women
"are the mainstay of the oral tradition" (15). As Filomina Steady
and others contend, the black woman throughout Africa and the
diaspora "represents the ultimate value in life, namely the continuation of the group" (32). It can be argued that part of the
cultural achievement of Africans in the Americas has come from
the diaspora women who "mothered" African-American culture
into being (Reagon 177). For Morrison and other contemporary
black women writers, the attention to the role of women in
passing on the traditions comes directly from their African and
African-American foremothers. Morrison, in her role as storyteller, creates an environment within the context of the novel
for the stories of women, especially Pilate's, to be recognized and
privileged. Macon's stories direct Milkman to unrewarding ends;
it is Pilate's rendition of their past which helps Milkman grow.
Moreover, the stories of his sister Lena, his mother, Ruth, and
his distant cousin Susan Byrd, along with Pilate, help Milkman
learn how to be "a single, separate Afro-American person . . .
while also connected to a family, a community, and a culture"
(Skerrett 200).

Morrison's attention to storytelling traditions reflects specific
aspects of women's role in African culture; *Song of Solomon* employs
other African artistic traditions as well. By leaving out the "mothers" in her dedication, Morrison has not necessarily forgotten
them; rather, it is up to us through our reading of the book—
and our own understanding of how women are often left out
of recorded history—to fill in what is missing. Morrison comments:

> My writing expects, demands participatory reading, and that I
> think is what literature is supposed to do. It's not just about
> telling the story; it's about involving the reader . . . My lan-
> guage has to have holes and spaces so the reader can come
> into it. . . . Then we [you, the reader, and I, the author] come
> together to make this book, to feel this experience. (Tate 125)

As Morrison's community of readers, we are constantly called to
question values as well as supply information—in short, to read
with an Afrocentric approach. Morrison's engagement with her
readers (community) in this interrogative text may very well be
based on the concept of the artist's role and responsibility in
African societies: the "artist in the traditional African milieu spoke
for and to his [or her] community" (Chinweizu and Maduibuike
241). Certain genres of African orature, particularly the dilemma
tales, have unresolved endings which call for community response; moreover, the participation of the community/audience
is often ensured by a "chorus" designed to engage them. In writing village literature, Morrison emphasizes the use of a chorus in
making the "story appear oral, meandering, effortless spoken. . . .
The real presence of a chorus. *Meaning the community or the reader at
large, commenting on the action as it goes ahead*" ("Rootedness" 341; emphasis added).

One of the questions raised in *Song of Solomon* has plagued African Americans since emancipation—that of one's place in
American society. From Du Bois's "double self" to Ralph Ellison's
"invisible man," the question of identity in a hostile and antag-
onistic world has been paramount. Often, this search for identity
has led to one of two opposite approaches: mainstream assimi-
lation/accommodation or radical separatism. Two characters in
the novel illustrate these warring factions: Macon Dead, Milkman's father (assimilation), and Guitar Bains, Milkman's friend
(separatism). In addition, Milkman's mother, Ruth, appears to
symbolize the death of the genteel, bourgeois, light-skinned black
who is isolated from her community. Through the characterization of Pilate, a female ancestor, Morrison emphasizes the dead-
end of both mainstream assimilation and radical separatism by

offering an alternative—perhaps not a reconciliation but a more clearly articulated dialectic of the double self by the acceptance of one's African values and cultural heritage.

African values and African culture, exemplified in Pilate, are privileged in the text. Like the woman in yellow in *Tar Baby*, Pilate has all the qualities Morrison associates with an ideal African woman: she has stature, strength, presence. Pilate is tall, as tall as her brother Macon, with black skin and wine-colored lips; moreover, she constantly has a "chewing stick" between her lips, much like a West African market woman. And even if those images are missed by the casual reader, one easily notes Macon's statement to his son: "If you ever have a doubt we from Africa, look at Pilate" (54). Pilate also has mystical powers. She was born without a navel, which allows her special privileges as a conjure woman, even though it separates her—like any religious figure— from her community. Pilate's house resembles one in a traditional African village compound: she has forgone gas and electricity and uses candles and kerosene, and she cooks over a three-stone fire-place.[7] Pilate lives "pretty much as though progress was a word that meant walking a little farther down the road" (27).

When Milkman and Guitar try to rob Pilate of what they think is the gold, they encounter in the ginger-smelling air a surreal middle passage back to the western coast of Africa from whence their ancestors were stolen:

> Breathing the air that could have come straight from a mar-
> ketplace in Accra, they stood for what seemed to them a very
> long time. Although they had stood deliberately in the dark
> of the pine trees, they were unprepared for the deeper darkness
> that met them there in that room. Neither had seen that kind
> of blackness, not even behind their own eyes. (186)

Pilate's house reflects her African heritage in other ways. Her house appears to her in-law Ruth as "an inn, a safe harbor" (135), and "true to the palm oil that flowed in her veins," Pilate offers both food and hospitality to all who enter (150). Even Macon, who deserted his sister, sees the house as a place of music, warmth, and caring, not realizing that he has destroyed the music in his own house. The two houses stand in stark contrast. In the Deads' house, built by Ruth's acerbic and bourgeois father, the women cower and Milkman is bored. Ruth suffers under Macon's rule, her creativity stunted, her flowers dying. The two daughters, Magdalene, called Lena, and First Corinthians, pine for lack of love and life, since no man in the community is good enough for Macon Dead's daughters. In contrast to this "dead" house, three generations' worth of women in Pilate's house can live and breathe and sing in harmony (28). There is deep consanguineous bonding between grandmother Pilate, mother Reba, and daughter Hagar. The grandmother, as sociologists Wilhemina Manns and Niara Sudarkasa note, has had a profound influence on the socialization of children in both African and African-American cultures, based on African family organization.[8] Grandmother Pilate is certainly the head of this household. Ironically, Milkman, brought into existence through Pilate's powers, practically destroys the foundation of these women's lives.

Pilate has been called a "primal mother goddess" (Lee 357), and her role as conjurer is well documented throughout the book. Revealingly, she is also the one who attempts to rebuild her extended family as well as pass on the knowledge of her heritage to her nephew/son so that he can recover their roots. I have noted the importance of women in transmitting the stories of the past to maintain the culture within an Afrocentric world view; here generational continuity (passing on the stories of the family) becomes cultural continuity as well. Much of the focus of generational continuity, especially for contemporary writers, has centered on the (grand)mother-daughter relationship, so it is interesting, in light of this context, that Morrison chooses the son to make the search rather than any of the daughters of the novel. Perhaps it is because Morrison herself has two sons, but this choice may also illustrate the dominant role the female ancestor/mother plays in passing on cultural knowledge and values to *both* male and female children in the family. Pilate, in this case, also reflects practices in many West African cultures where the education of the children—until the boys' initiation—is done by

the women of the compound (Nwoga). Pilate seems to understand the necessity of Milkman's life before he is born. Returning
to find her brother a "hard man" and her sister-in-law dying from
lack of love, she gives Ruth a greenish-grey powder to put in
Macon's food so as to revive their sex lives (131). When Pilate
finds out later that Macon is trying to abort the child conceived
in deception, she reminds him of her obeah powers: she puts a
male doll with a chicken bone stuck between its legs in his office.
After that, Macon leaves Ruth alone (132).

As one in touch with the continuum of ancestors/descendants,
Pilate holds posthumous conversations with her own father and
has an uncanny knowledge of events she has not witnessed. She
knows her mother's history and the color of her mother's hair
ribbons even though her mother died with Pilate's birth. Moreover, after Milkman and Guitar steal the bones they believe to be
gold, Pilate goes to the police station and weaves a "sambo" story
to save them, incorporating knowledge to which she should not
have been privileged. Later Macon remarks to Milkman: "Who
knows what Pilate knows" (207). To get her bag of bones back,
Pilate takes on the changeable characteristics of Legba, the African
deity worshiped throughout the Caribbean and parts of the
South.[9] Almost the height of Macon, she shrinks herself in front
of the police, turning her strong powerful African presence into
a stereotypic imitation of Aunt Jemima (208).

Pilate is omnipresent in the novel, and many of her values and
powers are passed on to her daughter and granddaughter. Reba,
for example, wins every contest she enters in spite of her lack of
interest in the prizes. The image of the three generations of
women living in harmony, plaiting hair, and singing songs revisions an ideal African village compound, yet the realities of
African-American life and its constraints shatter this image. For
all her powers, Pilate is unable to bring her extended family back
together as a force to confront racial oppression, nor is she able
to save Hagar from the imposition of the white dominant culture's definition of beauty after Hagar and Milkman's incestuous
relationship ends in disaster.

Exogamy, in most African societies, ensures that the children from an upcoming marriage will be healthy, productive members of society. According to sociologist Kamene Okonjo, it is one of the most important considerations in mate selection and helps justify the involvement of the extended family in that selection, since the elders would know who was a relative (8). The sexual relationship between Milkman and his cousin Hagar is doomed at the start since it breaks this African cultural practice. Our perceptions of this relationship, which destroys Hagar and Pilate's dream of an extended family are shaped by this taboo in many African cultures; it is that reality which determines the breakdown. Pilate foreshadows the disastrous end to their relationship by referring to Milkman as Hagar's brother rather than cousin. When both Reba and Hagar correct her, Pilate questions the difference between the two words: "I mean what's the difference in the way you act towards 'em? Don't you have to act the same way to both? . . . Then why they got two words for it 'stead of one, if they ain't no difference?" (44). Moreover, when Hagar sets out to kill Milkman after being humiliated and dropped by him, the community comments that he's getting what he deserves for "messing with his own cousin" (129).

Another African practice, prolonged breast feeding, functions antithetically in the novel. In Western medical practice, breast feeding is recommended up to six months whereas, within traditional communities, it can extend up to two years or more. (It is interesting that contemporary Western women's groups like the La Leche League are now suggesting that women breast feed as long as they like.) In the novel, Ruth's breast feeding is a source of embarrassment for both Milkman and Macon and shows her intense loneliness and apparent uselessness. But Milkman's prolonged breast feeding also highlights the conflict of values in the novel. When the yardman Freddie witnesses one of Milkman's afternoon sucklings, his comments reflect both the knowledge of this traditional practice and the dominant culture's view that the experience is somehow obscene: "I be damn, Miss Rufie. . . . I don't even know the last time I seen that. I mean, ain't nothing wrong with it. I mean, old folks swear by it" (14).

This African practice connects with another as Freddie dubs

the young Macon a "milk man." Freddie's renaming of Milkman represents a major occurrence in Milkman's life—and it sticks. Melville Herskovits, in *The Myth of the Negro Past*, focuses on the importance of naming in African-American culture. He associates this naming practice with that of their African forebears and comments:

> Names are of great importance in West Africa. . . . That is why, among Africans, a person's name may in so many instances change with time, a new designation being assumed on the occasion of some striking occurrence in his life, or when he goes through one of the rites marking a new stage in his development. (191)

The significance of names and naming in the novel is the subject for a separate essay, but naming as a method of resisting the hegemony of white society through African cultural practices is of primary concern here. The power of a name is so strong in much of Africa and the diaspora that often people kept a secret name so that an enemy could not use it for evil intent. In the New World, a name could also be employed in opposition to the oppressor, as slaves were wont to do. The biblical names used in the novel present a "secret" name since they rarely fit the person named, thus transforming the Old Testament (Pilate, of course, is the most obvious example). Morrison comments: "I used the Biblical names to show the impact of the Bible on the lives of Black people, their awe and respect for it coupled with their ability *to distort it for their own purposes*" (LeClair 28; emphasis added). From Sing Dead's insistence that her husband Jake should keep the misguided name he was given by an illiterate white man to Pilate's wearing of her name in her ear, a constant process of oppositional naming and renaming occurs in the novel. In this context, it is evident that naming can be a method of regaining control of one's life. Moreover, this process demonstrates the pattern of passing on the unique cultural traits of Africa within the context of the African-American community. In line with Asante's comment about black Americans retaining "the basic components of the African experience" ("African" 21), I would further suggest that, in reference to Morrison's dedication, it may not be necessary to learn one's original African name; it is the *process* of naming which must survive.

Explicit aspects of African cultural heritage in *Song of Solomon* are the supernatural occurrences throughout the novel. Morrison's attention to the "discredited" knowledge of African Americans and to the African notion of reincarnation both attest to the alternate reality presented in the cultural discourse of the novel. The acceptance of the supernatural is treated, for the most part, very differently in African and Western cultures. Morrison emphasizes this aspect of black Americans' African heritage in comments about *Song of Solomon*:

> [With that novel], I could blend the acceptance of the supernatural and a profound rootedness in the real world at the same time with neither taking precedence over the other. It is indicative of the cosmology, the way in which Black people looked at the world. We are very practical people . . . but within that practicality we also accepted what I suppose could be called superstition and magic, which is another way of knowing things. . . . And some of those things were "discredited knowledge" that Black people had; discredited only because Black people were discredited therefore what they *knew* was "discredited. . . ." That knowledge has a very strong place in my work. ("Rootedness" 342)

It is this special, "discredited" knowledge that Pilate has. Macon tells Milkman to stay away from Pilate because she is a "snake" and explains the way of the world to him in hard-core materialist terms: "After school come to my office; work a couple of hours there and learn what's real. Pilate can't teach you a thing you can use in this world. *Maybe the next, but not this one*" (55; emphasis added). Macon makes a sharp division between the material and spiritual worlds, privileging the material, but there are other characters, deeply rooted in the African-American tradition, who have a more integrated world view. These people, mostly women, ex-

tend their knowledge of African-American life to include an Afrocentric perspective in which there is dialogue with the ancestors, extended longevity, and perceptions of "things" outside a
narrow, literalist vision. Paul Carter Harrison points out that this
is not surrealism within a modernist context:

> Dialogue between living and dead members of the community
> should not be misconstrued as surrealism: What is important
> to the mode here is simply the materialization of the ancestral
> spirit so that one is able to identify the precise source of a
> particular piece of wisdom. (19)

Therefore, the presence of an ancestor (alive or dead) and the
wisdom one receives from that source are seen within the context
of the African continuum.

Both of Milkman's "mothers" (Ruth and Pilate) speak with
their dead fathers. Ruth, who was "pressed small" by a society
which would not allow her to grow, believed her father to be the
only friend that she had (124). Unfortunately, her father added
to Ruth's "smallness" and alienation so that her love for him has
become distorted with profanity. Still, her trips to his grave to
"speak" with him reflect the ongoing continuum from the ancestors to the descendants. Pilate's relationship with her dead father is clearly more sustaining than Ruth's. Unlike Ruth's father,
Jake (the first Macon Dead) is a proud and connected member
of his community. Before his murder, he was a successful farmer,
but he did not set himself apart from others in the community;
moreover, in death, he still directs Pilate and helps her to understand her life and her heritage. She explains to Ruth: "He's
helpful to me, real helpful. Tells me things I need to know. . . .
It's a good feeling to know he's around. I tell you he's a person
I can always rely on" (141). Through the words and actions of
her father and the prenatal knowledge she gains from her
mother, Pilate begins to unravel the family history which she
passes on to the next generation through Milkman.

Milkman is comfortable with waking dreams, ghosts, and supernatural occurrences, for he states: "Pilate did not have a navel.

Since that was true, anything could be, and why not ghosts as well?" (294). It is this ability which separates him from the stark materialism of his father and allows him to understand and respect Pilate's powers. And although it takes him almost twenty years to truly comprehend the importance of what she says, his initial meeting with Pilate and her daughters was "the first time in his life that he remembered being completely happy" (47). The relationship between Pilate and Milkman is the focal one of the novel, and Milkman's beginnings reveal further evidence of the supernatural as part of Morrison's cultural discourse. As noted earlier, Pilate prepares a potion for Macon so that he will sleep with his wife. But Pilate is not only thinking of solving the loneliness of Ruth; she is also worried that the family males may end with the alienated Macon. She tells Ruth: "[Macon's] as good as anybody. . . . Besides you'll get pregnant and your baby ought to be his. He ought to have a son. Otherwise this be the end of us" (125). Pilate's interest in the continuation of her family is typical of most human yearnings, but in another way Pilate seems to prophesy Milkman's becoming not only a repository for the family's history but also a reincarnation of his great-grandfather Solomon, the flying African. Pilate's statement to Ruth might appear idle guessing, but since Pilate's powers are well documented in the novel, it seems as if she willed Milkman to come or at least acted as the liaison between the ancestors and the unborn. In *Beloved*, Morrison returns to this theme. The daughter "Beloved," throat slashed by a fugitive slave mother, is "reincarnated" as a young woman who reenters her mother's postslavery life.

Reincarnation, as it functions in the diaspora, remains a powerful concept within an Afrocentric world view. African scholar Donatus Nwoga comments that, although this concept, as "rationally valid acceptable knowledge," is yet to be analyzed, both traditional religion and contemporary literature explore reincarnation in the black world.[10] By the end of the novel, Milkman's flight, which mirrors his great-grandfather's, appears predestined. Milkman, who is born under the blue satin wings of Robert Smith's suicide/flight, is imprinted with the desire to fly: "Mr. Smith's blue silk wings must have left their mark, because when the little boy discovered, at four, the same thing that Mr. Smith had learned earlier—that only birds and airplanes could fly—he lost all interest in himself" (9). Morrison gives us the flight of Robert Smith as the reason Milkman wants so desperately to fly. But later in this detective-like, interrogative novel, it is evident that Smith's "blue wings" are only one small part of the story. By the end of the novel, Milkman's yearning for flight is intricately connected with the history of his great-grandfather. If indeed he is the reincarnation of this African, the desire to fly would have been there whether he felt the prenatal flapping of his mother's stomach or not. I am not suggesting that Robert Smith, the insurance agent who may also have been flying to escape his form of slavery, is not at all connected with Milkman's propensity for flight or the alternative reality of the novel; rather, Smith's takeoff from Mercy Hospital appears to echo the flight of Solomon (Shalimar) and this collective myth of freedom throughout the African diaspora.

Milkman's penchant for flight leads him to seek the gold his father wants retrieved. Macon sends his son because he still thinks the gold is in the cave in which Pilate and he hid after their father was killed. Milkman's own search, however, reaches beyond the gold which is the final aim for both his father and Guitar. On the airplane, he thinks: "In the air, away from real life, he felt free, but on the ground . . . the wings of all those other people's nightmares flapped in his face and constrained him" (222). Milkman envisions this trip back east as an escape from the drudgery of his life, but through the remembered instructions of Pilate, the search for gold becomes a greater search for family history and African heritage. Milkman's search takes him farther than his grandfather's farm in Pennsylvania; he returns to the world the slaves made—the South.

The American South, in spite of its iniquitous history of racial segregation and slavery, has become for many African-American writers a source of heritage, a familial home. This may seem, and perhaps is, ironic, but the fact remains that this is where African-America began and where the relationship to one's African roots is the strongest. From Harrison's *The Great MacDaddy* (in *Kuntu*

Drama), in which the protagonist travels from Los Angeles to the Sea Islands in South Carolina to find the "source," to the work of contemporary women writers such as Bambara, Marshall, and Naylor, who center healing experiences and awareness of one's heritage in southern coastal regions, movement south reaffirms a connection to the African diaspora. Morrison is no exception, and Milkman's trip south—this time to Virginia—finally leads him to an understanding of himself, his family, and his culture. Milkman's growing comprehension that rural life differs extensively from the life he has known in the city starts when he visits his grandfather's community in Pennsylvania. As he hears stories about his family heritage, he realizes a strength in his culture that he had paid little attention to in the past: "It was a good feeling to come into a strange town and find a stranger who knew your people. All his life he'd heard the tremor in the word. . . . But he hadn't known what it meant: links" (231). Milkman's appreciation that people may be more important than material goods, that family and community are strengths, and that knowing one's heritage is a power separate from the power of money affects him in both conscious and subconscious ways. To search for the gold surreptitiously, Milkman makes up a story that he is going to look for his grandfather's remains (251). Yet it is the search for his ancestors, not necessarily for the remains but for the remainder of the story, that directs Milkman to Virginia. He follows not the gold of his farther but the song and story of his aunt: "Macon didn't even try to get to Virginia. Pilate headed straight for it" (297).

Milkman's journey south is a learning experience for him as he pieces together the different stories and lore of his family. There are aspects of his culture of which he, from an isolated, assimilated family, knows nothing. What little he has gleaned comes from the presence of his aunt Pilate. He notices that the women do not carry purses, and their walk and carriage reflect a personal strength that the overly made-up city women have lost. He thinks: "That's the way Pilate must have looked as a girl, looked even now. . . . Wide sleepy eyes that tilted up at the corners, high cheekbones, full lips blacker than their skin, berry-stained, and long, long necks" (266). In addition to the slow pace and sense of community that he finds in Shalimar (pronounced Shallimone/Solomon—another renaming), he realizes that he is unlearned in rural customs. He alienates the men around him by his garish display of money. Before they accept him, he has to go through an initiation consisting of hunting and fighting. Moreover, he has to reconnect with the natural world before he can clearly see what is right in front of him.

Milkman's awareness of the community, the culture, and the natural world around him leads him to reassess his family as well as his own selfishness. He sees all of his extended family in a different light and is sympathetic to both his father's distorted ambition and his mother's pathetic helplessness. His understanding encompasses both those he hurt and ignored and those who were out to "kill" him. However, his perception centers on his two "mothers," who never wanted to take his life, but had given it to him—one physically, the other spiritually: "The two exceptions were both women, both black, both old. From the beginning, his mother and Pilate had fought for his life and he had never so much as made either of them a cup of tea" (335).

In "Rootedness," Morrison states that Pilate functions as the ancestor for Milkman, and it is under her guidance that he becomes responsible and humane (343–44). Moreover, it is her stories and songs, passed on to all of her children, which not only lead him to unravel his family history but implant in him the desire to know. Although she cannot save her own granddaughter from the imposing environment which inevitably destroys Hagar, she manages to protect both Ruth and Milkman. In the end, she bequeaths to Milkman not only his birthright but a legacy which allows him, too, to fly: "She had told him stories, sang him songs, fed him bananas and cornbread, and on the first cold day of the year, hot nut soup" (211). More than the traditional West African peanut soup fed to him, Pilate gives Milkman back his heritage through her African-based orature, although it takes him years to understand the true value of the tales and songs. Most important, the children's song, turned into a woman's blues by Pilate, is what leads Milkman to the legacy of his great-grandfather and the flying Africans.

From the homophone of Pilate's name to Robert Smith's flying on his own wings and the Shalimar children's rendition of the folksong with the sounds of an airplane, the desire to fly and its execution, much discussed by critics, is a major motif in *Song of Solomon*. This motif markedly augments the alternative reality of an Afrocentric world view presented in the novel. The song in Pilate's voice that accompanies Milkman's birth and which he hears throughout his life helps Milkman to realize that he is descended from the flying Africans who refused to exist under the confines and humiliation of slavery. As Milkman listens to the ancient words of the song sung by children who do not even understand the African words like *yaruba* (possibly *Yoruba*), he begins to piece together his family history as told to him by Pilate, Circe, and his grandmother Sing's niece, Susan Byrd, a Native American. Byrd (her name a further configuration of the flying motif) not only confirms Milkman's thoughts about the song, but tells him about the flying. Milkman asks her incredulously, "Why did you call Solomon a flying African?" She answers: "Some of those Africans they brought over here as slaves . . . flew back to Africa. The one around here who did was this same Solomon" (326). When Milkman returns to his lover Sweet, with whom sex is also a dream of flying (302), he is vibrant as he tells her what he has always felt but never before known—that somewhere in his ancestry, someone could fly: "No more cotton! No more bales! No more orders! No more shit! He flew, baby. Lifted his beautiful black ass up in the sky and flew on home" (331–32).

Our enjoyment as readers at Milkman's elation is marred by the death of Hagar (chapter 13), sandwiched in between the two chapters on Milkman's comprehension and acceptance of his birthright. Evidently, Morrison is quick to remind us that the man flying away leaves people behind, most often women and their children. Both Ryna, Solomon's wife, and Hagar, Milkman's spurned lover and cousin, cannot function after being left, and basically die of broken hearts. Hagar unfortunately has inherited the weakness of her great-grandmother, and this trait is further exacerbated by the imposition of the dominant culture, the lack of a truly extended family, and Milkman's selfishness. But there is another female tradition which is exhibited in the myth of the flying Africans—the tradition of women left to tell the tale. These women pass on the stories so that the children will know their names. In this context, Morrison states: "There is a price to pay and the price is the children. . . . All the men have left someone, and it is the children who remember it, sing about it, make it a part of their family history" (Watkins 50).

As illustrated in the novel, it is the women who have kept track of the names and stories so that the men could soar and the children could learn and remember. Pilate hears the words from her father, "You just can't fly off and leave a body," and she lives her life that way—a lament for those who left and a commitment, from the bones of her father to the name that is pierced in her ear, to bear witness. Pilate tells the tale to the young ones who would not even have guessed without her. Indeed, the men who fly off have a price to pay for disappearing without a thought to the women and children left behind. The novel reveals, however, that not all women are destroyed by an oppressive system's dissolution of their family (for the men would not have had to fly away if they were not subject to slavery). Just as the spirituals transformed the slaves' misery into music, Pilate and the other women storytellers turn their "plea into a note" (321) and pass on the memory of the names that were stolen and the stories suppressed.

Germane to this transformational aspect of the storytelling which uncovers the words hidden by the dominant culture is Morrison's statement: "If you come from Africa, your name is gone. It is particularly problematic because it is not just *your* name but your family, your tribe. When you die how can you connect with your ancestors if you have lost your name?" (LeClair 28). The concept of knowing ones's name, tribe, and cultural heritage is paramount to the novel, but Morrison takes it one step further. She shows the necessity of stripping off the layers of hegemonic discourse which have hidden both the names and values of "that civilization which exists underneath." Morrison catches us in our own Eurocentric assumptions to expose one of that civilization's legends. Most readers even vaguely familiar with the Bible will immediately assume the title of the novel relates in some way to the song in the Old Testament, but as the plot unravels, we realize the song is about the flying African Solomon. As in the earlier examples of the use of naming, Morrison emphasizes the ability of black people to subvert images of dominant white Christian values to expose underlying cosmologies while taking on some of the characteristics of the original.

Not only does Morrison demonstrate the ability black people have in turning around the mythologies of the West, but closing her novel in the form of an African dilemma tale's participatory ending compels us to focus on another hegemonic Western notion—science as the sole explanation of the universe. The end of *Song of Solomon* has evoked much critical discussion about what happens to Milkman at Solomon's Leap. After witnessing Pilate's murder by Guitar, Milkman offers his life to his friend and leaps: "As fleet and bright as a lodestar, he wheeled toward Guitar and it did not matter which one of them would give up his ghost in the killing arms of his brother. For now he knew what Shalimar knew: If you surrendered to the air, you could *ride* it" (341). One question which has been raised is whether Milkman lives or dies. Reynolds Price, in a *New York Times* review, asks, "Does Milkman survive to use his new knowledge, or does he die at the hands of a hateful friend?" (48). The ending of the novel is unresolved, but the question the reader should ponder in this interrogative text is not whether Milkman lives or dies, but whether Milkman dies or flies! Which perception of reality are we to believe?

As shown by slavers' reports, many slaves committed suicide by jumping overboard during the Middle Passage. Yet in the southern United States and throughout the Caribbean, legends abound which tell us that the slaves flew back to Africa. If Morrison is ending this novel in the style of an African dilemma tale, there is both a question and a caveat for the reader. In a multicultural society, there may be other perceptions of reality, other values, and other ways of interpretation than the ones ordained by the dominant culture. In this case, Morrison exposes the conflict of Western and African cultural perceptions, revealing the importance of African heritage and values for black Americans. In the reincarnation of his great-grandfather, and through the instructions of his female ancestor and aunt, Milkman flies as his ancestors flew, leaving a legacy for women's tales and children's songs.

In "Towards Dialectical Criticism," Fredric Jameson states, "The process of criticism is not so much an interpretation of content as it is a revealing of it, a laying bare, a restoration of the original message, the original experience beneath the distortions of the various kinds of censorship that have been at work on it" (404). *Song of Solomon* is a text that lends itself to precisely this kind of critical methodology. And Morrison has provided guideposts along the way, at least for readers who also strip bare their Eurocentric perceptions. In so visibly layering her novel, she directs us to the original message that has been censored, almost effaced, by the language of slavery, oppression, and hegemonic discourse. But the novel makes it clear that we must do the work to uncover the civilizations underneath. Morrison, in the manner of African women storytellers, weaves a tale to confound our notions of reality and leaves us with a dilemma that, in finishing the novel, we have to solve. Her aim, of course, is to catch us (whatever our ethnic background) in our easy acceptance of Euro-American cultural hegemony; her discourse is based in the values and traditions of an African heritage which informs the African-American community and its writers.

Notes

1. Most African writers and critics (as well as other African artists) refer to the participatory nature of their art. See, for example, Achebe, "The Writer," and Soyinka.

2. In addition to Holloway's *Africanisms in American Culture*, see Van Sertima's *They Came before Columbus* and Magubane's *The Ties That Bind*. Literary criticism like Henry Louis Gates, Jr.'s *The Signifying Monkey* and conferences such as "The Black Woman and the Diaspora," held at Michigan State University in 1986—and the ensuing conference proceedings in the Mar.–Apr. 1986 *Black Scholar*—also reflect this trend.

3. See, for example, Jean Strouse, "Toni Morrison's Black Magic," *Newsweek*, 30 Mar. 1981, p. 52. Fortunately, the privileging of Western culture and written text over African cultural traditions and orature has begun to change since black feminist and cultural critics have been exploring these works.

4. There is evidence that the novel has its development in orature as well as in literature. Chinweizu and Maduibuike argue that the modern African novel has evolved from the African epic in terms of structure, content, and the world it creates. Moreover, Russian theorist M. M. Bakhtin, in *The Dialogic Imagination*, persuasively states that even the traditional European novel incorporated its oral antecedents.

5. Most essays dealing with folklore in *Song of Solomon* do not examine the African basis of those folk traditions. One article which does specifically is Susan L. Blake's "Folklore and Community in *Song of Solomon*." In addition to the studies cited in the text, works which address myth/ folk heritage and, to some extent, African carryovers include De Weever, Samuels, and Harns. See also Samuels and Hudson-Weems, and Smith.

6. Caribbean writer and scholar Wilson Harris referred to the extensiveness of this phenomenon throughout the New World in a seminar at the University of Texas, Spring 1983. Most African-American folktale collections include tales of flying Africans. References to this legend are found in *Drums* and *Shadows* and in Caribbean studies like Monica Schuler's *Alas, Alas, Congo*. For a more developed study of the flying Africans in literature, see Gay Wilentz, "If You Surrender to the Air: Folk Legends of Flight and Resistance in African-American Literature," *MELUS* 18, no. 1 (1989–1990): 21–32.

7. The three-stone fireplace is a direct carryover from the Bakongo peoples in Central Africa. The stones not only are practical in terms of designing the fire, but they also have religious significance. I am grateful to C. Daniel Dawson, director of special projects at the Caribbean Culture Center, New York City, for bringing this to my attention.

8. For discussion of the role of the grandmother in African-American society and its connections to African family organization, see Manns and Sudarkasa.

9. For a fuller examination of Eshu Elegba, see Consentino.

10. Discussion with African critic and philosopher Donatus Nwoga, University of Nigeria, Nsukka, Feb. 1983. At the time, Dr. Nwoga was working on an article seriously appraising the concept of reincarnation within the context of modern African society. In addition to *Beloved*, Buchi Emecheta's *The Joys of Motherhood* and John Edgar Wideman's *Dam-*

ballah offer examples of contemporary African and African-American novels which incorporate reincarnation.

Works Cited

Abrahams, Roger. *African Folktales*. New York: Pantheon, 1983.

Achebe, Chinua. *Morning Yet on Creation Day*. London: Heinemann, 1972.

————. "The Writer and His Community." In *Hopes and Impediments*, 47–61. Garden City, N.Y.: Doubleday, 1988.

Arthin, Kwame. "The Political and Military Role of Akan Women." In *Female and Male in West Africa*, edited by Christine Oppong, 92–98. London: George Allen, 1983.

Asante, Molefi Kete. "African Elements in African American English." In *Africanisms in American Culture*, edited by Joseph E. Holloway, 19–33. Bloomington: Indiana University Press, 1990.

————. *The Afrocentric Idea*. Philadelphia, Pa.: Temple University Press, 1987.

Bakhtin, Mikhail M. *The Dialogic Imagination: Four Essays*. Edited by Caryl Emerson and Michael Holquist. Translated by Michael Holquist. Austin: University of Texas Press, 1989.

Bambara, Toni Cade. *The Salt Eaters*. New York: Random, House, 1980.

Belsey, Catherine. *Critical Practice*. London: Methuen, 1980.

Blake, Susan L. "Folklore and Community in *Song of Solomon*." MELUS 7, no. 3 (1980): 77–82.

Chinweizu, Onwuchekwa Jernie, and Ihechukwu Maduibuike. *Toward the Decolonization of African Literature*. Washington, D.C.: Howard University Press, 1983.

Christian, Barbara. *Black Feminist Criticism*. New York: Pergamon, 1985.

Consentino, Donald. "Who Is That Fellow in the Many-Colored Cap? Transformations of Eshu in Old and New World Mythologies." *Journal of American Folklore* 100 (1987): 261–75.

De Weever, Jacqueline. "Toni Morrison's Use of Fairy Tale, Folk Tale, and Myth in *Song of Solomon.*" *Southern Folklore Quarterly* 44 (1980): 131–44.

Emecheta, Buchi. *The Joys of Motherhood*. New York: Braziller, 1979.

Evans, Mari. *Black Women Writers (1950–1980)*. Garden City, N.Y.: Doubleday, 1984.

Gates, Henry Louis, Jr. *The Signifying Monkey*. New York: Oxford University Press, 1988.

Harris, Leslie A. "Myth as Structure in Toni Morrison's *Song of Solomon*." *MELUS* 7, no. 3 (1980): 69–76.

Harrison, Paul Carter, ed. *Kuntu Drama: Plays of the African Continuum*. New York: Grove, 1974.

Herskovits, Melville. *The Myth of the Negro Past*. Boston: Beacon, 1941.

Holloway, Joseph E., ed. *Africanisms in American Culture*. Bloomington: Indiana University Press, 1990.

Jameson, Fredric. *Marxism and Form*. Princeton, N.J.: Princeton University Press, 1971.

LeClair, Thomas. "The Language Must Not Sweat." *New Republic*, 21 Mar. 1981, pp. 25–32.

Lee, Dorothy, H. "The Quest for Self: Triumph and Failure in the Works of Toni Morrison." In *Black Women Writers (1950–1980)*, edited by Mari Evans, 346–50. Garden City, N.Y.: Doubleday, 1984.

McAdoo, Harriette, ed. *Black Families*. Beverly Hills, Calif.: Sage, 1981.

Magubane, Bernard Makhosezwe. *The Ties That Blind: African-American Consciousness of Africa*. Trenton, N.J.: Africa World Press, 1987.

Manns, Wilhemina. "Support Systems of Significant Others in Black Families." In *Black Families*, edited by Harriette McAdoo, 237–49. Beverly Hills, Calif.: Sage, 1981.

Marshall, Paule. *Praisesong for the Widow*. New York: Putnam's, 1983.

Mere, Ada. "The Unique Role of Women in Nation Building." Unpublished paper, University of Nigeria, 1984.

Morrison, Toni. *Beloved*. New York: Knopf, 1986.

———. "Rootedness: The Ancestors as Foundation." In *Black Women Women Writers (1950–1980)*, edited by Mari Evans, 339–45. Garden City, N.Y.: Doubleday, 1984.

———. *Song of Solomon*. New York: Knopf, 1977.

———. *Tar Baby*. New York: Knopf, 1981.

Naylor, Gloria. *Mama Day*. New York: Ticknor, 1988.

Nwoga, Donatus. Personal interview, Mar. 1983.

Okonjo, Kamene. "Aspects of Continuity and Change in Mate Selection among the Igbo West of the River Niger." Unpublished paper, University of Nigeria, 1978.

Ong, Walter J. *Orality and Literacy*. London: Methuen, 1982.

Price, Reynolds. Review of *Song of Solomon*. *New York Times Book Review*, 11 Sept. 1977, pp. 48–50.

Reagon, Bernice Johnson. "African Diaspora Women: The Making of Cultural Workers." In *Women in Africa and the Diaspora*, edited by Rosalyn Terborg-Penn, Sharon Harley, and Andrea Benton Rushing, 167–80. Washington, D.C.: Howard University Press, 1987.

Reed, Ishmael. *Flight to Canada*. New York: Random House, 1976.

Samuels, Wilfred D. "Liminality and the Search for Self in Toni Morrison's *Song of Solomon*." *Minority Voices* 5 (Spring–Fall 1981): 59–68.

Samuels, Wilfred D., and Clenora Hudson-Weems, eds. *Toni Morrison*. Boston: Twayne, 1990.

Savannah Unit, Georgia's Writers Project. *Drums and Shadows: Survival Studies among the Georgia Coastal Negroes*. Athens: Georgia University Press, 1940.

Schuler, Monica. *Alas, Alas, Congo: A Social History of Indentured Africans in Jamaica*. Baltimore, Md.: Johns Hopkins University Press, 1980.

Skerrett, Joseph T. "Recitations to the Griot: Storytelling and Learning in Toni Morrison's *Song of Solomon*." In *Conjuring: Black Women, Fiction, and the Literary Tradition*, edited by Marjorie Pryse and Hortense Spillers, 192–202. Bloomington: Indiana University Press, 1985.

Smith, Valerie A. *Self-Discovery and Authority in Afro-American Narrative*. Cambridge, Mass.: Harvard University Press, 1987.

Soyinka, Wole. *Myth, Literature and the African World View*. Cambridge: Cambridge University Press, 1979.

Steady, Filomina Chioma, ed. *The Black Woman Cross-Culturally*. Boston: Schenkman, 1981.

Strouse, Jean. "Toni Morrison's Black Magic," *Newsweek*, 30 March 1981, pp. 52–57.

Sudarkasa, Niara. "Interpreting the African Heritage in Afro-American Family Organization." In *Black Families*, edited by Harriette McAdoo, 38–50. Beverly Hills, Calif.: Sage, 1981.

Tate, Claudia. "Toni Morrison." In *Black Women Writers at Work*, 117–31. New York: Continuum, 1983.

Van Sertima, Ivan. *They Came before Columbus*. New York: Random House, 1976.

Watkins, Mel. "Talk with Toni Morrison." *New York Times Book Review*, 11 Sept. 1977, pp. 48, 50.

Wideman, John Edgar. *Damballah*. New York: Avon, 1981.

Wilentz, Gay. "If You Surrender to the Air: Folk Legends of Flight and Resistance in African American Literature," *MELUS* 18, no. 1 (1989–1990): 21–32.

Toni Morrison's *Song of Solomon*

A Blues Song

JOYCE M. WEGS

◆　◆　◆

FOR THOSE INTERESTED in Toni Morrison and her work, a valuable side effect of her recent critical and popular success is the rush of interviewers to query her about her interests, themes, and purpose in writing fiction. One of the most valuable interviews is by Thomas LeClair in the *New Republic* for March 21, 1981. When LeClair asked Morrison how she conceived of her function as a writer, she replied by describing how her writing belongs to the continuing traditions of black communal life:

> I write what I have recently begun to call village literature, fiction that is really for the village, for the tribe. Peasant literature for *my* people, which is necessary and legitimate but which also allows me to get in touch with all sorts of people. I think long and carefully about what my novels ought to do. They should clarify roles that have become obscured; they ought to identify those things in the past that are useful and those things that are not; and they ought to give nourishment. ... peasants don't write novels because they don't need them.

They have a portrait of themselves from gossip, tales, music, and some celebrations. That is enough.[1]

Morrison continued her answer by noting that the novel form developed in response to a need of the middle class at the beginning of the industrial revolution for "a portrait of itself" because the old one did not fit any longer: "their roles were different." Morrison's own audience, she believes, is in a similar situation: they have come from the country, from a peasant life, to the city where they find new values, and the resulting "confrontation" of values leaves many confused. Her response as a writer is to try to do for the community what music used to do:

> There has to be a mode to do what the music did for blacks, what we used to be able to do with each other in private and in that civilization that existed underneath the white civilization. . . . I am not explaining anything to anybody. My work bears witness and suggests who the outlaws were, who survived under what circumstances and why, what was legal in the community as opposed to what was legal outside it. All that is in the fabric of the story in order to do what the music used to do. The music kept us alive, but it's not enough anymore. My people are being devoured.

This essay will explore how Morrison seeks in fiction to enliven and replenish the function music used to serve in its clarification of roles and its comparison of old and new values. Specifically, it will demonstrate how Morrison as novelist takes on the role of a blues singer in order both to explore how folk values buried in the past may contribute to a better future for all her people and to describe variations on traditional male and female roles in order that her readers may analyze for themselves which ones appear most valuable. As Sherley A. Williams notes, "The blues singer strives to create an atmosphere in which analysis can take place."[2] Similarly, in his study of Afro-American culture, Lawrence Levine describes the dual (individual and group) nature of the blues as "a perfect instrument for voicing the internal group problems, the individual personal difficulties and experiences."[3]

Creating a climate for analysis may seem disloyal to a cultural heritage, but Morrison appears both conscious of this possible criticism and ready to meet it. A twice-repeated line, evidently speaking for the author, protests: *"What else but love. Can't I love what I criticize?"*[4] Her protagonist elucidates the function of such criticism in another key speech: "You have to know what's wrong before you can find what's right" (p. 295).

Morrison provides several clues that the black music she emulates in this novel is the blues and not, for instance, jazz. The "song" of Solomon is modeled on an old blues song about Sugarman. This particular song appears in at least three variations during the novel. Although a complete analysis of characters' names would itself require an essay, Morrison's naming often contains clear links to the blues. For instance, her protagonist's best friend, his "main man," is named Guitar, which is the principal blues instrument. Also, Guitar frequently criticizes black women, and thus he acts as a counterweight to the kinds of criticisms of contemporary black men which Morrison, the female blues singer, is suggesting. More tellingly, Morrison's protagonist near the novel's end meditates on the significance of names in this fashion: "Their names. Names they got from yearnings, gestures, flaws, events, mistakes, weaknesses. Names that bore witness" (p. 334). He then begins to list names. These include not only those of all the principal characters in the novel but also those of such blues greats as Muddy Waters, Leadbelly, and Bo Diddley.

Like Morrison's blue-noted novel, "most blues lyrics provide the listener with a poetic yet starkly realistic look at relationships between the sexes."[5] Morrison's novel and many blues lyrics image the basic difference between the male and the female response to harsh experience in strikingly similar terms: men run away from trouble while women complainingly endure it. A popular blues lyric, which, according to Levine, "generations of Negroes" repeated with variations, makes the point succinctly:

when a woman takes the blues.
She tucks her head and cries;
But when a man catches the blues
He catches er freight and rides.[6]

Most of the principal male and female figures in *Song of Solomon* fit this model of men who flee and women who lament; more specifically, the men fly away and leave their women to sing the blues.

These similarities occur because they are rooted in the black experience. In an interview with Toni Morrison, Robert Stepto noted that "most of the major male characters in black literature are in motion."[7] Morrison agreed with this observation: "I think that one of the major differences between black men's work— the major black characters—and black women's work is precisely that. The big scene is the traveling Ulysses scene, for black men. They are moving."[8] She attributes the motivation for this travel to their lack of a land—"they don't have dominion"—and to curiosity. The result of these travels is that, in the process, "they are also making themselves." As these observations suggest, Morrison does not share the sociological opinion that this trait is the "major failing of black men." Rather, "that has always been to me one of the most attractive features about black male life. I guess I'm not suppose to say that. But the fact that they would split in a minute just delights me."[9] Despite her personal attraction to their life style, the treatment she gives to the traveling men of her novel is highly mixed.

The opening scene of the novel prefigures the essential roles of men and women (flying and singing) that will be developed by each generation of the Dead family. As chapter 1 begins, Robert Smith (not a member of the Dead family) is attempting a suicidal flight from the roof of Mercy Hospital to the other side of Lake Superior—Morrison sounds the dominion theme early[10]— on "his own wings" (p. 1). In the public announcement of his plans, which he tacks to his office door two days in advance, he pleads for forgiveness and protests, "I loved you all" (p. 91). Many pages later, the reader realizes that the flyer is apologizing for his role as assassin, not his suicidal flight.

Publicly, Smith has been selling life insurance, but privately he has been ensuring death, making sure that murders of blacks by whites are avenged. As a member of the Seven Days, a secret society of killers devoted to evening the balance when white justice fails to function, he has been responsible for selecting at random a white victim and killing him. This killing is supposed to be carried out in the same manner the unavenged black person had been killed. Each of the seven members has a day assigned to him, and each avenges murders falling on that day. This bizarrely superior group has no interest in finding the actual murderer; their logic insists that since all whites are naturally evil (p. 156), what is important is keeping the numbers even. Morrison's depiction of these men's sense of moral superiority shows that their personal sacrifices of forgoing a wife and children and living lonely lives serve no good purpose, that their murdered fellows deserve a better revenge. Their solution, after all, does not add to the store of love in the world but emphasizes hatred; worst of all, their roles estrange them from those they claim to care about. For instance, the scheme of Milkman's friend Guitar, who becomes a Seven Days assassin, to dynamite "four innocent white girls" (p. 334) strikes Milkman as unworthy: "The Sunday-school girls deserved better than to be avenged by that *hawk*-headed, *raven*-skinned Sunday man" (p. 334; emphases mine). The bird imagery serves to remind the reader of male flight once again. Robert Smith's plunge to his death graphically indicates the deadly consequences of placing one's self above others. Tragically, he seems unaware that his community does not appreciate his sacrifices, that a solo flight is not the way to show love for others. The name of the group recalls the seven days of creation and suggests these men are trying to play God with others' lives; their grasp of "dominion" is a destructive one.

Several key figures witness Smith's flight. Of most interest besides the pregnant Ruth Dead, who is about to bear the protagonist Macon Dead III (aka Milkman), is a singing woman, who introduces the blues motif of the novel:

> O Sugarman done fly away
> Sugarman done gone

> Sugarman cut across the sky
> Sugarman gone home. (p. 5)

The singer is Pilate Dead, the ragged bootlegger who is the coming baby's aunt and the potion maker who has insured his advent, and she tells Ruth that "a little bird'll be here with the morning" (p. 8).

The bird image does not predict the coming child's gender, for the image simultaneously offers connections to both flight and song. In the context of this novel, however, flight seems associated only with extraordinary women just as song is associated only with extraordinary men. When the novel abruptly and characteristically cuts from the opening scene to a time four years later, Morrison reveals that the little bird was male and reminds the reader of the blues framework in this way:

> Mr. Smith's blue silk wings must have left their mark, because when the little boy discovered, at four, the same thing Mr. Smith had learned earlier—that only birds and airplanes could fly—he lost all interest in himself. To have to live without that single gift saddened him and left his imagination so bereft that he appeared dull. (p. 9)

In other words, Milkman, like Mr. Smith, will later try to shake off his case of the blues by flying, but that flight, like the other aspects of the novel, will have a mixed significance.

Milkman's middle-class parents are cut off from their culture and so repeat the painful male and female patterns in a less obvious fashion. When Ruth tells her grown son the story of her difficult life with her vain father and her equally vain husband, Milkman thinks of it as "his mother's sad sad song" (p. 165). Macon Dead, Ruth's husband, never flies, but he does consider himself far above Ruth because he suspects her of an incestuous attachment to her father. Macon lives in the same house with her but leaves her sexually abandoned for most of their married life: from the time that Ruth is twenty, Macon returns to her for only the four days of potion-induced sexual enchantment that produce Milkman. Constantly criticized by Macon for her deficient housekeeping, Ruth is a pitiable figure in her thoroughgoing ineptitude, yet at least part of her silliness, soggy cakes, and lumpy mashed potatoes seems to be calculated to annoy Macon. Her self-destructive revenge only occasions violent outbursts from him. Milkman finally realizes late in the novel that she might have been far different if his father had loved her (p. 304). The malignant influence of the unloving Macon Dead on his family illustrates that there is no automatic virtue in not flying away.

True to the familial pattern, the adult Milkman soars away from his Michigan hometown in an airplane bound for Pennsylvania. He leaves his long-time "honey-pot" and cousin Hagar to sicken with despair and die after she fails first to rewin him, then to kill him. Before her fatal fever, her conversation with her mother and her grandmother forms a traditionally African cry-and-response pattern as her blues lament is answered by a reassuring lullaby from Reba and Pilate:

> He loves silky hair.
> Hush, Hagar.
> Penny-colored hair.
> Please, honey.
> And lemon-colored skin.
> Shhh.
> And gray-blue eyes.
> Hush, now, hush.
> And thin nose.
> Hush, girl, hush.
> He's never going to like my hair.
> Hush. Hush. Hush, girl, hush. (pp. 319–20)

The third generation of Deads contains a significant break in the four-generation progression of flying men and blues-singing women. Milkman's grandfather, Jake (also known as Macon Dead I), marries a beautiful part-Indian girl he had grown up with— Singing Bird, usually called Sing. Because Sing is overfond of her man, old Circe compares her to a pheasant hen with her "watchful," "nervous" (p. 245) love. Like so many of the women Morrison has described, Sing is overly concerned about her nest, but she neither sings the blues nor goes mad. Instead, she dies as a result of her love in a far more conventional and natural way—in childbirth. Twice abandoned, by both his own father and his wife, Jake does not willingly, leave his children. Instead, he is killed, blown into the air by a gunblast from the whites who covet his legendary farm, Lincoln's Heaven. Even his ghost continues to mourn, ambiguously protesting, "You just can't fly on off and leave a body" (p. 336).

Jake embodies for Morrison the ideal aspects of traditional male traits. An old acquaintance still remembers him towering above others in a most positive way:

> Head and shoulders above all of it was the tall, magnificent Macon Dead, whose death, it seemed to him, was the beginning of their own dying even though they were young boys at the time. Macon Dead was the farmer they wanted to be, the clever irrigator, the peach-tree grower, the hog slaughterer, the wild-turkey roaster, the man who could plow forty in no time flat and sang like an angel while he did it. (p. 237)

This extraordinary man combines both an admirable ability to rise above others and the capacity for song. As Morrison noted in her description of male roles cited earlier, one reason for male travel is the lack of land and dominion. Jake's farm, modeled on one in Morrison's own family,[11] gives him dominion: he need not travel.

Morrison's ideal father figure and his farm serve as a reminder to others that this "is what a man can do if he puts his mind to it and his back in it" (p. 238). Jake's farm says to the other men: "Stop sniveling. . . . Stop picking around the edges of the world. Take advantage. And if you can't take advantage, take disadvantage. We live here. On this planet, in this nation, in this country, right here. No where else! . . . Grab this land. . . . Pass it on!" (pp. 238–39). Morrison's call to labor does not endorse some Puritan work ethic. Rather, it pays tribute to the documented imagination and productivity of black men both during and after slavery. In Morrison's "Rediscovering Black History," she includes a long list of significant advances by black inventors. Two of these inventions, John Pickering's 1900 invention of an airship and A. Miles's 1887 patent on the elevator,[12] may serve as historical sources for the male desire to soar that she endorses in part of the novel's epigraph, "The fathers may soar."

Milkman Dead only gradually becomes a real blues man, for he needs first to find his own identity and then to find a sense of community with his people. The structure of the novel reflects these steps: part I chronicles Milkman's private story (his relationships with his family, his best friend Guitar, and his cousin Hagar), while part II covers his search for a lost treasure during which he also discovers his lost family heritage. As Charles Keil points out, when a black man searches for his identity, he is not trying "so much to discover or create a new identity as, first to accept an identity that is already available and, second, to transform into working assets whatever crippling liabilities may be associated with that identity."[13] Morrison indicates that the crippling liability for Milkman is not a physical defect of having one leg shorter than the other, a deformity that is "mostly in his mind. Mostly but not completely" (p. 68). Rather, the crippling results from his loss of family heritage, so that once he finally discovers his roots and his faults, both his boredom and his limp disappear: "he found himself exhilarated by simply walking the earth. . . . And he did not limp" (p. 284).

Late in the novel, Milkman discovers both his personal and his cultural heritage in the rhymes of a children's game set to an old blues song. When Milkman first sees his own heritage played out in front of him in the tableau of the game which the children of Shalimar, Virginia, play, he does not recognize it. After undergoing such initiation experiences as the hunt and interviewing a number of people, he watches the game again. This time he connects it to his own heritage. It takes him even longer before he understands its contradictory significances. His experience parallels that of the reader, who is introduced to several generations of the Dead family before it gradually becomes clear that there are both positive and negative aspects in a pattern which each generation unconsciously repeats.

Varying a traditional blues song about the flying Sugarman, the Shalimar children over the years have altered their game's lyrics to fit the cultural hero after whom almost everyone and everything in their isolated mountain community is named—Solomon. The town remembers Solomon chiefly for his fathering epic numbers of children and his being able to fly. The game's central figure thus must always be a boy, who spins around in the middle of the circling children "like an airplane" (p. 297). His motions recall the leap Solomon (Milkman's great-grandfather) made from a cliff as he abandoned his wife, Ryna, and his twenty-one children (whose names form many of the song's lyrics) to get free of orders and picking cotton, flying back to Africa alone. The rest of the children play Ryna's role by beginning the blues plea for him not to "leave me here" when the spinning boy's finger points out "the last one Jake" (p. 307), the youngest child Solomon tried at the last minute to take with him. As Milkman later learns from Susan Byrd, Solomon could not hold on to baby Jake (Milkman's grandfather) and dropped him near Heddy, an Indian who reared him as her own.

Even the form of the children's game reflects Milkman's cultural heritage because it has its origins in similar ring games played by both slave and African children.[14] Divorced from his cultural and personal heritage, the watching Milkman ruefully recollects that in his own childhood his mother's folly of sending him to school in a velvet suit had made him such a pariah that he "was never asked to play those circle games, those singing games, to join in anything" (p. 267). The children's game also resembles the shout, an ancestor of the blues utilized by field slaves whose knowledge of English was minimal. Both the shout and the Shalimar game contain "only a few English words," the rest being "composed of Africanized English words or some patois-like language."[15] Out of touch with his cultural past, Milkman predictably describes these non-English sections as "nonsense words" (p. 267).

Morrison uses the children's game to dramatize the folk

knowledge that black people were once able to fly. In her interview with LeClair, Morrison indicates her feeling that recovering this knowledge, which many contemporary urban dwellers have forgotten, is important:

> The myths get forgotten. Or they may not have been looked at carefully. Let me give you an example: the flying myth in *Song of Solomon*. If it means Icarus to some readers, fine: I want to take credit for that. But my meaning is specific. It is about black people who could fly. That was part of the folklore of my life; flying was one of our gifts. I don't care how silly it may seem. It is everywhere—people used to talk about it, it's in the spirituals and gospels. Perhaps it was wishful thinking—escape, death, and all that. But suppose it wasn't. What might it mean? I tried to find out in *Song of Solomon*.[16]

One of the difficulties of discovering the meaning of this heritage is that folk wisdom usually comes in several variants; folk proverbs, for instance, often directly contradict one another in the wisdom they offer. Searchers for a heritage, therefore, must recognize which elements provide life and nourishment, as roots should, and which are destructive and deserving of burial. Two quite different folktales about the flying Africans illustrate this point. In one version of tales about slaves from Africa who fly back home, male slaves, abused by a hard overseer significantly named Mr. Blue, fly off in an all-male group.[17] The teller of the tale mentions no women and children left behind; only a hoe is left sticking up out of the ground to bear witness to their former presence. A more communal version of the tale, one Morrison evidently sees as more worthy of emulation, is retold in Langston Hughes and Arna Bontemps's collection of folklore under the title. "All God's Chillun Got Wings."[18] This tale contains an exemplary elderly male figure, but instead of being a lone eagle, like the Solomon figure Milkman admires,[19] he helps his community to remember their power to fly, and "like a flock of crows," they all fly away from oppression together. As in Morrison's version, the women sing, but certainly not the blues, for men, women, and children all form a celebratory whole: "The men went clapping their hands and the women went singing; and those who had children gave them their breasts, and the children laughed and sucked as their mothers flew, and were not afraid."[20]

Although *Song of Solomon* pays tribute to the sort of father suggested by the affectionately simple dedication to "Daddy," Morrison also aims many criticisms specifically at men, not just at negative characters who happen to be male. Their frequent urination in public places illustrates a danger of man's love of flight: undeservedly placing one's self above others may simply exploit the many "ways to pee on people" (p. 215). Milkman's repeated urination in inappropriate contexts symbolizes his self-concern, his indifference to others, and his childishness. His name also has as one of its overtones an implication of immaturity. As a small child, he innocently sprays his older sister, Lena, when she startles him by walking up behind him after a flower-gathering foray into the woods. Yet his subsequent behavior as an adult makes his childish act take on a more negative, premonitory cast. Years later Milkman condescendingly decides that his other sister, Corinthians, is having an affair with someone not good enough for her and tells their father about it. As she defends their fortyish sister's last chance for love, the angry Lena spells out in blunt terms how undeserved his dominion is. She associates the "kinds of ways to pee on people" with male arrogance as she asks, "Where did you get the *right* to decide our lives?" (p. 217). In answer to her own question, she attributes his smug superiority to the "hog's gut that hangs down between your legs" (p. 217). Finally, she announces that his attempts to take over the family, which he began by hitting his father, ostensibly in defense of his mother, are over: he has "pissed" his "last" in their house (p. 218). The urinary imagery graphically illustrates the negative aspects of the novel's dominion theme and contains links to the image of a bird in flight: the birds menace those below them.

Other references to male urination all link it to a desire to dominate others or to a lack of self-control. Morrison foreshadows Macon Dead's later role as a callous slumlord in her description of his behavior after he has evidently killed a man and found a hoard of gold nuggets in the man's cave: "like a burglar out on his first job Macon stood up to pee," excited by his vision of "life, safety, and luxury" (p. 171). Macon's vision of the future does not include love or sharing his wealth with others. Milkman later exhibits a similar lack of self-control and concern for others when he is thrown out of a house party for urinating in the kitchen sink (p. 213).

In another key passage that illustrates Milkman's self-absorption, he is dreaming of flying while asleep in Sweet's arms. Although the dream occurs in an erotic context, Milkman none-theless flies alone in his dream: "He was alone in the sky but somebody was applauding him, watching him and applauding. He couldn't see who it was" (p. 302). His inability to see the on-looker comes not only because he faces skyward—he is "in the relaxed position of a man lying on a couch reading a newspaper" (p. 302)—but also because he lacks real interest in others except as he can use them. Similarly, when he rides he rides on an airplane, he wants to "go solo. In the air, away from real life, he . . . [feels] free, but on the ground the wings of all those other peoples' nightmares . . . [flap] in his face and . . . [constrain] him" (p. 222). Since only his own dreams are important to him, he labels those of others "nightmares." Flight also gives Milkman an unrealistic feeling of "invulnerability" from error. So strong is this feeling that "it was not possible to believe he had ever made a mistake or could" (p. 222).

Just as Milkman's aunt Pilate rescues him from his brush with the police, so too she cures him of his illusion of lofty perfection. When he elatedly returns to Michigan to tell her of his marvelous discoveries, she breaks a bottle over his head as her greeting to her granddaughter's killer. Brought low to Pilate's cellar, he faces his guilt and accepts Pilate's "version of punishment" when "somebody took another person's life" (p. 336). This punishing memento turns out to be a box of Hagar's hair, an appropriate reminder of Milkman's guilt since Hagar mourned before her death that Milkman could not love her because of her hair, be-cause of her blackness. Pilate comforted her then by saying that if he hated her hair, he must hate himself. When Milkman takes the box of hair, therefore, he also acknowledges his true self, a self not immune to mistakes. He realizes his selfish cruelty to Hagar: "While he dreamt of flying, Hagar was dying" (p. 336). When he bragged to his new lover, Sweet, about his great grandfather's ability to fly, he had not understood the implications of her question. "Who'd he leave behind?" (p. 332). Then, he had exulted in his answer to her query: "Everybody!" But now he sees the selfishness in Solomon's desertion: "Who looked after those twenty children? Jesus Christ, he left twenty-one children!" (p. 336). Both Pilate and her ghostly adviser, her father, Jake— the two guiding figures and true role models in the novel—have long realized what Milkman now finally understands: "A human life is precious. You shouldn't fly off and leave it" (p. 209).

As long as Milkman emulates his great-grandfather's lonely flight, he too deserves Morrison's scorn as a "solo man." With Pilate's guidance, Milkman finally realizes that a genuine bluesman does not really fly solo since he is connected musically to the other musicians, to their shared pasts; only as each bluesman adds his personal history to that shared past may he be said to launch into a solo flight.

While Morrison excoriates male arrogance, selfishness, isolation, and immaturity, she also recognizes that the blues-singing woman is far from perfect. Posterity remembers Ryna, the archetypal blues singer who goes mad after Solomon's desertion, and only for her excesses of mourning. She has a moaning ditch named after her—Ryna's Gulch. Susan Byrd's description of such women suggests that their devotion is self-destructive: "You don't hear about women like that anymore, but there used to be more—the kind of woman who couldn't live without a particular man. And when the man left, they lost their minds, or died or something. Love, I guess" (p. 327). Her dubious tone suggests that such behavior is more self-indulgence than love, just as Guitar's tirades harshly criticize black women's notions of love:

> And black women, they want your whole self. Love, they call it, and understanding. "Why don't you *understand* me?" What

they mean is, Don't love anything on earth except me. They say, "Be responsible," but what they mean is. Don't go anywhere where I ain't. You try to climb Mount Everest, they'll tie up your ropes. Tell them you want to go to the bottom of the sea—just for a look—they'll hide your oxygen tank. Or you don't even have to go that far. Buy a horn and say you want to play. Oh, they love the music, but only after you pull eight at the post office. (p. 224)

Morrison notes not only men's flight but also the reason they left: the women hung on too tightly. Guitar's lecture addressed to Hagar, a "doormat woman" (p. 306) with an "anaconda love" (p. 137) that destroys her self, continues a condemnatory theme in Morrison's work—a smothering possessiveness in women, often disguised as domesticity, which works against their keeping their men and which is totally unrelated to any meaningful concept of love. Warning Hagar against the incompatibility of love and possession, Guitar also points out that their love is not great simply because the loss of their men drives them mad. These conceited women who "think they [are] so lovable" are in fact greedy, and their "stingy little love" eats "everything in sight" (p. 306).

Milkman's rejection of both his mother and Hagar stems largely from their attempts to own him, to have dominion over him. As Guitar tells Milkman, "There's nothing wrong with controlling yourself, but can't nobody control other people" (p. 117). After many years of an "on-again, off-again" affair which keeps Milkman interested, the aging Hagar panics and places "duty squarely in the middle of their relationship" (p. 98). Predictably, he reacts by trying "to think of a way out" (p. 98). His rejection launches her on a series of attempts to kill what she cannot have. When his mother finally learns of Hagar's attempts to kill Milkman, she visits Hagar. In their conversation, Hagar calls Milkman her "home in this world" (p. 137) while Ruth calls herself Milkman's home. After overhearing this conversation, the more realistic Pilate scolds them in pungent terms which reiterate the novel's themes of male flight, arrogance, and excretion and female possessiveness: she reminds them that he "wouldn't give a pile of swan shit" for either of them and points out that "he ain't a house, he a man, whatever he need, don't none of you got it" (p. 138).

Although the novel focuses on Milkman, he is guided in his discoveries by Pilate, the wise old woman who has already arrived at peace with herself and the world. Her role in leading the Deads back to life is made explicit in the reaction of the Shalimar residents to Milkman's queries as to whether any of them has ever heard of his aunt: "Ha! Sound like a newspaper headline: Pilot Dead. She do any flying?" (p. 286). As the pun shows, Pilate has in fact piloted or guided Milkman to Virginia, for he has been following what he supposes to have been her path from the gold cave in Pennsylvania to the family home in Virginia. Although Milkman never finds the gold hoard, he does, Morrison implies, find a real treasure—his lost heritage.

Because Pilate is an extraordinary woman and in touch with her roots, Morrison links her to both singing and flying. Throughout the novel Pilate sings to comfort herself in her loneliness, to accompany work as she and her family make wine, to comfort Hagar, and to mourn Hagar at Hagar's funeral. Like that of her exemplary father, her singing also serves other purposes than singing the blues. Near the end of the novel, her unusual strengths are acknowledged in references to her as a flyer; at least in metaphor: when she dies, the grieving Milkman finally knows why "he loved her so. Without ever leaving the ground, she could fly" (p. 340). Reflecting Morrison's own interest in the blackmale's travel urge, Pilate spends much of her life traveling before she settles down for her granddaughter's sake: all God's children have wings, not just men.

Real strength means taking command of one's own life as Pilate did. When she realizes that her strange lack of a navel will always isolate her from other people, who consider her "unnatural" and class her with "mermaids," she throws "away every assumption" she has had and begins again at "zero": "Then she tackled the problem of trying to decide how she wanted to live and what was valuable to her. When am I happy and when am

I sad and what is the difference? What do I need to know to stay alive? What is true in the world?" (p. 149). These basic questions also outline the fundamental concerns of the novel: the need to identify life-affirming, loving behavior and to spot the dangers of false assumptions, behavior, and roles. Pilate's missing navel suggests her role as an Eve figure who marks a possible new beginning. Pilate is not, however, a sentimental figure in the novel, for just as Guitar berates black women for their foolish notions of love, she can indulge in humorous excoriations of black men, who fear her because of her harmless difference: "It occurred to her that although men fucked armless women, one-legged women, hunchbacks and blind women, drunken women, razor-toting women, midgets, small children, convicts, boys, sheep, dogs, goats, liver, each other, and even certain species of plants, they were terrified of fucking her—a woman with no navel" (pp. 148–49).

While Pilate is a strong, admirable figure, Morrison acknowledges that there are not many women like her. Milkman can only hope that there is "at least one more woman" (p. 341) like her. What most women need to be like Pilate is support from a broad spectrum of relatives and other women in their community, something Hagar, with her unusual mother and grandmother, lacks. Morrison makes this point explicit in her description of Hagar's plight after being abandoned by Milkman:

> Neither Pilate nor Reba knew that Hagar was not like them. Not strong enough, like Pilate, nor simple enough, like Reba, to make up her life as they had. She needed what most colored girls needed: a chorus of mammas, grandmammas, aunts, cousins, sisters, neighbors, Sunday school teachers best girl friends, and what all to give her the strength life demanded of her—and the humor with which to live it. (p. 311)

The importance of community to both men and women is illustrated by Hagar's tragedy and by Milkman's new awareness of links to other people as he discovers his roots in Shalimar: "He was curious about these people. He didn't feel close to them, but he did feel connected, as though there was some cord or pulse or information they shared. Back home he had never felt that way, as though he belonged to anyplace or anybody" (pp. 292–93).

The novel's conclusion reiterates the themes of flight, song, community, heritage, and the blues. Morrison unites the central male and female symbols of flight and song in connection with both Pilate and her pupil Milkman. When the dying Pilate, shot by the maddened and vengeful Guitar, asks Milkman to sing for her, he obliges out of love but shows that this blues-singing role is totally new to him: "Milkman knew no songs, and had no singing voice that anybody would want to hear, but he couldn't ignore the urgency in her voice. Speaking the words without the least bit of a tune, he sang for the lady" (p. 340). His plaintive spoken song about Sugargirl awakens some sleeping birds, which also unite the images of flight and song. One of them darts into the grave filled with the first Macon Dead's bones, the only family treasure. There the bird sees Pilate's earring box with her name in it, "something shiny" (p. 340) it snatches up in its beak. In this way, Pilate's name flies away. Milkman recognizes the significance when he says, "Without ever leaving the ground, she could fly" (p. 340). Then Milkman too becomes a guide or pilot, for he leaps from Solomon's Leap toward Guitar "as fleet and bright as a *lodestar*" (p. 341; emphasis mine).

To celebrate life-giving love over death, even the hills and rocks participate in echoing the novel's message as Milkman's shouts to Guitar reverberate this life-affirming statement about being black: *"Tar tar tar. . . . Am am am am. . . . Life life life life"* (p. 341). The novel chronicles the blues history of an individual, a family, and a people who are not really *Dead* but alive.

To be truly alive, one must love and act upon that love. Having finally learned to love, Milkman leaps toward Guitar to carry out his recent insight that "perhaps that's what all human relationships boiled down to: Would you save my life? Or would you take it?" (p. 334). Thus, he sails toward Guitar not necessarily to take his life but perhaps to save through active love the life of the man he still regards as "his brother" (p. 341). To Morrison, loss of familial, communal, and brotherly love may be reasons to sing the blues, but their presence can offer the power to soar.

Notes

1. Thomas LeClair, " 'The Language Must Not Sweat,' " *New Republic*, 21 March 1981, p. 26.

2. Sherley A. Williams, "The Blues Roots of Contemporary Afro-American Poetry," in *Chant of Saints*, ed. Michael S. Harper and Robert B. Stepto (Urbana: University of Illinois Press, 1979), p. 125.

3. Lawrence Levine, *Black Culture and Black Consciousness: Afro-American Folk Thought from Slavery to Freedom* (New York: Oxford University Press, 1977), p. 268.

4. Toni Morrison, *Song of Solomon* (New York: New American Library, 1977), pp. 225, 285. Subsequent references to the novel appear parenthetically in the text.

5. Charles Keil, *Urban Blues* (Chicago: University of Chicago Press, 1966), p. 53.

6. Levine, *Black Culture*, p. 262. Levine is citing from Newman Ivey White, *American Negro Folk-Songs* (Cambridge, Mass.: Harvard University Press, 1928), p. 394.

7. Robert B. Stepto, " 'Intimate Things in Place': A Conversation with Toni Morrison," in *Chant of Saints*, p. 226.

8. Ibid.

9. Ibid., p. 27.

10. Jane Bakerman. "The Seams Can't Show: An Interview with Toni Morrison," *Black American Literature Forum* 12 (1978): 60. Morrison says that "dominion" is the novel's theme.

11. Colette Dowling, "The Song of Toni Morrison," *New York Times Magazine*, 20 May 1979, p. 40.

12. Toni Morrison, "Rediscovering Black History," *New York Times Magazine*, 11 August 1974, p. 24.

13. Keil, *Urban Blues*, p. 15.

14. Mary F. Berry and John W. Blassingame, "Africa, Slavery, and the Roots of Contemporary Black Culture," *Massachusetts Review* 18 (1977): 509.

15. Leroi Jones, *Blues People: Negro Music in White America* (New York: Morrow, 1963), p. 63.

16. LeClair, "Language," p. 27.

17. J. Mason Brewer, "Flying People," in his *American Negro Folklore* (Chicago: Quadrangle, 1972), p. 309.

18. Langston Hughes and Arna Bontemps, eds., *The Book of Negro Folklore* (New York: Dodd Mead, 1958), p. 64.

19. Milkman tells Sweet that Solomon "sailed on off like a black eagle" (p. 332).

20. Hughes and Bontemps, *Book of Negro Folklore*, p. 64.

Names to Bear Witness

The Theme and Tradition of Naming
in Toni Morrison's Song of Solomon

LUCINDA H. MACKETHAN

◆　◆　◆

TONI MORRISON OPENS her 1977 novel, *Song of Solomon*, with an epigraph which reads, "The fathers may soar / And the children may know their names." In the first chapter of a novel full of ironic father-child relationships and complex searches for the meanings of names, the first discussion of names concerns the name of a street on which much of the action of the story will take place. "The only colored doctor in the city" had lived and died on a street officially listed as "Mains Avenue," but the doctor's patients, chiefly poor blacks living in the city's "Southside" section, called the street "Doctor Street," and this name had persisted for many years in spite of official disapproval. When the city fathers put up notices insisting that the street "had always been and would always be known as Mains Avenue and not Doctor Street," their attempt to humble the black citizenry backfires in a reaction that is both comic and wickedly sly: "It was a genuinely clarifying public notice," we are told, "because it gave Southside residents a way to keep their memories alive and please the city legislators as well. They called it Not Doctor

Street."¹ Though not particularly interested in whether their thoroughfare is called "Doctor" or "Not Doctor" Street, the Southside residents are determined that the name their street is given reflect themselves and their memories of one of their own who became "the first colored man of consequence in the city . . . when the odds were that he would be a yardman."

In this opening scene, Morrison begins her treatment of the central theme of her novel with a humorous example of how names come to be and have meaning. She is providing a kind of base note for a key idea that will be given richly varied expression as her story progresses—it is an idea which another black writer, Ralph Ellison, explored in a 1964 address entitled "Hidden Name and Complex Fate," in which he said, "Our names, being the gift of others, must be made our own."² The residents of Southside make the name of their street an announcement of their concern for their own identities as they rebel covertly against a system that would take title to their names and lives as well.

In an interview given in 1976 while she was still writing the work tentatively titled "Milkman Dead" which would become *Song of Solomon*, Morrison said, "The name thing is a very, very strong theme in the book that I'm writing, the absence of a name given at all, the odd names and the slave names, the whole business, the feeling of anonymity, the feeling of orphanage."³ The anecdote of the origin of the name of Not Doctor Street is the first of a series of narrative sections which probes the names of characters and places. Names define values in the novel because of the crucial ways that they both reveal and conceal true knowledge and true identity. The members of the novel's family received the richly ironic surname "Dead" during Reconstruction times, when a drunk Freedman Bureau official mistakenly scrawled the name "Macon Dead" on the freedom papers of Jake Solomon. From that time forward, all of Solomon's children inherit his struggle. They find that their names, being "gifts" of questionable value from others out of love or hate, ignorance or accident, must be made their own. Milkman Dead (christened Macon Dead III), Macon the first and Macon the second, Pilate Dead, Sing, Guitar, First Corinthians Dead, the family's progenitor

Solomon—all these and others are linked in a quest that is an archetype in the main body of black literature beginning with the slave narratives. It is a quest which Ralph Ellison eloquently defined in his essay:

> We must learn to wear our names within all the noise and confusion of the environment in which we find ourselves; . . . We must charge them with all our emotions, our hopes, hates, loves, aspirations. They must become our masks and our shields and the containers of all those values and traditions which we learn and/or imagine as being the meaning of our familial past.

Song of Solomon emphasizes names and naming in ways that place the novel squarely within black American literature's dominant tradition. Works in this tradition enact quests for identity within a culture which systematically denies the black person's right to both name and identity as a means of denying his or her humanity. In the slave narratives, in first-person initiation novels such as James Weldon Johnson's *Autobiography of an Ex-Coloured Man* or Ellison's *Invisible Man*, in autobiographies by Richard Wright and Malcolm X, to know one's name, to tell it, accept it, insist on it are measures of one's freedom and selfhood and fate. Morrison's use of the tradition and theme of naming encompasses all of these aspects of the power inherent in the right to name, yet she makes the theme her own through a marvelous originality of voice and freshness of scene, giving to the tradition perhaps its most celebrative expression to date.

In her 1976 interview, Morrison mentions that "just for sustenance, I read those slave narratives."[4] In her reading, she would necessarily find the beginnings of the black writer's historical interest in names, a phenomenon which Sidonie Smith notes in her study of black autobiography when she says that for the slave narrators relating their escapes to freedom, "the rite of naming came to symbolize the act of liberation."[5] Gilbert Osofsky, introducing a collection of slave narratives, writes, "The right to proscribe letters or command a man's name is understood as the power to subordinate. . . . The right to control it . . . is the power to order reality, to subjugate man himself."[6] The slave narrators' understanding of this power within the right to name is demonstrated repeatedly in their narratives. James Pennington, at the beginning of his work entitled *The Fugitive Blacksmith; or, Events in the History of James W. C. Pennington* (1849), bitterly denounced the "chattel principle" chiefly on the grounds that it took away the black man's name as a device for making a record of himself "as a man." Slavery, Pennington maintained, left the slave "without a single record to which he may appeal in vindication of his character, or honor," because when the slave looked for "any record of himself *as a man*," he could find only "his name on a catalogue with the horses, cows, hogs, and dogs."[7] William Wells Brown, reacting to the human right to show oneself through one's name, took back the name "William," which a master had changed to "Sandford." Because of the special emphasis he placed on the event of deciding what his name would be in his narrative, all the events involved with his struggle for freedom could be identified as part of what was symbolized through his taking back of his name. As he put it, "I was not only hunting for my liberty, but also hunting for a name."[8] His first and perhaps most important act, after arriving on free soil, was to decide to be William, a decision which indicated his entrance into a self-shaped world: "Traveling along the road, I would sometimes speak to myself, sounding my name over, by way of getting used to it, before I should arrive among civilized human beings."[9] This statement presents William Wells Brown as a free man fulfilled within his name, announcing the identity with which he would meet a new kind of world that he had humanized by his own humanity.

In "Hidden Name and Complex Fate," Ellison tells of hearing a black preacher exhort the brothers and sisters of his congregation to "let us make up our faces before the world, and our names shall sound throughout the land with honor! For we ourselves are our *true* names, not their epithets."[10] Surely this is how James Pennington resolved the problem of having a name that listed him with horses and hogs; he honored his idea of himself as a man enough to insist upon his right to a free condition consistent with his sense of self. William Wells Brown knew the truth of the preacher's statement and named himself to reflect who he felt himself to be. Richard Wright seems to have had a similar assertion of vision of self in mind when he titled his autobiography *Black Boy*, not in acceptance of an epithet but in an enactment of the idea suggested by Ellison that he could take a racial label and make it sound out his book's saga of struggle to achieve a voice and an identity on his own terms. In Ellison's *Invisible Man*, the naive, unenlightened narrator's lack of a name indicates not just lack of identity in the white world but also lack of sense of self; the Invisible Man who takes many labels but cannot name himself pinpoints his own incompleteness as he muses about one of his heroes, the orator and slave narrator Frederick Douglass. "What had his true name been?" wonders the Invisible Man. "Whatever it was it was as Douglass that he became himself, defined himself."[11] The Invisible Man understands that Douglass's ability to name himself and to define himself gave him freedom and honor. One last example of how "making a face" and naming are connected in black tradition is *The Autobiography of Malcolm X*, in which Malcolm Little's transformation from hoodlum and criminal to orator and black nationalist was keyed around his taking of the Muslim symbol "X" to signify his mastery of the problem of identity facing all blacks in America, a problem his brother explained when he said, "You don't even know who you are. . . . You don't even know your true family name, you wouldn't recognize your true language if you heard it."[12]

Toni Morrison's achievement in *Song of Solomon* is her ability to absorb these many facets of the tradition of naming, from James Pennington's lament to Malcolm X's defiance, and to shape her own artistic design from them. She explores the many options available within the power to name that belong rather uniquely to the black man and woman within American culture and emerges with a novel that affirms both the heritage of the name as a "gift of others" and the function of the name as "witness bearer" to an individual's treasure of selfhood.

Near the end of *Song of Solomon*, after a series of flights and evasions, Milkman Dead thinks of the names of all the people and places he has come to know, "Names they got from yearnings, gestures, flaws, events, mistakes, weaknesses. Names that bore witness" (330). The journey which teaches him that "when you know your name, you should hang on to it" is a journey which offers him all of the options that his status in America leaves open to him, a status which Ralph Ellison describes when he says, "We are reminded so constantly that we bear, as Negroes, names originally possessed by those who owned our enslaved grandparents."[13] Milkman Dead can, because of this constant reminder, acquiesce to the official notice that his name makes him the white man's chattel and so live by white definitions of success and failure; his father, the second Macon Dead, provides a model for this option. Milkman can reject his name as a burden of shame, as his grandmother had influenced the first Macon Dead to do. He can try to be totally unconcerned with individual names and to lose himself within a group consciousness of protest, as his friend Guitar does. Or, he can follow the most vital example offered by the novel, that of aunt Pilate Dead, who accepted a name that carried the awful connotation of Christ killer. The name P-i-l-a-t-e was just as often mistaken for the name P-i-l-o-t, the spelling and meaning of which are not insignificant for the role that Pilate plays in teaching Milkman how to regard himself within his own name. A study of Milkman's movement through this series of choices of how to live with his name and his familial past shows how at the last, he sees Pilate, who has treasured every aspect of her own identity from her tragic past to her family to all of her human relationships, as the one who has the best grasp of the power of naming. She is a dramatization of Ellison's point that "we take what we have and make of our names what we can," not in "mere forgiveness" or "obsequious insensivity" but in "conscious acceptance of the harsh realities of the human condition, of the ambiguities and hypocrisies of human history as they have played themselves out in the United States."[14]

Macon Dead III was rechristened "Milkman" by a local gossip who discovered that he was being nursed by his mother at an

age when the boy was old enough to suspect something unnatural in sitting on his mother's lap that way. His father was sure
that this nickname for his son, picked up with glee by the whole
community, had some "filthy connection" with his wife, whom
he despised, and so the name, which came into being as a joke,
evolved into a truth, not about Milkman himself but about his
parents, their diseased relationship, and their ambiguous feelings
about him. Many of the names in the novel grow into meaning
in this way, "begat" by accident or misunderstanding yet accruing
associations which articulate some truth about the name bearer.

Macon II does not try to find out how his son received a name
that to him sounds "dirty, intimate, and hot," but he does mourn
the fact that his own father had allowed an official "who couldn't
have cared less" to write the words "Macon Dead" on his "freedom" papers after the Civil War in a comedy of errors which
consigned all his issue "to this heavy name scrawled in perfect
thoughtlessness" (18). To Jake Solomon and his proud part-Indian
wife, the name "Macon Dead" could mean something very positive in 1869, in spite of the circumstances of its inception; to
Macon Dead II, the name means only a heritage of oppression
that his father was unable to master or even survive. Macon II
thinks that surely somewhere he must have had an ancestor
"who had a name that was real. A name given him at birth with
love and seriousness. A name that was not a joke, nor a disguise,
nor a brand name" (18). Indeed, there was such an ancestor, as
Milkman will be the one to discover. However, Macon Dead Two,
who hates his name yet abides by it, will never be able to acknowledge this ancestor, for in accepting *his* name he is actually
accepting the idea that the white man can determine his values
and control his life. After his father had been murdered by local
whites for his land, Macon Two managed to work his way up in
the white man's world as a slum landlord; he married the black
doctor's daughter, collected rents without mercy, watched land
values and stock markets, and on Sundays drove his late model
Packard (which his neighbors called "Macon Dead's hearse") out
to the wealthy white neighborhoods in a parody of white greed
and status seeking. As Milkman is told by his radical friend Guitar,

"He behaves like a white man, thinks like a white man" (223). The first Macon Dead's pride has been replaced by a lust for comfort and security in the second one, who tells his son, "The only important thing you'll ever need to know" is to "own things. And let the things you own own other things. Then you'll own yourself and other people too" (55).

Milkman has his father's example to go by in the matter of what to allow his name to mean. He can be the duplicate of his father in philosophy as in name, carrying on the father's belief that "money is freedom. . . . The only real freedom there is" (162). To choose this alternative would make Milkman dead, like his father, to the regenerative qualities of his family's past, yet through his father another alternative is made available to him— the example of his grandfather. This name bearer, who could not read, took the freedom papers with the ridiculous name scrawled on it in an affirmation of himself not unlike that of William Wells Brown, who reported that in his escape from slavery, he was not only hunting his liberty but also looking for a name. The grandfather had kept the name, although it was a callously made mistake, at his wife's insistence because she "said it was new and would wipe out the past. Wipe it all out" (54). Milkman at first thinks that his grandfather was a "sheep" to allow a "cracker" to name him, but he learns eventually that the name bore witness to his grandparents' determination to shape a new identity out of a past that had ranked his race, as James Pennington would say, with the horses, cows, hogs, and dogs. In an enactment of Ellison's preacher's idea that "we ourselves are our *true* names," the first Macon Dead carved a farm out of rock and so became known by an admiring community for his various achievements; he was "the farmer they wanted to be, the clever irrigator, the peach tree grower, the hog-slaughterer, the wild-turkey roaster" (235). The first Macon Dead's actions were his name, through which he said, "Never mind you can't tell one letter from another, never mind you born a slave, never mind you lose your name. . . . Here, this here, is what a man can do" (235).

From his father, Milkman learns that a name can be a title of ownership given gratuitously by those who would rule by force what they cannot know in love. From his grandfather, he learns that a name, though created as accidentally as life itself, can, again like life itself, be shaped to mean anything that a man decides he wants it to show. Yet Milkman's grandparents hoped to wipe out the past by denying their original name and accepting an arbitrary new one, and the murder of the grandfather showed the futility of that attempt. They could not shape who they wanted to be exclusively on the basis of courage for the present moment and dreams for the future, because their identities were rooted in a past steeped in oppression as well as love and accident.

Yet love is still the key to naming, and Milkman has two teachers to show him this truth, one whose message is love in death, the other whose lesson is that love keeps identity alive through roots in memory and responsibility. Guitar, a member of a secret sect which murders whites in retaliation for white brutalities on blacks, is Milkman's only friend. He received his name out of his desire to have, not his ability to play, the guitar. As a baby, "I cried for it," he explains, "and always asked about it" (45). Guitar's knowledge of the world grows from the desire and deprivation that were the twin sources of his name, and he is able to teach Milkman many facts of black life from them. In words similar to Ellison's, he tells Milkman, "Niggers get their names the way they get everything else—the best way they can." When Milkman whines in reply, "Why can't we get our stuff the right way?" Guitar answers simply, "The best way is the right way" (88).

Guitar's desire to be a man who can live with dignity leads him to confuse love with need and to accept killing and death as the answers to the problem of establishing black identity in a world that denies it. Milkman, after listening to Guitar's theory that all whites deserve to die, says, "You sound like the red-headed Negro named X. Why don't you join him and call yourself Guitar X?" (160). Guitar's reply is very close to Ralph Ellison's thoughts on the black Muslim rejection of names rooted in a slave past. Ellison wrote, "We have ... the example of ... the Black Muslims, discarding their original names in rejection of the bloodstained, the brutal, the sinful images of the past. Thus they would declare new identities, would clarify a new program of intention and destroy the verbal evidence of a willed and ritual- ized discontinuity of blood and human intercourse."[15] Milkman's grandmother, seeking to "wipe out the past," seems to be trying to reject her husband's "sinful past" and to declare a new identity in just this way. Ellison, in his essay, goes on to say, "Not all of us, actually only a few, seek to deal with our names in this man- ner. We take what we have and make of them what we can."[16] Guitar's reply to Milkman expresses a similar attitude: "X, Bains— what difference does it make? . . . Besides, I do accept it. It's part of who I am. Guitar is *my* name. Bains is the slave master's name. And I'm all of that. Slave names don't bother me; but slave status does" (160).

Guitar can accept his name as the expression of how his her- itage has shaped him; in addition he is committed to action to express who he is and what his status should be. But Guitar cannot make his acceptance of who he is a force to live by; his submergence of self in a group that lives by killing to show its love leads him to equate life with death: "*What* and how I die or when doesn't interest me," he says. "What I die for does. It's the same as what I live for" (159). Thus Milkman cannot use Guitar as a model for learning the value of his name to his life because Milkman is, in spite of his detachment from others, committed to living, and to living for himself. His selfishness, turned from self-gratification to self-knowledge, can be his salvation, and he is open to this possibility in part because of his heritage from the Dead side of the family: "Ain't but three Deads alive," Pilate tells Milkman, instilling in him a determination to be one of them. "I'm a Dead," he shouts (38).

Learning what it truly means to be one of the living Deads is Milkman's hidden assignment, and his aunt Pilate's first lesson, the one that makes her wisdom so different from Guitar's, is that "life is life. Precious" (208) and that "ain't nothin natural about death. It's the most unnatural thing they is" (140). Pilate's lessons and her wisdom are intimately connected to what her name sig- nifies and to her attitude toward it. The name was a confused gift of love from her father, who could not read the word but picked it out of the Bible for its visual shape, choosing "a group of letters that seemed to him strong and handsome, saw in them a large figure that looked like a tree hanging in some princely but protective way over a row of smaller trees" (18). Thus Pilate's father attempted to give his daughter a name that would be a blessing and a prophecy, so that the motherless child could protect herself and others. Pilate reveres the name as a gift and carries the piece of paper on which he wrote the name in an earring fashioned from her mother's snuffbox. Her name is her charm, symbolizing her love and acceptance of who she is and her resolution to live according to her own lights. The name must bear witness to her life, not her life to the name. The questions she is able to ask show a totally self-shaped, free individual: "She threw away every assumption she had learned and began at zero. . . . Then she tackled the problem of trying to decide how she wanted to live and what was valuable to her. When am I happy and when am I sad and what is the difference? What do I need to know to stay alive?" (149).

Trying to trace the path Pilate had taken as a girl of twelve after her father's murder, Milkman journeys south until he arrives at his grandfather's birthplace and also comes home to himself. Alone in dark, unknown, wooded mountain country, he finds that he cannot "see" himself with his eyes and that all the societal contexts and learned habits are of no use. He must, like Pilate, begin "at zero" at this point: "He was only his breath, coming slower now, and his thoughts" (277). Stripped of all external aids and assumptions, Milkman experiences one revelation after another concerning his own actions, his parents, and their shared inheritance. When he returns from the South to Michigan, he has none of the things he started with—no watch, clothes, money, or suitcase—but he knows his name.

Milkman's true family name is Solomon; his great-grandfather had escaped slavery in a magical flight that was recorded among his descendants in fable and song. Yet knowledge of name and past endows Milkman with no more than a beginning, a zero point from which to start; they bear witness to but do not fix or limit his life and way of living. What Milkman can learn from all his relationships is that the power to give a name is a trifle; the power to give a name its meaning is the power over life itself. The words of Ralph Ellison's essay, that "our names, being the gifts of others, must be made our own," fit Milkman's quest for a hidden name, as his experience, recorded in *Song of Solomon*, fits a long literary tradition examining the black American's complex fate.[17] "Under the recorded names," Milkman realizes at last, "were other names. . . . Names that had meaning. No wonder Pilate put hers in her ear. When you know your name, you should hang on to it, for unless it is noted down and remembered, it will die when you do" (329). Milkman's great-grandfather Solomon's song of flight to freedom was his and became his people's for all time because it was noted down and remembered, bearing witness to a dream that would not die.

Notes

1. Toni Morrison, *Song of Solomon* (New York: Knopf, 1977); 4. Subsequent references are cited parenthetically in the text.

2. Ralph Ellison, "Hidden Name and Complex Fate," in his *Shadow and Act* (New York: Random House, 1964), 147.

3. Robert Stepto, " 'Intimate Things in Place': A Conversation with Toni Morrison," in *Chant of Saints: A Gathering of Afro-American Literature, Art, and Scholarship*, edited by Michael Harper and Robert Stepto (Urbana: University of Illinois Press, 1979), 226.

4. Ibid., 229.

5. Sidonie Smith, *Where I'm Bound: Patterns of Slavery and Freedom in Black American Autobiography* (Westport, Conn.: Greenwood, 1974), 21.

6. Gilbert Osofsky, *Puttin' on Ole Massa* (New York: Harper and Row, 1969), 41.

7. James Pennington, "The Fugitive Blacksmith," in *Five Slave Narratives: A Compendium*, edited by William Loren Katz (New York: Arno, 1968), 30, xii.

8. William Wells Brown, "Narrative of William Wells Brown," in *Five Slave Narratives*, 98.

9. Ibid., 99.

10. Ellison, "Hidden Name and Complex Fate," 149.

11. Ralph Ellison, *Invisible Man* (New York: Random House, 1952), 381.

12. Malcolm X, *The Autobiography of Malcolm X* (New York: Grove, 1965), 161.

13. Ellison, "Hidden Name and Complex Fate," 148.

14. Ibid., 149.

15. Ibid., 148.

16. Ibid., 149.

17. For valuable studies of the black literary tradition that link naming to being, see Lloyd W. Brown, "Black Entitles: Names as Symbols in Afro-American Literature," *Studies in Black Literature* 1 (1970): 16–44; Michael Cooke, "Naming, Being, and Black Experience," *Yale Review* 68 (1978): 167–86; Kimberly W. Benston, "I Yam What I Am: The Topos of (Un)naming in Afro-American Literature," in *Black Literature and Literary Theory*, edited by Henry Louis Gates, Jr. (New York: Methuen, 1984), 151–72; Margaret M. Dunn and Ann R. Morris, "The Narrator as Nomenclator: Narrative Strategy through Naming," *CEA Critic* 46 (1983–1984): 24–30.

Part IV

◆ ◆ ◆

HISTORICAL PERSPECTIVES

Dead Teachers

Rituals of Manhood and Rituals of Reading in Song of Solomon

LINDA KRUMHOLZ

❖   ❖   ❖

The paradox of education is precisely this—that
as one begins to become conscious one begins to
examine the society in which he is being educated. The purpose of education, finally, is to create in a person the ability to look at the world
for himself, to make his own decisions, to say to
himself this is black or this is white, to decide
for himself whether there is a God in heaven or
not. To ask questions of the universe, and then
learn to live with those questions, is the way he
achieves his own identity. But no society is really
anxious to have that kind of person around. What
societies really, ideally, want is a citizenry which
will simply obey the rules of society. If a society
succeeds in this, that society is about to perish.
The obligation of anyone who thinks of himself
as responsible is to examine society and try to
change it and to fight it—at no matter what risk.
This is the only hope society has. This is the only
way societies change.

>   —James Baldwin, "The Negro Child—His
>   Self-Image"

It seems to me that the best art is political and
you ought to be able to make it unquestionably
political and irrevocably beautiful at the same
time.

>   —Toni Morrison, "Rootedness"

J AMES BALDWIN ARGUED THIRTY YEARS AGO for the importance of teaching black history in the United States for the construction of identity both of black and white students. He writes:

> So where we are now is that a whole country of people believe I'm a "nigger," and I *don't*, and the battle's on! Because if I am not what I've been told I am, then it means that *you're* not what you thought *you* were *either!* . . . What is upsetting this country is a sense of its own identity. If, for example, one managed to change the curriculum in all the schools so that Negroes learned more about themselves and their real contributions to this culture, you would be liberating not only Negroes, you'd be liberating white people who know nothing about their own history. (8)

Baldwin goes on to argue that the sense of identity in the United States is based on myths that have no basis in historical reality. His argument points out the power of pedagogues to control the definitions that shape identity, which today may be described as the perpetuation of hegemonic ideologies of oppression through the educational institutions.[1]

In Toni Morrison's *Song of Solomon* the politics of the novel and the politics of pedagogy are closely aligned. The novel's protagonist, Milkman Dead, acquires the knowledge and motivation for his self-creation and self-definition as a black man. In the process, the reader also learns both the pleasure in and the need for a creative and critical engagement of the imagination, based in black history and a black feminist subject position.[2] Thus Milkman's initiation into black manhood serves to initiate the reader in the "discredited knowledge" of African Americans.[3]

As in many of Morrison's novels, the politics of pedagogy are treated both as theme and as form in *Song of Solomon*. In the *Bluest Eye* the children's primer is interspersed throughout the novel, representing an idealized and inaccessible white middle-class model of reality as the source of the young black girls' basic reading skills. Pedagogical issues are also fundamental in *Tar Baby*, in which Jadine's education teaches her to shun her blackness, and in *Beloved*, in which the anonymous white schoolteacher epitomizes the physical and mental cruelties of slavery as he employs highly scientific and Manichean terms in his teaching that serve to obliterate black personhood. Schoolteacher represents the relationship between power and pedagogy; he teaches the rebellious slave Sixo, through physical beatings, that "definitions belonged to the definers—not the defined" (190), thus clarifying the urgency of black self-definition, either through teaching, as Denver chooses in the novel, or through writing, Morrison's own tool of artistry, pleasure, and pedagogy.

In *Song of Solomon*, Milkman Dead is a disengaged, self-centered young man, who has presumably been educated in a school system that offered him no point of connection or inspiration as a black man. In fact, as Milkman's quest begins in part 2 of the novel, when he is in his early thirties, he has no interest in finding links to his heritage; he seeks gold and all of the wealth, pride, and individual satisfaction gold signifies. On his quest, Milkman learns the "discredited knowledge" of African-American history and spirituality, and for the first time he sees some connection between obtaining knowledge, interpreting signs in the world, and constructing his sense of himself. The importance of this active engagement in the production of one's own meaning should not be underestimated, as Cornel West points out in his essay "Nihilism in Black America." West describes the destructiveness of nihilism for black people:

> *Nihilism is to be understood here not as a philosophic doctrine that there are no rational grounds for legitimate standards or authority; it is, far more, the lived experience of coping with a life of horrifying meaninglessness, hopelessness, and (most important) lovelessness.* The frightening result is a numbing detachment from others and a self-destructive disposition toward the world. Life without meaning, hope, and love breeds a coldhearted, mean-spirited outlook that destroys both the individual and others. . . . [A]s long as hope remains and meaning is preserved, the possibility of overcoming oppression stays alive. The self-fulfilling prophecy of the nihilistic

threat is that without hope there can be no future, that without meaning there can be no struggle. (14–15)

Milkman shows all the signs of the hopelessness and coldheartedness that result, according to West, from a lack of meaning. In *Song of Solomon*, Morrison demonstrates the necessity of producing meaning. In fact, in the novel Morrison suggests that the act of creating meaning is more important than the particular meaning (or, preferably, the multiplicity of meanings) produced, as long as it occurs with a spiritual and compassionate engagement.

Of course, this spiritual and compassionate engagement must have a cultural base. In *Song of Solomon*, Morrison provides for Milkman and the reader an African-American cultural literacy composed of folk stories and biblical stories, individual and collective history, and a spiritual openness and perception, all of which, in the hands of Morrison as author and Pilate as teacher, comprise the "subversive memory" and "love ethic" that West argues can counter nihilism by generating a sense of agency, increasing self-valuation, and encouraging political hope and resistance (West 19).[4] Morrison's novel provides the pleasure of interpretation, the richness of African-American cultural stories and voices, and a historical power—all of which culminate in the beauty and the politics of her art.

Revising Myths of Manhood

In *Song of Solomon*, Morrison revises the myth of the African-American man, just as in *Sula* she revises the myth of the African-American woman.[5] In *Sula*, Morrison both cherishes and criticizes the character Nel, who (ambiguously) embodies the myth of the black woman as a nurturing, self-sacrificing, infinitely strong burden bearer. Hortense Spillers describes the novel as a "countermythology" because it "abandon[s] the vision of the corporate good as a mode of heroic suffering [for black women]"; the novel shakes loose clear definitions between the good and the evil woman and thereby offers the possibility of subversion of and

liberation from the confining myth (Spillers 320, 319).[6] A countermythology can be offered as an alternative interpretation and
belief system, or it can be constructed, as I think Morrison does,
to open up multiple possibilities in the interplay between myths.
Sula is not the social "solution" to Nel; neither character signifies
an ideal image of black womanhood, nor do they offer an ideal
as a single joined entity (although they may complement one
another, one cannot live both as Sula does and as Nel does in
any simple sense). But in the spaces the novel creates between
the traditional myth of the black woman and the liberated, self-
centered, and contradictory Sula, there is a space for dispute,
reassessment, and instability of definitions vital to an ongoing
process of self-creation and self-definition for black women.

In both *Sula* and *Song of Solomon*, the reconceptualization of myth
deals with the contradictory impulses toward the assertion of individual identity in defiance of social rules of order, on the one
hand, and the need to ground identity in an integral sense of
connection to and responsibility for the collective, on the other.
Although the opposition between individual identity and social
order has been deconstructed by various theorists, and an awareness of the social construction of the subject in ideology has
proceeded apace, the individual-versus-society configuration still
shapes persisting gender mythologies. It has become an accepted
tenet of American gender myths that men find their freedom
and individuality by escaping the constraints of society, which are
represented by women and their ensnaring domestic demands.
Black women are also situated in this myth, but their position
is generally represented as inordinately powerful (the matriarchy
of the Moynihan report) and unusually powerless, as economic
victims and victims of male absence.[7] Black men are mythol-
ogized as violent and absent; what is represented as heroism in
white male individualism is considered antisocial in black male
behavior.[8]

The tension between black men's mobility, figured as flight in
Song of Solomon, and familial and communal responsibilities is sig-
naled in Morrison's epigraph to the novel: "The fathers may soar /
And the children may know their names." The fathers' flights

and the children's names are central aspects of Milkman's quest as he reproduces the ambiguously liberating flight of his great-grandfather Solomon by means of a rediscovery of his family names. In one interview, Morrison admires black men's mobility:

> [I]n the process of finding, they are also making themselves. Although in sociological terms that is described as a major failing of black men—they do not stay home and take care of their children, they are not there—that has always been to me one of the most attractive features about black male life. . . . [T]he fact that they would split in a minute just delights me. It's part of that whole business of breaking ground, doing the other thing. (" 'Intimate Things' " 486–87)

But in another interview, she describes the contradiction in the epigraph:

> It's a part of black life, a positive, majestic thing, but there is a price to pay—the price is the children. The fathers may soar, they may triumph, they may leave, but the children know who they are; they remember, half in glory and half in ac-cusation. That is one of the points of "Song" all the men have left someone, and it is the children who remember it, sing about it, mythologize it, make it a part of their family history. ("Talk with Toni Morrison")

In Morrison's revision of the myth of black men, she celebrates the independence, lawlessness, and self-invention represented by flight (all of these are also Sula's characteristics, suggesting that Morrison admires these characteristics in women as well), but she also shows the loss involved in abandoning the women and chil-dren. In *Song of Solomon*, Morrison seems to ask the same question about black men that her character Guitar asks about black women—"Can't I love what I criticize?" (225).[9]

Milkman's quest is to learn to fly *and* to find his name—in his pursuit, then, he straddles the two roles of father and son. But it is his aunt Pilate who exemplifies the combination of self-invention and responsibility, symbolized when Milkman realizes at her death that "without ever leaving the ground, she could fly" (340). As in many traditional male quests, Milkman seeks his origins through his paternal lineage, both overthrowing and taking on the name of the father. But although Milkman begins by seeking the gold his father considers his inheritance and ends by replicating the flight of his great-grandfather, it is Pilate who guides his quest. Pilate is, for Milkman, like the "black thread" she carries on her own peregrinations; in his quest for his heritage, "Milkman followed in her tracks" (145, 261).

Another important difference from many mythic and novelistic analogues is that in Milkman's quest the truth of his origins and the originary name is less important than the name he makes for himself and the way he invents himself. In our first introduction to Milkman, Morrison connects flight to his imagination: "when the little boy discovered, at four . . . that only birds and airplanes could fly—he lost all interest in himself. To have to live without that single gift saddened him and left his imagination . . . bereft" (9). In Danville, Milkman discovers men whose imaginations have also died when they saw Milkman's grandfather killed. For the first time, Milkman gains a sense of family pride and purpose because these men look to him to "rekindle the dream and stop the death they were dying" (238). Once Morrison connects flight with imagination, the liberation signified by flight becomes an act of self-creation rather than simply escape—one can fly without leaving the ground.

Imagination links Milkman's flight to the acquisition of his name. In the course of his quest, Morrison shifts the focus from the factual source of his name to the imaginative and spiritual constitution of his meaning in the world, without which Milkman would have considered the story of Solomon's flight to be merely "child's stories" and meaningless to him. From the beginning, Milkman's "real" or originary name proves elusive to him. For example, the story of the renaming of Milkman's grandfather (Jake) traces the origin of the name, Macon Dead, to the errors of an illiterate Yankee soldier who wrote in the wrong spaces in the registry of freed slaves, substituting the town Jake lived in and the fact that his father was dead, for his name (53). Milkman later finds out that Jake never lived in Macon (297), but this story continues to serve as a factual explanation for Milkman's father, who tells him this story. The name of Milkman's great-grandfather also shifts continually, among Sugarman, Charlemagne, Shalimar, and Solomon, with each name offering another context for self-invention.[10]

In the course of his ritual of initiation, Milkman makes his name meaningful. In chapter 1, Milkman's father, Macon Dead II, is disturbed by the name the community has given his son, wishing he had some ancient family name to pass on to him. In "thinking of names," Macon thinks in terms of unobtainable historical records:

> Surely, he thought, he and his sister had some ancestor, some lithe young man with onyx skin and legs as straight as cane stalks, who had a name that was real. A name given to him at birth with love and seriousness. A name that was not a joke, nor a disguise, nor a brand name. But who this lithe young man was, and where his cane-stalk legs carried him from or to, could never be known. No. Nor his name. (17–18)

Milkman's quest in part 2 of the novel, his hunt for gold, becomes an enactment of his father's dream, a hunt for an ancestral name and for his own "real" name. On the hunt, as Milkman connects to a natural and spiritual comprehension previously inaccessible to him, he *becomes* the "true" ancestor his father despaired of finding: "[Milkman] found himself exhilarated by simply walking the earth. Walking it like he belonged on it; like his legs were stalks, tree trunks, a part of his body that extended down down down into the rock and soil, and were comfortable there—on the earth and on the place where he walked" (284). Milkman becomes the true ancestor and the name the community gives him becomes his "true" name; through the new perceptions he learns on the hunt, Milkman reimagines himself and generates his own meaning.

In part 1, the meaning of Milkman's name seems evident—
Milkman Dead is a pampered mama's boy, suckled too long, and
the inheritor of a dead heritage, a culture dispersed and useless,
in which murder is the only solution (an analysis perfectly in
keeping with the Moynihan report). But in part 2, after Milkman
and the reader gain an African-American spiritual and cultural
framework for understanding, we can reinterpret his name with
greater complexity. Do we not discover that a connection to the
dead, to one's ancestors, is the essence of a vital cultural heritage?
Are we not led to believe that men must also recognize their role
as nurturers, as "mothers" supplying their "milk" to future generations? Did not Moses deliver his people from slavery to the
land of milk and honey? Is not a milkman also, in a more whim-
sical sense, a "deliverer" of his people? By the end of part 2, the
vitality of African-American culture is no longer in question; if
anything, it is the distinction between the living and the dead, a
distinction at the very basis of Western culture, that we are asked
to reconsider.

Milkman's Ritual of Initiation

In chapter 11, Milkman goes through a ritual of initiation. Although one could argue that the entirety of part 2 of the novel—
from Milkman's plane flight to Pittsburgh to his final flight at
Solomon's Leap—comprises his initiation, the events of chapter
11 enact most clearly the form and function of an initiation ritual.
Three parts of the chapter in particular—the fight with Saul, the
hunt with the older men, and the skinning of the cat—contain
the major elements of Milkman's manhood ritual. Corresponding
with this, from his chance arrival in Shalimar at the beginning
of the chapter to his lovemaking with Sweet at the end, Milkman
goes through a major transformation. An analysis of the ritual
and of the elements of Milkman's transformation will further
elucidate Morrison's revision of the myths of black manhood.

The anthropologist Victor Turner divides the ritual process

into three stages: rites of separation, rites of limen or margin, and rites of reaggregation ("Are There Universals?" 8–18). Turner theorizes "marginality" or "liminality" as a space and time within ritual in which social classifications break down and social relations are transformed. The rites of separation and reaggregation frame and mediate between the social structure and the status-free experience of liminality. Within the limen, a time and space outside of categories is created, a place where dangers have free play within the limits set by the ritual. This is the arena of the Other, where the "powers of the weak" are freed (and contained), and where the power of mystery supersedes the power of the social structure. Within the limen all participants, having temporarily put off their status will see the world differently. Ritual thus creates a time and space in which the nondifferentiation of *communitas* and the powers of Otherness (lawlessness, misrule, and so on) can break into, while being contained within, the preexisting power structures in the society (*Ritual Process* 128).[11]

The tripartite structure of ritual process, according to Turner's theories, can be usefully applied to Milkman's initiation ritual in chapter 11 of *Song of Solomon*. Milkman's fight with Saul functions as a rite of separation, the rite meant to divest the initiate of status and to separate him from the usual social order. The hunt with King Walker and the older men of Shalimar can be considered the liminal phase. During the hunt, Milkman goes through his most substantial transformation, in relations of equality with the hunters, and through contact with spiritual and natural forces made Other and mysterious within the prevailing social order. Finally, the skinning of the cat represents Milkman's rite of reaggregation, also called the rite of integration, when he moves back from the disorder of liminality to the social order, transformed both internally and in status. Symbolically, the ritual as a whole depicts a death and rebirth, and it conveys Milkman's lessons in the meaning of blackness as a form of existence and knowledge. Thus the ritual represents Milkman's rebirth as a black man.

Milkman's fight with Saul can best be described as a "cockfight" since their fight is presaged when "a black rooster strutted by, its blood-red comb draped forward like a wicked brow" and because both men spar verbally about the ultimate symbol of manhood, the cock (268, 270–71). Milkman's "cockiness," his thoughtless presumption of male privilege, is criticized in the last pages of part 1, as Lena excoriates Milkman for thinking "that [his] hog's gut that hangs down between [his] legs" gives him the right to treat the women in his family like servants (217). The rooster and the peacock, two flightless and domesticated male birds, represent masculine pride, vanity, and the desire for domination and material wealth. When Macon Dead II first sees gold, "Life, safety, and luxury fanned out before him like the tail-spread of a peacock" (171). When Guitar and Milkman plot to steal that same gold, they see a peacock, and Guitar explains that peacocks are "like vanity. Can't nobody fly with all that shit. Wanna fly, you got to give up the shit that weighs you down" (180).

The egg offers an opposing symbol to the cock, signifying ungendered potential, but it is also related to females since they contain and traditionally nurture the egg (though in the bird world the gender division of labor does not abide by these social stereotypes). The egg is a particularly apt symbol of Milkman's ritual rebirth and flight since he traces his ancestry to his Native-American grandmother, Singing Bird, and his great-grandfather Solomon, the flying African. Pilate is also associated with these symbols of rebirth and flight; Milkman remembers her from their first meeting as "an old black lady who had cooked him his first perfect egg, who had shown him the sky" (211).

The egg also signifies a "white" ideological vision from which Milkman must break free; the shell of white ideological vision is an external social encumbrance, the blindness of looking at externals for meaning. In a humorous argument, Milkman tells Guitar that he wants to be an egg, but Guitar argues that a black man cannot be an egg because eggs are white (115). When Milkman persists, Guitar responds, "Then somebody got to bust your shell" (116). Milkman's shell does crack off as he travels in the South; slowly he loses the material accoutrements of white existence—the clothes, the watch, the car, the possessions and protections that hide his own blackness from himself.

But Milkman's transformation from a white vision to a black one needs more than a shedding of externals; it requires the profound encounter with blackness that occurs on the hunt. Milkman provokes Saul to battle over symbols of manhood after Milkman's treatment of the men of Shalimar and his casual request for a woman strip them of their manhood and personhood. Morrison writes, "They looked at his skin and saw it was as black as theirs, but they knew he had the heart of the white men who came to pick them up in the trucks when they needed anonymous, faceless laborers" (269). Milkman must exchange the "heart of a white man" for the heart of a black man; his fight with Saul represents his first ritual death.

The hunt is the liminal phase of Milkman's initiation ritual in which unrecognized powers and mysteries teach and transform him. Turner describes liminality as a time and space of possibility:

> [T]he liminal phase [is] in the "subjunctive mood" of culture, the mood of maybe, might-be, as-if, hypothesis, fantasy, conjecture, desire. . . . Liminality can perhaps be described as a fructile chaos, a fertile nothingness, a storehouse of possibilities, not by any means a random assemblage but a striving after new forms and structure, a gestation process, a fetation of modes appropriate to and anticipating postliminal existence. ("Are There Universals?" 11–12)

This liminal or marginal state is figured in *Song of Solomon* as blackness.

Earlier in the novel, Pilate tries to teach Milkman about blackness as a cultural, physical, perceptual, and spiritual entity. The first time Milkman meets Pilate, she tells him:

> You think dark is just one color, but it ain't. There're five or six kinds of black. Some silky, some woolly. Some just empty. Some like fingers. And it don't stay still. It moves and changes from one kind of black to another. Saying something is pitch

black is like saying something is green. What kind of green? Green like my bottles? Green like a grasshopper? Green like a cucumber, lettuce, or green like the sky is just before it breaks loose to a storm? Well, night black is the same way. May as well be a rainbow. (40)

In Pilate's description, blackness is shifting and multiple, sensual and spiritual. Through his ritual experiences, Milkman learns Pilate's lesson; he learns to see in darkness, beneath the surface of things. By the end, "everybody kept changing right in front of him," because he has learned to see differently and, like Pilate, to see the shifting nature and multiple meanings inherent in the world (324). Thus blackness becomes an image for an African-American spiritual vision that "sees" past material forms to the spiritual and natural world beneath them.

At various stages of his quest, Milkman experiences an intense darkness: when he and Guitar rob Pilate's "treasure" (186), in the Hunters Cave (254), and on the hunt for the wildcat (276–83). In the darkness, Milkman is blinded to externals, and he must learn new skills. On the hunt, Milkman realizes:

His watch and his two hundred dollars would be of no help out here, where all a man had was what he was born with, or had learned to use. And endurance. Eyes, ears, nose, taste, touch—and some other sense that he knew he did not have: an ability to separate out, of all the things there were to sense, the one that life itself might depend on. (280–81)

As he recognizes his own egotism, selfishness, and manipulation of other people, he sheds the shell of his previous existence or, in another image of emergent flight, "his self—the cocoon that was 'personality'—gave way," revealing to him this "other sense" (280).

On the wildcat hunt, Milkman emerges from the shell or the cocoon of his past; he is reborn in the darkness, and he learns the sixth sense that will save his life. Milkman describes this "other sense" as a natural, preliterate language:

> It was all language. An extension of the click people made in their cheeks back home when they wanted a dog to follow them. No, it was not language: it was what there was before language. Before things were written down. Language in the time when men and animals did talk to one another. (281)

Only moments later he listens and hears it, and it saves his life: "He tried to listen with his fingertips, to hear what, if anything, the earth had to say, and it told him quickly that someone was standing behind him and he had just enough time to raise one hand to his neck and catch the wire that fastened around his throat" (282). Milkman's revelation is not transcendent; it is sensual, and it is a matter of survival. It is a recognition that something more is there, that animals, trees, and earth have a language and that spirits of the earth and of the ancestors exist.

Milkman is initiated into his own blackness. He realizes that through "[i]gnorance, he thought, and vanity," he "hadn't seen the signs" (279). Milkman's ability to understand the preliterate language and to "see" in the dark represent blackness as a way of seeing and a way of reading, as an ideology that constitutes knowledge as multiple, subjective, nonrational, and spiritual. Morrison describes this formulation of knowledge as "discredited knowledge," which

> blend[s] the acceptance of the supernatural and a profound rootedness in the real world at the same time with neither taking precedence over the other. It is indicative of the cosmology, the way in which Black people looked at the world. We are very practical people, very down-to-earth, even shrewd people. But within that practicality we also accepted what I suppose could be called superstition and magic, which is another way of knowing things. ("Rootedness" 342)

Milkman's new knowledge signals a stage in his rebirth. After the loss of his egotistic shell, he admits his fears, laughs at himself, and encourages the others to laugh with him, with the Shalimar hunters "egging him on" the whole way (284). This ushers in the third part of the initiation ritual, the integration into the community as a changed person with new status.

Like the wild cat who is killed during the hunt, Milkman acts as both the hunter and the hunted. At the beginning of the chapter, Milkman receives a message from Guitar, "Your day has come," the words the Seven Days utter as they kill their victims. On the hunt at the moment when Milkman feels like he finally really understands Guitar, who misses the South and the hunt, Guitar tries to kill him (with a guitar string?) (282). Milkman experiences another symbolic death and rebirth at Guitar's hands, and his presence stays with Milkman after the hunt, both as enemy and as brother.

The ritual of skinning the cat is written as a call and response between a description of the skinning process Milkman is watching and words Guitar said to Milkman earlier, presumably echoing now in Milkman's memory. The juxtaposition of the graphic evisceration of the cat and Guitar's words pulls together considerations of life and death, violence and love, around the theme of Guitar's words, *"Everybody wants a black man's life"* (285). The description of the skinning evokes all of the physical horrors of lynching, castration, and mutilation suffered by black men, while it also challenges Guitar's murderous solution to the situation of black men. At first, the act of skinning the cat reaffirms the love of the hunter for the hunted in the delicacy and precision of the description, and Guitar's words, *"It is about love. What else?"* are uttered just as Milkman is offered the cat's heart (285). But the echoing of the phrase *"What else? What else? What else?"* adds an urgency and a confusion to the question, suggesting that Guitar's eye-for-an-eye solution may not be the best expression of love. At this point Milkman pulls the cat's heart from its body: "The heart fell away from the chest as easily as yolk slips out of its shell" (286). Milkman receives the cat's heart, symbolizing his rebirth as a black man, aware now of the danger and the power this identity entails.

Revising the Mythic Hero

The richness of story and allusion in *Song of Solomon* has led critics to discuss the novel in relation to various mythic analogues. The analyses include comparisons between *Song of Solomon* and Judeo-Christian biblical sources, Greco-Roman myths, African-American folktales about flying Africans, and African ritual and oral traditions, such as the griot tradition.[12] I will add to this array of analogues two African epics, the Mwindo epic and the Kambili epic, both of which were available in English translations when Morrison was working on the novel.[13] Their inclusion as textual analogues to *Song of Solomon* reinforces non-Western interpretive frames for the novel and further informs reconsiderations of hero myths in relation to gender.

With the African myths, as with other analogues to the novel, Morrison's usage is both dynamic and critical. In "Unspeakable Things Unspoken," she writes about *Song of Solomon*, "Sotto (but not completely) is my own giggle (in Afro-American terms) of the proto-myth of the journey to manhood. Whenever characters are cloaked in Western fable, they are in deep trouble; but the African myth is also contaminated" (29). In both the Mwindo and the Kambili epics, the tension between the exceptional individualism of the hero and the values of collectivity is elaborated and situated to some extent within gender relations, thus suiting Morrison's own development of this tension. Nonetheless, the African epics also inscribe heroism as a specifically male province, and the relegation of women to the role of helper as well as discussions of co-wives and their jealous machinations against one another may be the "contamination" to which Morrison refers.[14]

The Mwindo epic is the story of the exploits of Mwindo, the son of the village chief Shemwindo (literally, "father of Mwindo").[15] Mwindo's father attempts to prevent his birth, then attempts to kill him after his birth. Mwindo overcomes his father with the help of his paternal aunt, and he becomes the savior and ruler of his people. As is usual in African epic, the story begins before the birth of the hero, and the birth is in some way extraordinary. After Shemwindo forbids his wives to have male children, the preferred wife delivers Mwindo through her middle finger. Mwindo travels through the underground world to find his father and supersede him, all the while attached to his powerful paternal aunt through a magic cord. Mwindo also has a friend and ally, Nkuba, who late in the epic brings him into the sky for a period of punishment and celestial suffering and berates Mwindo for his pride and his heroism. There are a number of superficial similarities with *Song of Solomon*. Milkman's birth is heralded by extraordinary events (the flight of Robert Smith); his father tries to force his mother to abort him; Milkman "overthrows" his father when he knocks him down at dinner; he is led by his paternal aunt Pilate in seeking his "fathers"; and Guitar Bains, like Nkuba, is both his friend and his enemy.

Perhaps most important in the comparison, though, is the nature of Mwindo's conversion from a proud boastful fighter to a wise, generous, and benevolent ruler who has learned humility and compassion through cosmic suffering. Editor Daniel Biebuyck explains in his notes to the epic, "The Nyanga have a profound dislike for boasting and megalomania," and that Mwindo's only justification for his behavior is the unjust treatment by his father (145). Mwindo's final period of great suffering and humility redeems Mwindo for his listeners. In this version, the epic ends with Mwindo passing laws for proper behavior, followed by a series of morals. The four morals are that no child should be rejected, that heroism must not include excessive callousness, that mutual agreement is the best form of leadership, and that even a hero who can surpass others will one day meet his match (144). It is clear that these morals correspond to Morrison's reconstruction of heroism in Milkman, who must also lose his self-centered conceit and his callous disconnection from others and learn to respect and seek relations of mutuality with women and children.

The relationship between individual ambition and collective values is also explored in the Kambili epic. An interesting characteristic of the Kambili epic is that much more time is spent in describing interpretive enterprises that precede events than in narrating the major events themselves. The epic begins with a long process by which Kanji, a general of Imam Samory Toure, the historical nationalist leader of the Maninka at the turn of the century, seeks aid from the leader in grilling the seers (who are called *kun-nyini-na*, literally, "the seeker of reasons") as to which of his nine wives will have a child.[16] The contest among the seers is won by Bari, "the Omen Reader," who tells Kanji that the despised wife Dugo will have the child, much to the pain and chagrin of the formerly favored wife. The extraordinary promise of the unborn child Kambili is exemplified by his ability to leave his mother's womb and go for walks at night. As a child, he proves to be an excellent hunter. He is sent by his father to learn survival from Bari, to become a "reason-seeker" himself. Kambili then marries Kumba, who was previously wife to Cekura, the lion man. After their marriage, Cekura begins to kill all the people of the village. Bari sends Kumba to Cekura, and she pretends to return to him in order to get hair from his head, arm, and crotch. She brings Cekura's hair to Kambili, who uses it to defeat Cekura. The song ends with a praise of Kumba.

The only plot similarity between *Song of Solomon* and the Kambili epic is the central event of the lion/cat hunt in each. But the role of the hunters and their philosophy in Maninka society make this parallel more pertinent. The hunters tend to be very traditional, rejecting Islamic religious laws and ethics for the traditional Maninka beliefs. The hunters form "societies [which] serve to initiate the young hunter into the secrets necessary for survival in the bush, as well as into the occult philosophical world of the hunter" (Bird, Koita, and Soumaoro vi). The hunt and the epic itself serve as initiation and as lessons in survival, thus making word and deed of equal import in the young hunter's initiation. In fact, the bard has a central role in "initiating, mediating and terminating acts" for the hunters (vi).

Another parallel is that in the Kambili epic the hero's main interest is in making a name for himself, as is indicated in a line repeated with variations more than a dozen times in the epic: "A name is a thing to be paid for; a name is not to be forced." But the Maninka beliefs raise again the issue central to Morrison's novel, the relationship between collective values and individual pursuits, and in the Maninka system the distinctions are clearly gendered. *Ba-den-ya* translates as "mother-child-ness," and it refers to the forces of social cohesion—accommodation, conciliation, and expressions of respect—associated with village life. *Fa-den-ya*, or "father-child-ness," describes the forces oriented toward "the gaining of a name" to be sung for posterity; these forces are associated with the bush, the milieu of the hunters, and with the hero. Translator Charles Bird explains the contradictory nature of the hero:

> When Seydou Camara sings:
>
>> Nana ma man di fo ko-jugu-lon
>> The hero is welcome only on troubled days.
>
> he captures the anamolous [sic] relationship between the hero and the society. The hero is asocial, capable of unrestricted cruelty and destructiveness, whose presence is always a threat to the stability of the collectivity. He is, however, perhaps the only member associated with the group who is capable of swift and conclusive action. Through his actions, the hero can enhance the collective reputation of the group and perhaps bring riches to it, even though his motivation is unqualifiedly selfish. The society is thus damned with the hero and damned without him. (Bird, Koita, and Soumauro vii)[17]

This passage makes an interesting juxtaposition to the first passage I cited by Baldwin. They both point to contradictions in society, but Bird stresses the asocial nature of the hero who disrupts the stability of the collective, while Baldwin describes social disruption as one's social obligation. Clearly this indicates a part of the contemporary dilemma—how can we espouse and valorize an ethics of collectivity and social responsibility *and* work to disrupt and challenge the social order? How do we define who "our people" are—by race, gender, class, sexuality; by commitment to certain values or politics; by different measures at different moments? Which traditions do we conserve and which do we alter or destroy? Which are "our" traditions, which are "theirs," and what do these designations mean? Does espousing an ethics of collectivity trap women in caretaking roles, or does it challenge the intense individualism in U.S. society with its emphasis on individual acquisition and pleasure? Can "blackness" offer an alternative epistemology and aesthetics to counter hopelessness and meaninglessness, or does it encourage divisive nationalisms and essentialisms?

Morrison's power as an author lies in her refusal to offer simple answers to these problems; she keeps the contradictions in play. But part of the dilemma of *Song of Solomon* is that in redefining black male heroism she comes up against obstinate and intractable values that inform "masculine" and "feminine" behavior in the United States. Again I will turn to a comparison with *Sula*. *Sula* presents a much more radical deconstruction of black women's definitions than *Song of Solomon* does of black men's, in part because our culture, in its more inclusive sense, still values "male" characteristics over "female." Thus, for Sula to "invent" herself, for her to experiment, to wander, to cast off sexual partners casually, is outrageous, alien, and dangerous, but we also glory in her "radical freedom." With Milkman, the "mother-child-ness" that gives him his name must be repudiated, and his masculinity reinforced, in order to situate him as hero, because the "feminized" man is not considered desirable or heroic. Morrison proceeds more cautiously in feminizing Milkman—in his mutual caring with Sweet, his attention to children's games, his use of women's gossip to unfold knowledge, and possibly his self-sacrificing act in the conclusion—than she does in masculinizing Sula. Nonetheless, I think Morrison does attempt to transform the definition of the hero in order to guide black men, and all of us, between the Scylla and Charybdis of meaninglessness, on one side, and overly simplified, static solutions, on the other; to affirm the necessity of both a collective basis for a sense of one's value and agency and a rebelliousness that continually challenges one's limits and the status quo; to somehow balance *ba-den-ya* and *fa-den-ya* and still create heroes.

The Reader's Ritual of Initiation

By the end of *Song of Solomon*, Milkman has been initiated; he can finally put together the children's song with the many stories he has heard to unriddle his history. In the course of Milkman's initiation, the reader is also called upon to apply her reading skills to interpret the signs and unriddle the mysteries. In *Song of Solomon*, the reader's initiation process parallels Milkman's initiation ritual, except instead of a hunt the reader's is composed of the fictional work itself. The central division in the novel, between parts 1 and 2, indicates for Milkman a gradual shift in the direction of his life, but for the reader it signals a more pronounced transition as the tone and content of the novel shift. In part 1, the reader is initiated into a reading practice that reflects the interpretive and signifying practices of northern urban black society—the irony of double consciousness, the jaded sociological perspective, and the critical political voices. In this section, Guitar is hero. In part 2, the move to the southern rural African-American folk culture is represented by a heightening of natural perception, a richness of symbolism, and the supernatural presence of natural and ancestral spirits that bring Milkman and the reader "beyond the veil" of the traditionally rational and empirical Euro-American discourse to an inspired and visionary African-American discourse. Although Pilate is absent through most of this section, this is her terrain.

In the first pages of *Song of Solomon*, Morrison establishes a reading practice based on the ironic and humorous inversions of white meaning from a black perspective. In the course of situating the reader physically in the town, she also situates us as readers with a pointed example of African Americans "signifying on" the white authorities when the authorities attempt to assert their naming power in an official proclamation.[18] The proclamation avers that the street in question, known as Doctor Street among the black residents, "had always been and would always be known as Mains Avenue and not Doctor Street" (4). The narrator replies in the voice of the community, "It was a genuinely clarifying public notice because it gave Southside residents a way to keep their memories alive and please the city legislators as well. They called it Not Doctor Street, and were inclined to call the charity hospital at its northern end No Mercy Hospital" (4). The mockery of the narrative voice illustrates, first of all, the blind pompousness of the white authorities who could announce that something "had always been and would always be" when it clearly was not so. It also illustrates the mask of humble self-effacement that wishes to "please the city legislators" while indeed laughing at anyone who would believe such a thing. What this notice "genuinely clarifies" is far different for the black readers of the official document than for the white writers, which indicates the differences in the reading practice and the practice of signification for black readers and white. By making central African-American signification and placing the black reader's subject position in the forefront, Morrison insists that—just as in "white" America, black people need a double consciousness—in the black world of her novel, a white reader needs a double consciousness, along with the ability to signify on his *own* status.

In part 1, Morrison constructs an African-American subjectivity based in double consciousness, folk humor, and a pleasure in the rebellious deployment of language. But the reader's interpretation is inadequate without the spiritual context supplied by part 2. Just as Milkman's experiences in the South make new demands on his imagination, part 2 makes new demands on the reader's imagination. In the first paragraph, Morrison invokes fairytale images, supernatural presences, and emotional extremes. She refers to Hansel and Gretel as they approach the witch's house—the fear and hunger, witches and magic—to create the setting for Milkman's encounter with Circe at the Butlers' house. In the second paragraph of part 2, nature overwhelms and eats away at the house, adding to the supernatural presence a vital and thriving natural life that Milkman is "oblivious to" (221). Morrison provokes us to interpret differently, to perceive a new relationship between the material and the spiritual, through our encounters with the supernatural in part 2. For example, in Milkman's encounter with Circe, he is presented with two conflicting facts:

"But Circe is dead. This woman is alive. That is as far as he got" (242). The solution of whether Circe is dead or alive is less important than a reassessment of the certainty with which we define and divide the living and the dead. The belief (or suspended disbelief) of the reader in the spiritual presences and magical occurrences of part 2 awaken our imaginations and complement the political and sociological perspective in part 1 to enable us to comprehend and interpret the world of the novel more fully.

Despite the reader's initiation, the conclusion of the novel remains enigmatic, especially the last two lines of the novel, after Guitar kills Pilate: "As fleet and bright as a lodestar [Milkman] wheeled toward Guitar and it did not matter which one of them would give up his ghost in the killing arms of his brother. For now he knew what Shalimar knew: If you surrendered to the air, you could *ride* it" (341). Although many have debated whether Milkman and/or Guitar die in the end, perhaps it is more important to consider the ways Morrison has challenged concepts of life and death. Guitar insists that what counts is what one dies for (160). Pilate tells Ruth, "Don't nobody have to die if they don't want to," and she uses her father's continuing presence after his death as example (141). Pilate also argues that you are responsible for those you kill, that "the dead you kill is yours" (210). And Milkman discovers a purpose when he wishes to reinvigorate the imaginations of the men of Danville and "stop the death they were dying" (238). Whether or not Milkman Dead dies in the end is less important, finally, than what the reader does with him after the novel ends, as our interpretive processes continue. He is our dead now, our textual ancestor to carry with us, to stimulate our imaginations.

Notes

1. Althusser, in his essay "Ideology and Ideological State Apparatuses," argues that educational institutions became the primary ideological state apparatus after the diminution of the power of the church.

2. I call the subject position of the novel feminist, first, because it

constructs a critique of European, African, and African-American models and myths of manhood and reevaluates gender roles and relations, and second, because the poetics of the novel favor multiple voices and interpretations and a participatory, nonauthoritarian narrative that are considered feminist in certain feminist literary theories. Morrison also treats the "simultaneity of oppressions," Barbara Smith's term for the struggles of black and Third World women in her introduction to *Home Girls* (xxviii), an idea embellished by bell hooks in *Feminist Theory*, in which feminism is defined as much by race, class, and sexual oppression as by gender since they are mutually constituted by an "ideology of domination" (24). Morrison's treatment of sexuality is primarily in terms of heterosexuality, although Smith argues for a lesbian reading of *Sula* in her signal article "Toward a Black Feminist Criticism." Morrison treats class issues in *Song of Solomon* in part through the conflicting value systems of Macon Dead, Jr., and his sister, Pilate. Although Morrison states in an interview that class is not a barrier between black men like Guitar and Milkman, we do hear Guitar's grandmother, when Macon Dead puts her out of her home because she cannot pay the rent, say, " 'A nigger in business is a terrible thing to see' " (22). See Willis for an extensive discussion of class in Morrison's work.

3. Morrison describes the "discredited knowledge" of black people in her essay "Rootedness" as "the acceptance of the supernatural and a profound rootedness in the real world" (342). I discuss this idea at some length in the second section of this essay.

4. I use the term "cultural literacy" advisedly, in an attempt to take back the meaning from E. D. Hirsch, Jr., who defines cultural literacy in terms of a normalized, Europeanized compendium of necessary data for children to learn in the United States in order to equalize access to economic opportunity. The problems with his theories are many, as are the responses, but see especially Helene Moglen's article, in which she raises issues important to our discussion here regarding student engagement, motivation, and imagination.

5. For definitions and discussions of myth in *Song of Solomon* see Awkward, Brenner, Davis, de Weever, Fabre, A. Leslie Harris, and Lee.

6. See also McDowell.

7. See Barbara Smith's refutation of the myths about black women in the introduction to *Home Girls*.

8. Morrison points out the irony of these divergent interpretations, writing, "If sociologists applied the same values to Ulysses (that classic absent father) as they do to black families, Penelope, a welfare mother,

would be damned for not getting a job, while Telemachus would have been persecuted in school as a product of a broken home and tracked into a class for slow readers with social adjustment problems" ("Rediscovering" 20).

9. As Michael Awkward suggests, this poetic line can be turned around to ask, Can't I criticize what I love? (493). In a similar vein, Awkward argues that "the author must produce narratives which clearly demonstrate her advocacy of afrocentric ideology, while simultaneously condemning myth's general failure to inscribe the possibilities of full female participation as subject in the story of black American self-actualization and cultural preservation" (487).

10. Morrison's grandfather's name is John Solomon, so in *Song of Solomon* she is paying tribute to, and playing with, her own paternal ancestral name. See "A Slow Walk of Trees."

11. Turner uses the word *communitas* rather than community to indicate an attitude among people rather than a mere proximity. *Communitas* is constituted by spontaneous, immediate, concrete relations rather than relations dictated by abstract structures (*Ritual Process* 128).

12. As textual and mythic analogues to *Song of Solomon*, A. Leslie Harris discusses Icarus, Aeneas, and Ulysses; Susan Blake discusses Gullah folktales; Dorothy Lee discusses Hermes, Apollo, Song of Songs, Solomon, and First Corinthians; Joseph Skerrett discusses the griot tradition; Gerry Brenner discusses African-American folktales and Rank's monomyth; Kathleen O'Shaughnessy discusses African dance, song, and ritual; and Kimberly Benston discusses Odysseus.

13. See Okpewho for an extended discussion of the African epic and its oral poetics. He describes the African epic much as Morrison describes African-American discredited knowledge—as a combination of the supernatural and the "real" world (15). Morrison also adapts some of the oral poetics associated with the African epic to her novel; in *Song of Solomon* she uses songs, riddles, chants, and call and response, as well as orally oriented conversation and a sense of the community as a choral voice. See also O'Shaughnessy in this regard.

14. Cynthia Davis considers *Song of Solomon* a reinscription of the male monopoly on heroism, but I think part of Morrison's work in the novel is to challenge and critique the basis of this monopoly, as I attempt to argue in this essay.

15. I want to thank Judylyn Ryan for leading me to the Mwindo epic as a textual relative of *Song of Solomon*. The Mwindo epic is part of the oral literature of the Nyanga, a Bantu-speaking people who live in

the eastern part of the Congo Republic. The published version of the epic was performed by She-karisi Rureke over the course of twelve days, an unusually long performance enacted specially for the anthropologist and translator Daniel Biebuyck, who, with Kahombo C. Mateene, translated and edited the epic, which was published in English in 1969. *Karisi*, as in Rureke's name, is also the word for the epic form and for a male spirit to whom the bards are devoted; Mwindo is the main character of the *karisi* (Biebuyck 11–12). For more information on the history of the Congo and the Bantu-speaking people before colonization, then under brutal Portuguese rule, and since independence in 1960, see Joseph E. Harris.

16. The Kambili epic is a hunter's epic of the Maninka people, who originate from the Mande, the geographical center of the thirteenth-century Mali Empire. They share ancestry, as well as language and culture, with the Mandinka, Malinke, Mandingo, Manya, Bambara, Dyula, Kuranko, and Wangara. The epic was performed by Seydou Camara of Mali, who makes his living as a singer for the hunters. It was translated by Charles S. Bird with Mamadou Koita and Bourama Soumaoro, and published in English in 1974. For more information on Samory Toure's role as a nationalist leader, see Joseph Harris, 172–73.

17. For further discussion of the Mande hero, see Bird and Kendall.

18. Henry Louis Gates, Jr., describes the African-American practice of "signifyin(g)" as "the language of trickery." Signifying is a verbal power play in which the signifier (in this case, a speaker, not a sound image), with an acute consciousness of status relationships and a greater sensitivity to possible interpretations of language, undermines a less self-conscious language act and deconstructs the coherence of an authoritative system of meaning.

Works Cited

Althusser, Louis. "Ideology and ideological State Apparatuses." In his *Lenin and Philosophy*, translated by Ben Brewster, 123–73. New York: Monthly Review Press, 1972.

Awkward, Michael. " 'Unruly and Let Loose': Myth, Ideology, and Gender in *Song of Solomon.*" *Callaloo* 13 (1990): 482–98.

Baldwin, James. "A Talk to Teachers." Previously titled "The Negro Child—His Self-Image." In *Multi-Cultural Literacy*, edited by Rick Simonson and Scott Walker, 3–12. Saint Paul, Minn.: Graywolf, 1988.

Benston, Kimberly W. "Re-Weaving the 'Ulysses Scene': Enchantment, Post-Oedipal Identity, and the Buried Text of Blackness in Toni Morrison's *Song of Solomon*." In *Comparative American Identities: Race, Sex, and Nationality in the Modern Text*, edited by Hortense Spillers, 87–109. New York: Routledge, 1991.

Biebuyck, Daniel, and Kahombo C. Mateene, eds. and trans. *The Mwindo Epic from the Banyanga (Congo Republic)*. Berkeley: University of California Press, 1969.

Bird, Charles S., with Mamadou Koita and Bourama Soumaoro, trans. *The Songs of Seydou Camara*. Vol. 1, *Kambili*. Bloomington: Indiana University African Studies Center, 1974.

Bird, Charles S., and Martha B. Kendall. "The Mande Hero." In *Explorations in African Systems of Thought*, edited by Ivan Karp and Charles S. Bird, 13–26. Bloomington: Indiana University Press, 1980.

Blake, Susan. "Folklore and Community in *Song of Solomon*." *MELUS* 7, no. 3 (1980): 77–82.

Brenner, Gerry. "*Song of Solomon*: Rejecting Rank's Monomyth and Feminism." In *Critical Essays on Toni Morrison*, edited by Nellie Y. McKay, 114–25. Boston: Hall, 1988.

Davis, Cynthia A. "Self, Society, and Myth in Toni Morrison's Fiction." *Contemporary Literature* 23 (1982): 323–42.

de Weever, Jacqueline. "Toni Morrison's Use of Fairy Tale, Folk Tale, and Myth in *Song of Solomon*." *Southern Folklore Quarterly* 44 (1980): 131–44.

Fabre, Genevieve. "Genealogical Archaeology; or, The Quest for Legacy in Toni Morrison's *Song of Solomon*." In *Critical Essays on Toni Morrison*, edited by Nellie Y. McKay, 105–14. Boston: Hall, 1988.

Gates, Henry Louis, Jr. "The Blackness of Blackness: A Critique of the Sign and the Signifying Monkey." In *Black Literature and Literary Theory*, edited by Henry Louis Gates, Jr., 285–321. New York: Methuen, 1984.

Harris, A. Leslie. "Myth as Structure in Toni Morrison's *Song of Solomon*." MELUS 7 (1980): 69–76.

Harris, Joseph E. *Africans and Their History*. New York: Penguin, 1987.

Hirsch, E. D., Jr. *Cultural Literacy: What Every American Needs to Know*. Boston: Houghton, 1987.

hooks, bell. *Feminist Theory: From Margin to Center*. Boston: South End Press, 1984.

Lee, Dorothy H. "*Song of Solomon*: To Ride the Air." *Black American Literature Forum* 16 (1982): 64–70.

McDowell, Deborah. "Boundaries: Or Distant Relations and Close Kin." In *Afro-American Literary Study in the 1990s*, edited by Houston A. Baker,

Jr., and Patricia Redmond, 51–70. Chicago: University of Chicago Press, 1989.

Moglen, Helene. "Allan Bloom and E. D. Hirsch: Educational Reform as Tragedy and Farce." In her *Profession 88*, 59–64. New York: MLA, 1988.

Morrison, Toni. *Beloved*. New York: Knopf, 1987.

———. " 'Intimate Things in Place': A Conversation with Toni Morrison." Interview with Robert B. Stepto. *Massachussetts Review* 18 (1977): 473–89.

———. "Rediscovering Black History." *New York Times Magazine*, 11 Aug. 1974, pp. 14ff.

———. "Rootedness: The Ancestor as Foundation." In *Black Women Writers (1950–1980)*, edited by Mari Evans, 339–45. New York: Anchor, 1984.

———. "A Slow Walk of Trees (as Grandmother Would Say) Hopeless (as Grandfather Would Say)." *New York Times Magazine*, 4 July 1976, 104–5, 150–64.

———. *Song of Solomon*. New York: New American Library, 1977.

———. *Sula*. New York: New American Library, 1973.

———. "Talk with Toni Morrison." Interview with Mel Watkins. *New York Times Book Review*, 11 Sept. 1979, p. 50.

———. "Unspeakable Things Unspoken: The Afro-American Presence in American Literature." *Michigan Quarterly Review* 33 (1989): 1–34.

Moynihan, Patrick D. "The Negro Family: The Case for National Action," issued by the Department of Labor. March 1965.

Okpewho, Isidore. *The Epic in Africa: Toward a Poetics of the Oral Performance*. New York: Columbia University Press, 1975.

O'Shaughnessy, Kathleen. " 'Life Life Life': The Community as Chorus in *Song of Solomon*." In *Critical Essays on Toni Morrison*, edited by Nellie Y. McKay, 125–33. Boston: Hall, 1988.

Skerrett, Joseph T., Jr. "Recitation to the Griot: Storytelling and Learning in Toni Morrison's *Song of Solomon*." In *Conjuring: Black Women, Fiction, and Literary-Tradition*, edited by Marjorie Pryse and Hortense Spillers, 192–202. Bloomington: Indiana University Press, 1985.

Smith, Barbara. Introduction. *Home Girls: A Black Feminist Anthology*, xix–lvi. New York: Kitchen Table, Women of Color Press, 1983.

———. "Toward a Black Feminist Criticism." In *All the Women Are White, All the Blacks Are Men, but Some of Us Are Brave*, edited by Gloria T. Hull, Patricia Bell-Scott, and Barbara Smith, 157–175. Old Westbury, N.Y.: Feminist Press, 1982.

Spillers, Hortense J. "A Hateful Passion, a Lost Love." *Feminist Studies* 9 (1983): 293–323.

Turner, Victor W. "Are There Universals of Performance in Myth, Ritual, and Drama?" In *By Means of Performance: Intercultural Studies of Theatre and Ritual*, edited by Richard Schechner and Willa Appel, 8–18. Cambridge: Cambridge University Press, 1989.

———. *Ritual Process: Structure and Anti-Structure*. 1969. Ithaca, N.Y.: Cornell University Press, 1991.

West, Cornel. "Nihilism in Black America." In his *Race Matters*, 9–20. Boston: Beacon, 1993.

Willis, Susan. "Eruptions of Funk: Historicizing Toni Morrison." In her *Specifying Black Women Writing the American Experience*, 83–109. Madison: University of Wisconsin Press, 1987.

Part V

◆ ◆ ◆

AN INTERVIEW

Toni Morrison

The Art of Fiction

ELISSA SCHAPPELL

◆   ◆   ◆

TONI MORRISON DETESTS being called a "poetic writer." She seems to think that the attention that has been paid to the lyricism of her work marginalizes her talent and denies her stories their power and resonance. As one of the few novelists whose work is both popular and critically acclaimed, she can afford the luxury of choosing what praise to accept. But she does not reject all classifications and embraces the title "black woman writer." Her ability to transform individuals into forces and idiosyncrasies into inevitabilities has led some critics to call her the "D. H. Lawrence of the black psyche." She is also a master of the public novel, examining the relationships between the races and genders and the struggle between civilization and nature, while at the same time combining myth and the fantastic with a deep political sensitivity.

Born Chloe Wofford in 1931 in Lorain, Ohio, a steel town on the banks of Lake Erie, Morrison sets many of her novels in the Midwest, in part because it is what she knows, but, more important, because the black experience she wants to dramatize is neither stereotypically inner-city ghetto nor Deep South plantation. It was in Lorain that she learned the importance of community, which she has described as being "both a support system and a hammer." She grew up hearing folktales of the supernatural, and her grandmother kept a dream book she believed enabled her to foretell the future. It was Morrison's father who taught her to look at the world critically and question white standards of beauty and success. He worked three jobs during the Depression and distrusted "every word and every gesture of every white man on earth."

After graduating from Howard University, where she acquired the nickname Toni, she went on to get a master's degree in English at Cornell University. She then taught at Texas Southern University and Howard University. While at Howard, she joined an informal writers' workshop to which she took "the old junk" she'd written in high school until her stockpile was depleted, and she was forced to compose a new story, a tale of a black girl who dreams of having blue eyes. This would become Morrison's first novel, *The Bluest Eye,* which was published in 1969. By the time her first book was published, Morrison was thirty-eight, divorced, and had left Howard for a job as a textbook editor at Random House. Later she became an editor in the trade book division, concentrating on bringing in books by black Americans like Toni Cade Bambara, Gayle Jones, Angela Davis, and Muhammad Ali. At the same time, she found time to write essays, criticism, and two novels. In 1977, her third novel, *Song of Solomon,* was chosen as a Book-of-the-Month Club selection (the first novel by a black writer to be chosen since Richard Wright's *Native Son* in 1940) and won the National Book Critics' Circle Award. It was only then that she decided to quit her day job and make a "genuine commitment" to writing. In 1988 her fifth novel, *Beloved,* won the Pulitzer Prize. Her most recent novel, *Jazz,* is a literary improvisation which has received great critical praise. Ms. Morrison, who has been teaching American literature and creative writing at Princeton University for the last four years, learned, just as this issue was going to press, that she had been named the recipient of the 1993 Nobel Prize for literature.

We talked with Ms. Morrison one summer Sunday afternoon on the lush campus of Princeton University. The interview took place in Ms. Morrison's office, which is decorated with a large Helen Frankenthaler print, pen-and-ink drawings that an architect did of all the houses that appear in her work, photographs, a few framed book-jacket covers, and an apology note to her from Hemingway—a forgery meant as a joke. On her desk is a blue glass tea cup emblazoned with the likeness of Shirley Temple filled with the number two pencils that she uses to write her first drafts. Pots of jade sit in a window, and a few more plants hang above. A coffeemaker and cups are at the ready. Despite the high ceilings, the big desk, and the high-backed black rocking chairs, the room had the warm feeling of a kitchen, maybe because talking to Morrison about writing is the intimate kind of conversation that often seems to happen in kitchens; or perhaps it was the fact that as our energy started flagging, she magically produced mugs of cranberry juice. We felt that she had allowed us to enter into a sanctuary, and that, however subtly, she was completely in control of the situation.

Outside, high canopies of oak leaves filtered the sunlight, dappling her white office with pools of yellow light. Morrison sat behind her big desk, which, despite her apologies for the "disorder," appeared well organized. Stacks of books and piles of paper resided on a painted bench set against the wall. She is smaller than one might imagine, and her hair, gray and silver, is woven into thin, steel-colored braids that hang just at shoulder length. Occasionally during the interview, Morrison let her sonorous, deep voice break into rumbling laughter and punctuated certain statements with a flat smack of her hand on the desktop. At a moment's notice, she can switch from raging about violence in the United States to joyfully skewering the hosts of the trashy TV talk shows through which she confesses to channel surfing late in the afternoon, assuming her work is done.

Interviewer: You have said that you begin to write before dawn. Did this habit begin for practical reasons, or was the early morning an especially fruitful time for you?

Toni Morrison: Writing before dawn began as a necessity—I had small children when I first began to write, and I needed to use the time before they said, "Mama"—and that was always around five in the morning. Many years later, after I stopped working at Random House, I just stayed at home for a couple of years. I discovered things about myself I had never thought about before. At first I didn't know when I wanted to eat, because I had always eaten when it was lunchtime or dinnertime or breakfast time. Work and the children had driven all of my habits. . . . I didn't know the weekday sounds of my own house; it all made me feel a little giddy.

I was involved in writing *Beloved* at that time—this was in 1983—and eventually I realized that I was clearer-headed, more confident, and generally more intelligent in the morning. The habit of getting up early, which I had formed when the children were young, now became my choice. I am not very bright or very witty or very inventive after the sun goes down.

Recently I was talking to a writer who described something she did whenever she moved to her writing table. I don't remember exactly what the gesture was—there is something on her desk that she touches before she hit the computer keyboard—but we began to talk about little rituals that one goes through before beginning to write. I, at first, thought I didn't have a ritual, but then I remembered that I always get up and make a cup of coffee while it is still dark—it must be dark—and then I drink the coffee and watch the light come. And she said, well, that's a ritual. And I realized that for me this ritual comprises my preparation to enter a space that I can only call nonsecular. . . . Writers all devise ways to approach that place where they expect to make the contact, where they become the conduit, or where they engage in this mysterious process. For me, light is the signal in the transition. It's not being *in* the light, it's being there *before it arrives*. It enables me, in some sense.

I tell my students one of the most important things they need to know is when they are their best, creatively. They need to ask themselves, What does the ideal room look like? Is there music? Is there silence? Is there chaos outside or is there serenity outside? What do I need in order to release my imagination?

Interviewer: What about your writing routine?

Morrison: I have an ideal writing routine that I've never experienced, which is to have, say, nine uninterrupted days when I wouldn't have to leave the house or take phone calls. And to have the space: a space where I have huge tables. I end up with this much space [*she indicates a small square spot on her desk*] everywhere I am, and I can't beat my way out of it. I am reminded of that tiny desk that Emily Dickinson wrote on, and I chuckle when I think "Sweet thing, there she was." But that is all any of us have—just this small space and no matter what the filing system or how often you clear it out, life, documents, letters, requests, invitations, invoices just keep going back in. I am not able to write regularly. I have never been able to do that—mostly because I have always had a nine-to-five job. I had to write either in between those hours, hurriedly, or spend a lot of weekend and predawn time.

Interviewer: Could you write after work?

Morrison: That was difficult. I've tried to overcome not having orderly spaces by substituting compulsion for discipline, so that when something is urgently there, urgently seen or understood, or the metaphor was powerful enough, then I would move everything aside and write for sustained periods of time. I'm talking to you about getting the first draft.

Interviewer: You have to do it straight through?

Morrison: I do. I don't think it's a law.

Interviewer: Could you write on the bottom of a shoe while riding on a train like Robert Frost? Could you write on an airplane?

Morrison: Sometimes, something that I was having some trouble with falls into place, a word sequence, say, so I've written on scraps of paper, in hotels on hotel stationery, in automobiles. *If* it arrives, you *know*. If you know it *really* has come, then you *have* to put it down.

Interviewer: What is the physical act of writing like for you?

Morrison: I write with a pencil.

Interviewer: Would you ever work on a word processor?

Morrison: Oh, I do that also, but that is much later when everything is put together. I type that into a computer, and then I begin to revise. But everything I write for the first time is written with a pencil, maybe a ballpoint [pen] if I don't have a pencil. I'm not picky, but my preference is for yellow legal pads and a nice number two pencil.

Interviewer: Dixon Ticonderoga number two soft?

Morrison: Exactly. I remember once trying to use a tape recorder, but it doesn't work.

Interviewer: Did you actually dictate a story into the machine?

Morrison: Not the whole thing, but just a bit. For instance, when two or three sentences seemed to fall into place, I thought I would carry a tape recorder in the car, particularly when I was working at Random House going back and forth every day. It occurred to me that I could just record it. It was a disaster. I don't trust my writing that is not written, although I work very hard in subsequent revisions to remove the writerliness from it, to give it a combination of lyrical, standard, and colloquial language. To pull all these things together into something that I think is much more alive, and representative. But I don't trust something that occurs to me, and then is spoken and transferred immediately to the page.

Interviewer: Do you ever read your work out loud while you are working on it?

Morrison: Not until it's published. I don't trust a performance. I could get a response that might make me think it was successful when it wasn't at all. The difficulty for me in writing—*among* the difficulties—is to write language that can work quietly on a page for a reader who doesn't hear anything. Now for that, one has to work very carefully with what is *in between* the words. What is not said. Which is measure, which is rhythm, and so on. So, it is what you don't write that frequently gives what you do write its power.

Interviewer: How many times would you say you have to write a paragraph over to reach this standard?

Morrison: Well, those that need reworking I do as long as I can. I mean, I've revised six times, seven times, thirteen times. But there's a line between revision and fretting, just working it to death. It is important to know when you are fretting it; when you are fretting it because it is not working, it needs to be scrapped.

Interviewer: Do you ever go back over what has been published and wish you had fretted more over something?

Morrison: A lot. Everything.

Interviewer: Do you ever rework passages that have already been published before reading them to an audience?

Morrison: I don't change it for the audience, but I know what it ought to be and isn't. After twenty-some years, you can figure it out; I know more about it now than I did then. It is not so much that it would have been different or even better; it is just that, taken into context with what I was trying to effect, or what consequence I wanted it to have on the reader, years later the picture is clearer to me.

Interviewer: How do you think being an editor for twenty years affected you as a writer?

Morrison: I am not sure. It lessened my awe of the publishing industry. I understood the adversarial relationship that sometimes exists between writers and publishers, but I learned how important, how critical an editor was, which I don't think I would have known before.

Interviewer: Are there editors who are helpful critically?

Morrison: Oh yes. The good ones make all the difference. It is like a priest or a psychiatrist; if you get the wrong one, then you are better off alone. But there are editors so rare and so important that they are worth searching for, and you always know when you have one.

Interviewer: Who was the most instrumental editor you've ever worked with?

Morrison: I had a very good editor, superlative for me—Bob Gottlieb. What made him good for me was a number of things: knowing what not to touch; asking all the questions you probably would have asked yourself had there been the time. Good editors are really the third eye. Cool. Dispassionate. They don't love you or your work; for me that is what is valuable—not compliments. Sometimes it's uncanny: the editor puts his or her finger on exactly the place the writer knows is weak but just couldn't do any better at the time. Or perhaps the writer thought it might fly, but wasn't sure. Good editors identify that place, and sometimes make suggestions. Some suggestions are not useful because you can't explain everything to an editor about what you are trying to do. I couldn't possibly explain all of those things to an editor, because what I do has to work on so many levels. But within the relationship, if there is some trust, some willingness to listen, remarkable things can happen. I read books all the time that I know would have profited from, not a copy editor, but somebody just talking through it. And it is important to get a great editor at a certain time, because if you don't have one in the beginning, you almost can't have one later. If you work well without an editor, and your books are well received for five or ten years, and then you write another one, which is successful but not very good, why should you then listen to an editor?

Interviewer: You have told students that they should think of the process of revision as one of the major satisfactions of writing. Do you get more pleasure out of writing the first draft, or in the actual revision of the work?

Morrison: They are different. I am profoundly excited by thinking up or having the idea in the first place . . . before I begin to write.

Interviewer: Does it come in a flash?

Morrison: No, it's a sustained thing I have to play with. I always start out with an idea, even a boring idea, that becomes a question I don't have any answers to. Specifically, since I began the *Beloved* trilogy, the last part of which I'm working on now, I have been wondering why women who are twenty, thirty years younger than I am are no happier than women who are my age and older. What on earth is that about, when there are so many more things that they can do, so many more choices? *All right*, so this is an embarrassment of riches, but so what. Why is everybody so miserable?

Interviewer: Do you write to figure out exactly how you feel about a subject?

Morrison: No, I know how I *feel*. My feelings are the result of prejudices and convictions like everybody else's. But I am interested in the complexity, the vulnerability of an idea. It is not "This is what I believe," because that would not be a book, just a tract. A book is "This may be what I believe, but suppose I am wrong, what could it be?" Or, "I don't know what it is, but I am interested in finding out what it might mean to me, as well as to other people."

Interviewer: Did you know as a child you wanted to be a writer?

Morrison: No. I wanted to be a reader. I thought everything that needed to be written had already been written or would be. I only wrote the first book because I thought it wasn't there, and I wanted to read it when I got through. I am a pretty good reader. I love it. It is what I do, really. So, if I can read it, that is the highest compliment I can think of. People say, "I write for myself," and it sounds so awful and so narcissistic, but in a sense if you know how to read your own work—that is, with the necessary critical distance—it makes you a better writer and editor. When I teach creative writing, I always speak about how you have to learn how to read your work. I don't mean enjoy it because you wrote it. I mean, go away from it, and read it as though it is the first time you've ever seen it. Critique it that way. Don't get all involved in your thrilling sentences and all that . . .

Interviewer: Do you have your audience in mind when you sit down to write?

Morrison: Only me. If I come to a place where I am unsure, I have the characters to go to for reassurance. By that time, they are friendly enough to tell me if the rendition of their lives is authentic or not. But there are so many things only I can tell. After all, this is my work. I have to take full responsibility for doing it right as well as doing it wrong. Doing it wrong isn't bad, but doing it wrong and thinking you've done it right is. I remember spending a whole summer writing something I was very impressed with, but couldn't get back to until winter. I went back confident that those fifty pages were really first-rate, but when I read them, each page of the fifty was terrible. It was really ill conceived. I knew that I could do it over, but I just couldn't get over the fact that I thought it was so good at the time. And that is scary because then you think it means you don't know.

Interviewer: What about it was so bad?

Morrison: It was pompous. Pompous and unappetizing.

Interviewer: I read that you started writing after your divorce as a way of beating back the loneliness. Was that true, and do you write for different reasons now?

Morrison: Sort of. Sounds simpler than it was. I don't know if I was writing for that reason or some other reason, or one that I don't even suspect. I do know that I don't like it here if I don't have something to write.

Interviewer: Here, meaning where?

Morrison: Meaning out in the world. It is not possible for me to be unaware of the incredible violence, the willful ignorance, the hunger for other people's pain. I'm always conscious of that though I am less aware of it under certain circumstances—good friends at dinner, other books. Teaching makes a big difference, but that is not enough. Teaching could make me into someone who is complacent, unaware, rather than part of the solution. So what makes me feel as though I belong here, out in this world, is not the teacher, not the mother, not the lover but what goes on in my mind when I am writing. Then I belong here, and then all of the things that are disparate and irreconcilable can be useful. I can do the traditional things that writers always say they do, which is to make order out of chaos. Even if you are reproducing the disorder, you are sovereign at that point. Struggling through the work is extremely important—more important to me than publishing it.

Interviewer: If you didn't do this, then the chaos would . . .

Morrison: Then I would be part of the chaos.

Interviewer: Wouldn't the answer to that be either to lecture about the chaos or to be in politics?

Morrison: If I had a gift for it. All I can do is read books and write books, and edit books and critique books. I don't think that I could show up on a regular basis as a politician. I would lose interest. I don't have the resources for it, the gift. There are people who can organize other people, and I cannot. I'd just get bored.

Interviewer: When did it become clear to you that your gift was to be a writer?

Morrison: It was very late. I always thought I was probably adept, because people used to say so, but their criteria might not have been mine. So, I wasn't interested in what they said. It meant nothing. It was by the time I was writing *Song of Solomon*, the third book, that I began to think that this was the central part of my life. Not to say that other women haven't said it all along, but for a woman to say, "I am a writer," is difficult.

Interviewer: Why?

Morrison: Well, it isn't so difficult *anymore*, but it certainly was for me, and for women of my generation or my class or my race. I don't know that all those things are folded into it, but the point is you're moving yourself out of the gender role. You are not saying, "I am a mother, I am a wife." Or, if you're in the labor market, "I am a teacher, I am an editor." But when you move to "writer," what is that supposed to mean? Is that a job? Is this the way you make your living? It's an intervention into terrain that you are not familiar with—where you have no provenance. At the time, I certainly didn't personally know any other women writers who were successful; it looked very much like a male preserve. So you sort of hope you're going to be a little minor person around the edges. It's almost as if you needed permission to write. When I read women's biographies and autobiographies, even accounts of how they got started writing, almost every one of them had a little anecdote which told about the moment someone gave them permission to do it. A mother, a husband, a teacher . . . somebody said, "Okay, go ahead—you can do it." Which is not to say that men have never needed that; frequently when they are very young, a mentor says, "You're good," and they take off. The entitlement was something they could take for granted. I couldn't. It was all very strange. So, even though I knew that writing was central to my life, that it was where my mind was, where I was most delighted and most challenged, I couldn't say it. If someone asked me, "What do you do?" I wouldn't say, "Oh I'm a writer." I'd say, "I'm an editor, or a teacher." Because when you meet people and go to lunch, if they say, "What do you do?" and you say, "I'm a writer," they have to think about that, and then they ask, "What have you written?" Then they have to either like it, or not like it. People feel obliged to like or not like and say so. It is perfectly all right to hate my work. It really is. I have close friends whose work I loathe.

Interviewer: Did you feel you had to write in private?

Morrison: Oh yes, I wanted to make it a private thing. I wanted to own it myself. Because once you say it, then other people become involved. As a matter of fact, while I was at Random House, I never said I was a writer.

Interviewer: Why not?

Morrison: Oh, it would have been awful. First of all, they didn't hire me to do that. They didn't hire me to be one of *them*. Second, I think they would have fired me.

Interviewer: Really?

Morrison: Sure. There were no in-house editors who wrote fiction. Ed Doctorow quit. There was nobody else—no real buying, negotiating editor in trade who was also publishing her own novels.

Interviewer: Did the fact that you were a woman have anything to do with it?

Morrison: That I didn't think about too much. I was so busy. I only know that I will never again trust my life, my future, to the whims of men, in companies or out. Never again will their judgment have anything to do with what I think I can do. That was the wonderful liberation of being divorced and having children. I did not mind failure, ever, but I minded thinking that someone male knew better. Before that, all the men I knew *did* know better, they really did. My father and teachers were smart people who knew better. Then I came across a smart person who was very important to me who *didn't* know better.

Interviewer: Was this your husband?

Morrison: Yes. He knew better about his life, but not about mine. I had to stop and say, let me start again and see what it is like to be a grown-up. I decided to leave home, to take my children with me, to go into publishing and see what I could do. I was prepared for that not to work either, but I wanted to see what it was like to be a grown-up.

Interviewer: Can you talk about that moment at Random House when they suddenly realized that they had a writer in their midst?

Morrison: I published a book called *The Bluest Eye*. I didn't tell them about it. They didn't know until they read the review in the *New York Times*. It was published by Holt. Somebody had told this young guy there that I was writing something, and he had said in a very offhand way, if you ever complete something, send it to me. So I did. A lot of black men were writing in 1968, 1969, and he bought it, thinking that there was a growing interest in what black people were writing and that this book of mine would also sell. He was wrong. What was selling was "Let me tell you how powerful I am and how horrible you are," or some version of that. For whatever reasons, he took a small risk. He didn't pay me much, so it didn't matter if the book sold or not. It got a really horrible review in the *New York Times Book Review* on Sunday and then got a very good daily review.

Interviewer: You mentioned getting permission to write. Who gave it to you?

Morrison: No one. What I needed permission to do was to succeed at it. I never signed a contract until the book was finished because I didn't want it to be homework. A contract meant somebody was waiting for it, that I *had* to do it, and they could ask me about it. They could get up in my face, and I don't like that. By not signing a contract, I do it, and if I want you to see it, I'll let you see it. It has to do with self-esteem. I am sure for years you have heard writers constructing illusions of freedom, anything in order to have the illusion that it is all mine, and only I can do it. I remember introducing Eudora Welty and saying that nobody could have written those stories but her, meaning that I have a feeling about most books that at some point somebody would have written them *anyway*. But then there are some writers without whom certain stories would never have been written. I don't mean the subject matter or the narrative but just the way in which they did it—their slant on it is truly unique.

Interviewer: Who are some of them?

Morrison: Hemingway is in that category, Flannery O'Connor. Faulkner, Fitzgerald.

Interviewer: Haven't you been critical of the way these authors depicted blacks?

Morrison: No! Me, critical? I have been revealing how white writers imagine black people, and some of them are brilliant at it. Faulkner was brilliant at it. Hemingway did it poorly in places and brilliantly elsewhere.

Interviewer: How so?

Morrison: In not using black characters, but using the aesthetic of blacks as anarchy, as sexual license, as deviance. In his last book, *The Garden of Eden*, Hemingway's heroine is getting blacker and blacker. The woman who is going mad tells her husband, "I want to be your little African Queen." The novel gets its charge that way: "Her white white hair and her black, black skin" . . . almost like a Man Ray photograph. Mark Twain talked about racial ideology in the most powerful, eloquent, and instructive way I have ever read. Edgar Allan Poe did not. He loved white supremacy and the planter class, and he wanted to be a gentleman, and he endorsed all of that. He didn't contest it, or critique it. What is exciting about American literature is that business of how writers say things under, beneath, and around their stories. Think of *Pudd'nhead Wilson* and all these inversions of what race is, how sometimes nobody can tell, or the thrill of discovery. Faulkner in *Absalom, Absalom!* spends the entire book tracing race, and you can't find it. No one can see it; even the character who *is* black can't see it. I did this lecture for my students that took me forever, which was tracking all the moments of withheld, partial, or disinformation, when a racial fact or clue *sort of* comes out but doesn't quite arrive. I just wanted to chart it. I listed its appearance, disguise, and disappearance on every page. I mean, every phrase! Everything, and I delivered this thing to my class. They all fell asleep! But I was so fascinated, technically. Do you know how hard it is to withhold that kind of information but hinting, pointing all of the time? And then to reveal it in order to say that it is *not* the point anyway? It is technically just astonishing. As a reader, you have been forced to hunt for a drop of black blood that means everything and nothing. The insanity of racism. So the structure is the argument. Not what this one says, or that one says . . . it is the *structure* of the book, and you are there hunting this black thing that is nowhere to be found, and yet makes all the difference. No one has done anything quite like that ever. So, when I critique, what I am saying is, I don't care if Faulkner is a racist or not; I don't personally care, but I am fascinated by what it means to write like this.

Interviewer: What about black writers . . . how do they write in a world dominated by and informed by their relationship to a white culture?

Morrison: By trying to alter language, simply to free it up, not to repress it or confine it, but to open it up. Tease it. Blast its racist straitjacket. I wrote a story entitled "Recitatif," in which there are two little girls in an orphanage, one white and one black. But the reader doesn't know which is white and which is black. I use class codes, but no racial codes.

Interviewer: Is this meant to confuse the reader?

Morrison: Well, yes. But to provoke and enlighten. I did that as a lark. What was exciting was to be forced as a writer not to be lazy and rely on obvious codes. Soon as I say, "black woman . . ." I can rest on or provoke predictable responses, but if I leave it out, then I have to talk about her in a complicated way—as a person.

Interviewer: Why wouldn't you want to say, "The black woman came out of the store"?

Morrison: Well, you can, but it has to be important that she is black.

Interviewer: What about *The Confessions of Nat Turner*?

Morrison: Well, here we have a very self-conscious character who says things like, "I looked at my black hand." Or "I woke up and I felt black." It is very much on Bill Styron's mind. He feels charged in Nat Turner's skin . . . in this place that feels exotic to him. So it reads exotically to us, that's all.

Interviewer: There was a tremendous outcry at that time from people who felt that Styron didn't have a right to write about Nat Turner.

Morrison: He has a right to write about whatever he wants. To suggest otherwise is outrageous. What they should have criticized, and some of them did, was Styron's suggestion that Nat Turner hated black people. In the book, Turner expresses his revulsion over and over again . . . he's so distant from blacks, so superior. So the fundamental question is, why would anybody follow him? What kind of leader is this who has a fundamentally racist contempt that seems unreal to any black person reading it? Any white leader would have some interest and identification with the people he was asking to die. That was what these critics meant when they said Nat Turner speaks like a white man. That racial distance is strong and clear in that book.

Interviewer: You must have read a lot of slave narratives for *Beloved*.

Morrison: I wouldn't read them for information because I knew that they had to be authenticated by white patrons, that they couldn't say everything they wanted to say because they couldn't alienate their audience; they had to be quiet about certain things. They were going to be as good as they could be under the circumstances and as revelatory, but they never say how terrible it was. They would just say, "Well, you know, it was really awful, but let's abolish slavery so life can go on." Their narratives had to be very understated. So while I looked at the documents and felt *familiar* with slavery and overwhelmed by it, I wanted it to be truly *felt*. I wanted to translate the historical into the personal. I spent a long time trying to figure out what it was about slavery that made it so repugnant, so personal, so indifferent, so intimate, and yet so public.

In reading some of the documents, I noticed frequent references to something that was never properly described—*the bit*. This thing was put into the mouth of slaves to punish them and shut them up without preventing them from working. I spent a long time trying to find out what it looked like. I kept reading statements like "I put the bit on Jenny" or, as Equiano says, "I went into a kitchen and I saw a woman standing at the stove, and she had a brake [b-r-a-k-e, he spells it] in her mouth," and I said, "What is that?" and somebody told me what it was, and then I said, "I never saw anything so awful in all my life." But I really couldn't image the thing—did it look like a horse's bit or what?

Eventually, I did find some sketches in one book in this country, which was the record of a man's torture of his wife. In South America, Brazil, places like that, they kept such mementos. But while I was searching, something else occurred to me, namely, that this bit, this item, this personalized type of torture, was a direct descendant of the Inquisition. And I realized that of course you can't buy this stuff. You can't send away for a mail-order bit for your slave. Sears doesn't carry them. So you have to make it. You have to go out in the backyard and put some stuff together and construct it and then affix it to a person. So the whole process had a very personal quality for the person who made it, as well as for the person who wore it. Then I realized that describing it would never be helpful, that the reader didn't need to *see* it so much as *feel* what it was like. I realized that it was important to imagine the bit as an active instrument, rather than simply as a curio or a historical fact. And in the same way, I wanted to show the reader what slavery *felt* like, rather than how it looked.

There's a passage in which Paul D. says to Sethe, "I've never told anybody about it, I've sung about it sometimes." He tries to tell her what wearing the bit was like, but he ends up talking about a rooster that he swears smiled at him when he wore it— he felt cheapened and lessened and that he would never be worth as much as a rooster sitting on a tub in the sunlight. I make other references to the desire to spit, to sucking iron, and so on, but it seemed to me that describing what it *looked* like would distract the reader from what I wanted him or her to experience, which was what it *felt* like. The kind of information you can find between the lines of history. It sort of falls off the page, or it's a glance and a reference. It's right there in the intersection where an institution becomes personal, where the historical becomes people with names.

Interviewer: When you create a character, is it completely created out of your own imagination?

Morrison: I never use anyone I know. In *The Bluest Eye*, I think I used some gestures and dialogue of my mother in certain places, and a little geography. I've never done that since. I really am very conscientious about that. It's never based on anyone. I don't do what many writers do.

Interviewer: Why is that?

Morrison: There is this feeling that artists have—photographers more than other people, and writers—that they are acting like a succubus ... this process of taking from something that's alive and using it for one's own purposes. You can do it with trees, butterflies, or human beings. Making a little life for oneself by scavenging other people's lives is a big question, and it does have moral and ethical implications.

In fiction, I feel the most intelligent, and the most free, and the most excited, when my characters are fully invented people. That's part of the excitement. If they're based on somebody else, in a funny way it's an infringement of a copyright. That person *owns* his life, has a patent on it. It shouldn't be available for fiction.

Interviewer: Do you ever feel like your characters are getting away from you, out of your control?

Morrison: I take control of them. They are very carefully imagined. I feel as though I know all there is to know about them, even things I don't write—like how they part their hair. They are like ghosts. They have nothing on their minds but themselves and aren't interested in anything but themselves. So you can't let them write your book for you. I have read books in which I know that has happened—when a novelist has been totally taken over by a character. I want to say, "You can't do that. If those people could write books, they would, but they can't. *You* can." So, you have to say, "Shut up. Leave me alone. I am doing this."

Interviewer: Have you ever had to tell any of your characters to shut up?

Morrison: Pilate, I did. Therefore she doesn't speak very much. She has this long conversation with the two boys, and every now and then she'll say something, but she doesn't have the dialogue the other people have. I had to do that, otherwise she was going to overwhelm everybody. She got terribly interesting; characters can do that for a little bit. I had to take it back. It's *my* book; it's not called *Pilate*.

Interviewer: Pilate is such a strong character. It seems to me that the women in your books are almost always stronger and braver than the men. Why is that?

Morrison: That isn't true, but I hear that a lot. I think that our expectations of women are very low. If women just stand up straight for thirty days, everybody goes, "Oh! How brave!" As a matter of fact, somebody wrote about Sethe and said she was this powerful, statuesque woman who wasn't even human. But at the end of the book, she can barely turn her head. She has been zonked; she can't even feed herself. Is that tough?

Interviewer: Maybe people read it that way because they thought Sethe made such a hard choice slashing Beloved's throat. Maybe they think that's being strong. Some would say that's just bad manners.

Morrison: Well, Beloved surely didn't think it was all that tough. She thought it was lunacy. Or, more important, "How do you know death is better for me? You've never died. How could you know?" But I think Paul D., Son, Stamp Paid, even Guitar, make equally difficult choices; they are principled. I do think we are too accustomed to women who don't talk back or who use the weapons of the weak.

Interviewer: What are the weapons of the weak?

Morrison: Nagging. Poison. Gossip. Sneaking around instead of confrontation.

Interviewer: There have been so few novels about women who have intense friendships with other women. Why do you think that is?

Morrison: It has been a discredited relationship. When I was writing *Sula*, I was under the impression that, for a large part of the female population, a woman friend was considered a secondary relationship. A man and a woman's relationship was primary. Women, your own friends, were always secondary relationships when the man was not there. Because of this, there's that whole cadre of women who don't like women and prefer men. We had to be taught to like one another. *Ms.* magazine was founded on the premise that we really have to stop complaining about one another, hating, fighting one another, and joining men in their condemnation of ourselves—a typical example of what dominated people do. That is a big education. When much of the literature was like that—when you read about women together (not lesbians, or those who have formed long relationships that are covertly lesbian, like in Virginia Woolf's work), it is an overtly male view of females together. They are usually male dominated—like some of Henry James's characters—or the women are talking about men, like Jane Austen's girlfriends . . . talking about who got married and how to get married, and are you going to lose him, and I think she wants him, and so on. To have heterosexual women who are friends, who are talking only about themselves to each other, seemed to me a very radical thing when *Sula* was published in 1973 . . . but it is hardly radical now.

Interviewer: It is becoming acceptable.

Morrison: Yes, and it's going to get boring. It will be overdone, and as usual it will all run amok.

Interviewer: Why do writers have such a hard time writing about sex?

Morrison: Sex is difficult to write about because it's just not sexy enough. The only way to write about it is not to write much. Let the reader bring his own sexuality into the text. A writer I usually admire has written about sex in the most off-putting way. There is just too much information. If you start saying, "the curve of . . ." you soon sound like a gynecologist. Only Joyce could get away with that. He said all those forbidden words. He said *cunt*, and that was shocking. The forbidden word can be provocative. But after a while it becomes monotonous rather than arousing. Less is always better. Some writers think that if they use dirty words they've done it. It can work for a short period and for a very young imagination, but after a while it doesn't deliver.

When Sethe and Paul D. first see each other, in about half a page they get the sex out of the way, which isn't any good anyway—it's fast, and they're embarrassed about it—and then they're lying there, trying to pretend they're not in that bed, that they haven't met, and then they begin to think different thoughts, which begin to merge so you can't tell who's thinking what. That merging to me is more tactically sensual than if I had tried to describe body parts.

Interviewer: What about plot? Do you always know where you're going? Would you write the end before you got there?

Morrison: When I really know what it is about, then I can write that end scene. I wrote the end of *Beloved* about a quarter of the way in. I wrote the end of *Jazz* very early and the end of *Song of Solomon* very early on. What I really want is for the plot to be *how* it happened. It is like a detective story in a sense. You know who is dead and you want to find out who did it. So, you put the salient elements up front, and the reader is hooked into wanting to know. How did that happen? Who did that and why? You are forced into having a certain kind of language that will keep the reader asking those questions. In *Jazz*, just as I did before with *The Bluest Eye*, I put the whole plot on the first page. In fact, in the first edition, the plot was on the cover, so that a person in a bookstore could read the cover and know right away what the book was about, and could, if they wished, dismiss it and buy another book. This seemed a suitable technique for *Jazz* because I thought of the plot in that novel—the threesome—as the melody of the piece, and it is fine to follow a melody—to feel the satisfaction of recognizing a melody whenever the narrator returns to it. That was the real art of the enterprise for me: bumping up against that melody time and again, seeing it from another point of view, seeing it afresh each time, playing it back and forth.

When Keith Jarrett plays "Ol' Man River," the delight and satisfaction is not so much in the melody itself but in recognizing it when it surfaces and when it is hidden and when it goes away completely, what is put in its place. Not so much in the original line as in all the echoes and shades and turns and pivots Jarrett plays around it. I was trying to do something similar with the plot in *Jazz*. I wanted the story to be the vehicle which moved us from page 1 to the end, but I wanted the delight to be found in moving away from the story and coming back to it, looking around it, and through it, as though it were a prism, constantly turning.

This playful aspect of *Jazz* may well cause a great deal of dissatisfaction in readers who just want the melody, who want to know what happened, who did it, and why. But the jazzlike structure wasn't a secondary thing for me—it was the raison d'être of the book. The process of trial and error by which the narrator revealed the plot was as important and exciting to me as telling the story.

Interviewer: You also divulge the plot early on in *Beloved*.

Morrison: It seemed important to me that the action in *Beloved*—the fact of infanticide—be immediately known, but deferred, unseen. I wanted to give the reader all the information and the consequences surrounding the act, while avoiding engorging myself or the reader with the violence itself. I remember writing the sentence where Sethè cuts the throat of the child very, very late in the process of writing the book. I remember getting up from the table and walking outside for a long time—walking around the yard and coming back and revising it a little bit and going back out and in and rewriting the sentence over and over again . . . Each time I fixed that sentence so that it was exactly right, or so I thought, but then I would be unable to sit there and would have to go away and come back. I thought that the act itself had to be not only buried but also understated, because if the language was going to compete with the violence itself it would be obscene or pornographic.

Interviewer: Style is obviously very important to you. Can you talk about this in relation to *Jazz*?

Morrison: With *Jazz*, I wanted to convey the sense that a musician conveys—that he has more but he's not gonna give it to you. It's an exercise in restraint, a holding back—not because it's not there, or because one had exhausted it, but because of the riches, and because it can be done again. That sense of knowing when to stop is a learned thing, and I didn't always have it. It was probably not until after I wrote *Song of Solomon* that I got to feeling secure enough to experience what it meant to be thrifty with images and language and so on. I was very conscious in writing *Jazz* of trying to blend that which is contrived and artificial with improvisation. I thought of myself as like the jazz musician: someone who practices and practices and practices in order to be able to invent and to make his art look effortless and graceful. I was always conscious of the constructed aspect of the writing process, and that art appears natural and elegant only as a result of constant practice and awareness of its formal structures. You must practice thrift in order to achieve that luxurious quality of wastefulness—that sense that you have enough to waste, that you are holding back—without actually wasting anything. You shouldn't overgratify, you should never satiate. I've always felt that that peculiar sense of hunger at the end of a piece of art—a yearning for more—is really very, very powerful. But there is at the same time a kind of contentment, knowing that at some other time there will indeed be more because the artist is end-lessly inventive.

Interviewer: Were there other . . . ingredients, structural entities?

Morrison: Well, it seems to me that migration was a major event in the cultural history of this country. Now I'm being very spec-ulative about all of this—I guess that's why I write novels—but it seems to me something modern and new happened after the Civil War. Of course, a number of things changed, but the era was most clearly marked by the disowning and dispossession of ex-slaves. These ex-slaves were sometimes taken into their local labor markets, but they often tried to escape their problems by migrating to the city. I was fascinated by the thought of what the city must have meant to them, these second- and third-generation ex-slaves, to rural people living there in their own number. The city must have seemed so exciting and wonderful, so much the place to be.

I was interested in how the city worked. How classes and groups and nationalities had the security of numbers within their own turfs and territories, but also felt the thrill of knowing that there were other turfs and other territories, and felt the real glamour and excitement of being in this throng. I was interested in how music changed in this country. Spirituals and gospel and blues represented one kind of response to slavery—they gave voice to the yearning for escape, in code, literally on the underground railroad.

I was also concerned with personal life. How did people love one another? What did they think was free? At that time, when the ex-slaves were moving into the city, running away from something that was constricting and killing them and dispossessing them over and over and over again, they were in a very limiting environment. But when you listen to their music—the beginnings of jazz—you realize that they are talking about something else. They are talking about love, about loss. But there is such grandeur, such satisfaction in those lyrics . . . they're never happy—somebody's always leaving—but they're not whining. It's as though the whole tragedy of choosing somebody, risking love, risking emotion, risking sensuality, and then losing it all didn't matter, since it was their choice. Exercising choice in who you love was a major, major thing. And the music reinforced the idea of love as a space where one could negotiate freedom.

Obviously, jazz was considered—as all new music is—to be devil music, too sensual and provocative and so on. But for some black people, jazz meant claiming their own bodies. You can image what that must have meant for people whose bodies had been owned, who had been slaves as children, or who remembered their parents being slaves. Blues and jazz represented ownership of one's own emotions. So of course it is excessive and overdone: tragedy in jazz is relished, almost as though a happy ending would take away some of its glamour, its flair. Now, advertisers use jazz on television to communicate authenticity and modernity, to say "trust me" and to say "hip."

These days, the city still retains the quality of excitement it had in the jazz age, only now we associate that excitement with a different kind of danger. We chant and scream and act alarmed about the homeless; we say we want our streets back, but it is from our awareness of homelessness and our employment of strategies to deal with it that we get our sense of the urban.

Feeling as though we have the armor, the shields, the moxie, the strength, the toughness, and the smarts to be engaged and survive encounters with the unpredictable, the alien, the strange, and the violent is an intrinsic part of what it means to live in the city. When people "complain" about homelessness, they are actually bragging about it: "New York has more homeless than San Francisco"—"No, no, no, San Francisco has more homeless"—"No, you haven't been to Detroit." We are almost competitive about our endurance, which I think is one of the reasons why we accept homelessness so easily.

Interviewer: So the city freed the ex-slaves from their history?

Morrison: In part, yes. The city was seductive to them because it promised forgetfulness. It offered the possibility of freedom— freedom, as you put it, from history. But although history should not become a straitjacket, which overwhelms and binds, neither should it be forgotten. One must critique it, test it, confront it, and understand it in order to achieve a freedom that is more than license, to achieve true, adult agency. If you penetrate the seduction of the city, then it becomes possible to confront your own history—to forget what ought to be forgotten and use what is useful—such true agency is made possible.

Interviewer: How do visual images influence your work?

Morrison: I was having some difficulty describing a scene in *Song of Solomon* . . . of a man running away from some obligations and himself. I used an Edvard Munch painting almost literally. He is walking, and there is nobody on his side of the street. Everybody is on the other side.

Interviewer: *Song of Solomon* is such a painted book in comparison with some of your others like *Beloved*, which is sepia toned.

Morrison: Part of that has to do with the visual images that I got being aware that, in historical terms, women, black people in general, were very attracted to very bright-colored clothing. Most people are frightened by color anyway.

Interviewer: Why?

Morrison: They just are. In this culture, quiet colors are considered elegant. Civilized Western people wouldn't buy blood-red sheets or dishes. There may be something more to it than what

I am suggesting. But the slave population had no access even to what color there was, because they wore slave clothes, hand-me-downs, work clothes made out of burlap and sacking. For them, a colored dress would be luxurious; it wouldn't matter whether it was rich or poor cloth . . . just to have a red or a yellow dress. I stripped *Beloved* of color so that there are only the small moments when Sethe runs amok buying ribbons and bows, enjoying herself the way children enjoy that kind of color. The whole business of color was why slavery was able to last such a long time. It wasn't as though you had a class of convicts who could dress themselves up and pass themselves off. No, these were people marked because of their skin color, as well as other features. So color is a signifying mark. Baby Suggs dreams of color, and says, "Bring me a little lavender." It is a kind of a luxury. We are so inundated with color and visuals. I just wanted to pull it back so that one could feel that hunger and that delight. I couldn't do that if I had made it the painterly book *Song of Solomon* was.

Interviewer: Is that what you are referring to when you speak about needing to find a controlling image?

Morrison: Sometimes, yes. There are three or four in *Song of Solomon*. I knew that I wanted it to be painterly, and I wanted the opening to be red, white, and blue. I also knew that in some sense, he would have to "fly." In *Song of Solomon*, it was the first time that I had written about a man who was the central, the driving engine of the narrative; I was a little unsure about my ability to feel comfortable inside him. I could always look at him and write from the outside, but those would have been just perceptions. I had to be able not only to look at him but to feel how it really must have felt. So in trying to think about this, the image in my mind was a train. All the previous books have been women-centered, and they have been pretty much in the neighborhood and in the yard; this was going to move out. So, I had this feeling about a train . . . sort of revving up, then moving out as he does, and then it sort of highballs at the end; it speeds up, but it doesn't brake, it just highballs and leaves you sort of suspended. So that image controlled the structure for me, although that is not something I articulate or even make reference to; it only matters that it works for me. Other books look like spirals, like *Sula*.

Interviewer: How would you describe the controlling image of *Jazz*?

Morrison: *Jazz* was very complicated because I wanted to represent two contradictory things—artifice and improvisation—where you have an artwork planned, thought through, but at the same time [it] appears invented, like jazz. I thought of the image being a book. Physically a book, but at the same time it is writing itself. Imagining itself. Talking. Aware of what it is doing. It watches itself think and imagine. That seemed to me to be a combination of artifice and improvisation—where you practice and plan in order to invent. Also the willingness to fail, to be wrong, because jazz is performance. In a performance, you make mistakes, and you don't have the luxury of revision that a writer has; you have to make something out of a mistake, and if you do it well enough it will take you to another place where you never would have gone had you not made that error. So, you have to be able to risk making that error in performance. Dancers do it all the time, as well as jazz musicians. *Jazz* predicts its own story. Sometimes, it is wrong because of faulty vision. It simply did not imagine those characters well enough, admits it was wrong, and the characters talk back the way jazz musicians do. It has to listen to the characters it has invented, and then learn something from them. It was the most intricate thing I had done, though I wanted to tell a very simple story about people who do not know that they are living in the jazz age, and to never use the word.

Interviewer: One way to achieve this structurally is to have several voices speaking throughout each book. Why do you do this?

Morrison: It's important not to have a totalizing view. In American literature, we have been so totalized—as though there is only one version. We are not one indistinguishable block of people who always behave the same way.

Interviewer: Is that what you mean by "totalized?"

Morrison: Yes. A definitive or an authoritarian view from somebody else or someone speaking for us. No singularity and no diversity. I try to give some credibility to all sorts of voices, each of which is profoundly different. Because what strikes me about African-American culture *is* its variety. In so much of contemporary music everybody sounds alike. But when you think about black music, you think about the difference between Duke Ellington and Sidney Bechet or Satchmo or Miles Davis. They don't sound anything alike, but you know that they are all black performers, because of whatever that quality is that makes you realize, "Oh yes, this is part of something called the African-American music tradition." There is no black woman popular singer, jazz singer, blues singer who sounds like any other. Billie Holiday does not sound like Aretha [Franklin], doesn't sound like Nina [Simone], doesn't sound like Sarah [Vaughan], doesn't sound like any of them. They are really powerfully different. And they will tell you that they couldn't possibly have made it as singers if they sounded like somebody else. If someone comes along sounding like Ella Fitzgerald, they will say, "Oh we have one of those." It's interesting to me how those women have this very distinct, unmistakable image. I would like to write like that. I would like to write novels that were unmistakably mine, but nevertheless fit first into African-American traditions and, second of all, this whole thing called literature.

Interviewer: First African American?

Morrison: Yes.

Interviewer: Rather than the whole of literature?

Morrison: Oh yes.

Interviewer: Why?

Morrison: It's richer. It has more complex sources. It pulls from something that's closer to the edge; it's much more modern. It has a human future.

Interviewer: Wouldn't you rather be known as a great exponent of literature rather than as an African-American writer?

Morrison: It's very important to me that my work be African American; if it assimilates into a different or larger pool, so much the better. But I shouldn't be *asked* to do that. Joyce is not asked to do that. Tolstoy is not. I mean, they can all be Russian, French, Irish, or Catholic; they write out of where they come from, and I do too. It just so happens that that space for me is African

American; it could be Catholic, it could be midwestern. I'm those things too, and they are all important.

Interviewer: Why do you think people ask, "Why don't you write something that we can understand?" Do you threaten them by not writing in the typical Western, linear, chronological way?

Morrison: I don't think that they mean that. I think they mean, "Are you ever going to write a book about white people?" For them, perhaps, that's a kind of a compliment. They're saying, "You write well enough, I would even let you write about me." They couldn't say that to anybody else. I mean, could I have gone up to André Gide and said, "Yes, but when are you going to get serious and start writing about black people?" I don't think he would know how to answer that question. Just as I don't. He would say, "What? I will if I want" or "Who are you?" What is behind that question is, there's the center, which is white, and then there are these regional blacks or Asians, or any sort of marginal people. That question can only be asked from the center. Bill Moyers asked me that when-are-you-going-to-write-about question on television. I just said, "Well, maybe one day . . ." but I couldn't say to him, you know, you can only ask that question from the center. The center of the world! I mean, he's a white male. He's asking a marginal person, "When are you going to get to the center? When are you going to write about white people?" I can't say, "Bill, why are you asking me that question?" or "As long as that question seems reasonable is as long as I won't, can't." The point is that he's patronizing; he's saying, "You write well enough. You could come on into the center if you wanted to. You don't have to stay out there on the margins." And I'm saying, "Yeah, well, I'm gonna stay out here on the margin, and let the center look for me."

Maybe it's a false claim, but not fully. I'm sure it was true for the ones we think of as giants now. Joyce is a good example. He moved here and there, but he wrote about Ireland wherever he was, didn't care where he was. I am sure people said to him. "Why?" Maybe the French asked, "When you gonna write about Paris?"

Interviewer: What do you appreciate most in Joyce?

Morrison: It is amazing how certain kinds of irony and humor travel. Sometimes Joyce is hilarious. I read *Finnegans Wake* after graduate school, and I had the great good fortune of reading it without any help. I don't know if I read it right, but it was hilarious! I laughed constantly! I didn't know what was going on for whole blocks, but it didn't matter because I wasn't going to be graded on it. I think the reason why everyone still has so much fun with Shakespeare is because he didn't have any literary critic. He was just doing it, and there were no reviews except for people throwing stuff on stage. He could just do it.

Interviewer: Do you think if he had been reviewed he would have worked less?

Morrison: Oh, if he'd cared about it, he'd have been very self-conscious. That's a hard attitude to maintain, to pretend you don't care, pretend you don't read.

Interviewer: Do you read your reviews?

Morrison: I read everything.

Interviewer: Really? You look deadly serious.

Morrison: I read everything written about me that I see.

Interviewer: Why is that?

Morrison: I have to know what's going on!

Interviewer: You want to see how you're coming across?

Morrison: No, no. It's not about me or my work, it's about what is going on. I have to get a sense, particularly of what's going on with women's work, or African-American work, contemporary work. I teach a literature course. So I read any information that's going to help me teach.

Interviewer: Are you ever really surprised when they compare you to the magic realists, such as Gabriel García Márquez?

Morrison: Yes, I used to be. It doesn't mean anything to me. Schools are only important to me when I'm teaching literature. It doesn't mean anything to me, when I'm sitting here with a big pile of blank yellow paper. . . . What do I say? I'm a magic realist? Each subject matter demands its own form, you know.

Interviewer: Why do you teach undergraduates?

Morrison: Here at Princeton, they really do value undergraduates, which is nice because a lot of universities value only the graduate school or the professional research schools. I like Princeton's notion. I would have loved that for my own children. I don't like freshmen and sophomores being treated as the staging ground or the playground or the canvas on which graduate students learn how to teach. They need the best instruction. I've always thought the public schools needed to study the best literature. I always taught *Oedipus Rex* to all kinds of what they used to call remedial or development classes. The reason those kids are in those classes is that they're bored to death, so you can't give them boring things. You have to give them the best there is to engage them.

Interviewer: One of your sons is a musician. Were you ever musical, did you ever play the piano?

Morrison: No, but I come from a family of highly skilled musicians. Highly skilled, meaning most of them couldn't read music, but they could play everything that they heard ... instantly. They sent us, my sister and me, to music lessons. They were sending me off to learn how to do something that they could do naturally. I thought I was deficient, retarded. They didn't explain that perhaps it's more important that you learn how to *read* music ... that it's a good thing, not a bad thing. I thought we were sort of lame people going off to learn how to walk while, you know, they all just stood up and did it naturally.

Interviewer: Do you think there is an education for becoming a writer? Reading perhaps?

Morrison: That has only limited value.

Interviewer: Travel the world? Take courses in sociology, history?

Morrison: Or stay home. ... I don't think they have to go anywhere.

Interviewer: Some people say, "Oh I can't write a book until I've lived my life, until I've had experiences."

Morrison: That may be—maybe they can't. But look at the people who never went anywhere and just thought it up. Thomas Mann. I guess he took a few little trips ... I think you either have or you acquire this sort of imagination. Sometimes you do need a stimulus. But I myself don't ever go anywhere for stimulation. I don't want to go anywhere. If I could just sit in one spot, I would be happy. I don't trust the ones who say I have to go do something before I can write. You see, I don't write autobiographically. First of all, I'm not interested in real-life people as subjects for fiction—including myself. If I write about somebody who's a historical figure like Margaret Garner, I really don't know anything about her. What I knew came from reading two interviews with her. They said, Isn't this extraordinary. Here's a woman who escaped into Cincinnati from the horrors of slavery and was not crazy. Though she'd killed her child, she was not foaming at the mouth. She was very calm. She said, "I'd do it again." That was more than enough to fire my imagination.

Interviewer: She was sort of a *cause célèbre*?

Morrison: She was. Her real life was much more awful than it's rendered in the novel, but if I had known all there was to know about her, I never would have written it. It would have been finished; there would have been no place in there for me. It would be like a recipe already cooked. There you are. You're already this person. Why should I get to steal from you? I don't like that. What I really love is the process of invention. To have characters move from the curl all the way to a full-fledged person, that's interesting.

Interviewer: Do you ever write out of anger or any other emotion?

Morrison: No. Anger is a very intense but tiny emotion, you know. It doesn't last. It doesn't produce anything. It's not creative . . . at least not for me. I mean these books take at least three years!

Interviewer: That is a long time to be angry.

Morrison: Yes. I don't trust that stuff anyway. I don't like those little quick emotions, like, "I'm lonely, *ohhh*, God . . ." I don't like those emotions as fuel. I mean, I have them, but . . .

Interviewer: They're not a good muse?

Morrison: No, and if it's not your brain thinking cold, cold thoughts, which you can dress in any kind of mood, then it's nothing. It has to be a cold, cold thought. I mean cold, or cool at least. Your brain. That's all there is.

Note

Additional material for this essay was supplied by Claudia Brodsky Lacour.

Chronology

African-American History, 1865–1977

1865 The Thirteenth Amendment, abolishing slavery, was ratified on December 18.

1866 The Ku Klux Klan held its first meeting, in Tennessee.

1868 The Fourteenth Amendment, granting equal rights to all persons, was ratified on June 13.

1870 The Fifteenth Amendment, giving blacks the right to vote, was ratified on March 30.

1875 Congress passed a Civil Rights bill that banned discrimination in places of public accommodation.

   The first African-American senator, Hiram R. Revels, Republican of Mississippi, took his seat. He served one year.

1883 On October 15, the Supreme Court declared the Civil Rights Act of 1875, which banned discrimination in places of public accommodation, unconstitutional.

1895   Frederick Douglass, African-American leader, activist, and statesman, died on February 20.

Booker T. Washington delivered his famous "Atlanta Compromise" speech on September 18 at the Atlanta Cotton States Exposition. He assured southern whites that blacks wanted to concentrate on economic advancement and not on political or social equality.

1896   On May 18, in *Plessy v. Ferguson*, the Supreme Court gave legal support to the concept of separate but equal public facilities for blacks.

1898   The black-owned North Carolina Mutual and Provident Insurance Company and the National Benefit Life Insurance Company of Washington, D.C., were established.

1899   The Afro-American Council designated June 4 as a national day of fasting to protest lynchings and massacres. In the late 1800s, more than 3,000 blacks were lynched as were hundreds more throughout the South in the early 1900s.

1903   W. E. B. Du Bois's *The Souls of Black Folk* was published. Du Bois was a sociologist and historian at Atlanta University who opposed Booker T. Washington's program by refusing to accept racial segregation.

1906   In Brownsville, Texas, on August 13, black troops rioted against segregation. President Theodore Roosevelt discharged three companies of black soldiers involved in the protest.

1909   On February 12, the National Association for the Advancement of Colored People (NAACP) was formed.

1910   In April, the National Urban League was established.

1913   Jubilee, the fiftieth anniversary of the Emancipation Proclamation, was celebrated all year.

1915	Booker T. Washington died on November 14.
1919	On February 19–21, the first Pan-African Congress met in Paris, France, under the leadership of W. E. B. Du Bois.
1920	On August 1, Marcus Garvey's Universal Improvement Association held its national convention in Harlem, New York. Garvey urged the establishment of a new homeland in Africa for dissatisfied blacks.
1920–1929	This was the decade of the Harlem Renaissance.
1925	On May 8, A. Philip Randolph organized the Brotherhood of Sleeping Car Porters.
1931	In Scottsboro, Alabama, nine black youths, accused of raping two white women on a freight train, went on trial.
1936	Jesse Owens won four gold medals at the Summer Olympics in Berlin, Germany.
1939	The Daughters of the American Revolution denied Marian Anderson permission to sing at Constitution Hall in Washington, D.C., because she was black. Eleanor Roosevelt resigned from the DAR and helped arrange a performance for Anderson at the Lincoln Memorial on Easter Sunday. More than 75,000 people attended.
1939–1945	Nearly a million African Americans served in the military. Most were in segregated units.
1940	Benjamin O. Davis became the first black brigadier general in the U.S. Army. His son, Benjamin O. Davis, Jr., later became the first black lieutenant general in the Air Force.
1941	The Supreme Court ruled that separate facilities for white and black railroad passengers must be significantly equal.

1942   The Congress of Racial Equality (CORE) was founded in Chicago.

1944   The Supreme Court ruled that southern white primaries, which barred black voters, were unconstitutional.

1947   Jackie Robinson of the Brooklyn Dodgers became the first black player in modern major league baseball.

1948   President Harry S. Truman issued an executive order desegregating the military.

1950   Gwendolyn Brooks was awarded the Pulitzer Prize for poetry for *Annie Allen*. She was the first African American to win.

Ralph J. Bunche was awarded the Nobel Peace Prize for his work as United Nations mediator in the Arab-Israeli dispute in Palestine.

1955   Rosa Parks refused to move to the back of a bus in Montgomery, Alabama. She was arrested, and blacks boycotted buses for 382 days, until the city changed the bus law.

Emmett Till, a fourteen-year-old boy from Chicago visiting relatives in Money, Arkansas, was savagely beaten to death and his body thrown into the Tallahatchie River. Roy Blanton and his brother-in-law, J. W. Milam, who had bragged about committing the crime, were acquitted by a jury, which deliberated for less than an hour.

1957   The Southern Christian Leadership Conference (SCLC) was established by Martin Luther King, Jr., and others to promote civil rights.

President Dwight D. Eisenhower ordered federal troops into Little Rock, Arkansas, in response to Governor Orval Faubus's efforts to block desegregation at Central High.

On August 29, Congress passed the Voting Rights Bill.

1960 The sit-in movement was launched at Greensboro, North Carolina, when black college students insisted on service at a segregated lunch counter.

1963 In Birmingham, Alabama, police commissioner Eugene "Bull" Connor used fire hoses and dogs against civil rights activists.

A dynamite bomb exploded at the Sixteenth Street Baptist Church in Birmingham. An eleven-year-old and three fourteen-year-old girls were killed. Fourteen years later, Robert Chambliss was convicted of the murder; he died in prison. Another suspect died before he was charged. Thomas Blanton was convicted and sentenced to life in prison thirty-eight years later. In 2002, the final suspect, Bobby Frank Cherry, was also convicted.

In August, more than 200,000 people took part in a march on Washington for civil rights.

President John F. Kennedy was assassinated in November. Vice President Lyndon B. Johnson became president.

1964 Congress passed Kennedy's Civil Rights Act, which prohibited discrimination in public places and called for equal opportunity in education and employment.

Martin Luther King, Jr., won the Nobel Peace Prize for leading nonviolent demonstrations for civil rights.

1965 King led about 30,000 people on a march from Selma, Alabama, to Montgomery.

Congress passed the Voting Rights Act, which gave the vote to thousands of southern blacks who had never voted.

In the Watts neighborhood of Los Angeles, riots erupted during the summer. Thirty-four people were killed, and more than a thousand were injured. The Kerner Commission, which studied the riot, put much of the blame on racial prejudice, poverty, police abuse, and the effects of segregation.

Malcolm X, a Black Muslim leader, was assassinated. Three black men were convicted of the murder.

1967   Thurgood Marshall became the first black associate justice of the Supreme Court.

1968   King was assassinated in Memphis on April 4. James E. Ray, a white man, was convicted and sentenced to ninety-nine years in prison.

1968   Shirley Chisholm became the first black woman to be elected to the U.S. Congress.

1969   The Supreme Court ruled that racial segregation in schools had to end.

1971   Angela Davis was arraigned on charges of murder, kidnapping, and conspiracy for her alleged participation in an attempted escape from the Hall of Justice in Marin County, California, in 1970.

1973   Thomas Bradley was elected the first black mayor of Los Angeles.

1975   Elijah Mohammed, leader of the Nation of Islam, died.

1977   Alex Haley's *Roots: The Saga of an American Family* (1976) was adapted for television. The miniseries aired eight nights and was reported to have had the highest ratings on record for a single program.

Selected Bibliography

Benston, Kimberly W. "Re-weaving the 'Ulysses Scene': Enchantment, Post-Oedipal Identity, and the Buried Text of Blackness in Toni Morrison's *Song of Solomon*." In *Comparative American Identities: Race, Sex, and Nationality in the Modern Text*, edited by Hortense J. Spillers, 87–109. New York: Routledge, 1991.

Bloom, Harold. *"Song of Solomon": Modern Critical Perspectives*. Broomall, Pa.: Chelsea House, 1999.

Branch, Eleanor. "Through the Maze of the Oedipal: Milkman's Search for Self in *Song of Solomon*." *Literature and Psychology* 41, nos. 1–2 (1995): 52–84.

Brenkman, John. "Politics and Form in *Song of Solomon*." *Social Text* 39 (Summer 1994): 57–82.

Brown, Joseph A. "To Cheer the Weary Traveler: Toni Morrison, William Faulkner, and History." *Mississippi Quarterly* 49 (Fall 1996): 709–26.

Butler, Robert James. "Open Movement and Self-hood in Toni Morrison's *Song of Solomon*." *Centennial Review* 28, no. 1 (1984–1985): 58–75.

Clarke, Deborah L. " 'What There Was before Language': Preliteracy in

Toni Morrison's *Song of Solomon*." In *Anxious Power: Reading, Writing, and Ambivalence in Narrative by Women*, edited by Carol J. Singley and Susan Elizabeth Sweeney, 265–78. Albany: State University of New York Press, 1993.

Coleman, James W. "Beyond the Reach of Love and Caring: Black Life in Toni Morrison's *Song of Solomon*." *Obsidian II* 1 (Winter 1986): 151–61.

Cowart, David. "Faulkner and Joyce in Morrison's *Song of Solomon*." *American Literature* 62 (March 1990): 87–100.

Ellis, Kate. "Text and Undertext: Myth and Politics in Toni Morrison's *Song of Solonom*." *Literature Interpretation Theory* 6 (April 1995): 35–45.

Fabre, Genevieve. "Genealogical Archaeology of the Quest for Legacy in Toni Morrison's *Song of Solomon*." In *Critical Essays on Toni Morrison*, edited by Nellie Y. McKay, 104–14. Boston: Hall, 1988.

Furman, Jan. *Toni Morrison's Fiction*. Columbia: University of South Carolina Press, 1996.

Gates, Henry Louis, Jr., and K. A. Appiah. *Toni Morrison: Critical Perspectives Past and Present*. New York: Amistad, 1993.

Harris, A. Leslie. "Myth and Structure in Toni Morrison's *Song of Solomon*." *MELUS* 7 (1980): 69–76.

Harris, Trudier. *Fiction and Folklore: The Novels of Toni Morrison*. Knoxville: University of Tennessee Press, 1991.

Holloway, Karla, and Stephanie Demetrakopoulos. *New Dimensions of Spirituality: A Biracial and Bicultural Reading of the Novels of Toni Morrison*. Westport, Conn.: Greenwood, 1987.

Hubbard, Dolan. "In Quest of Authority: Toni Morrison's *Song of Solomon* and the Rhetoric of the Black Preacher." *CLA Journal* 35, no. 3 (March 1992): 288–302.

Kang, Ja Mo. "Toni Morrison's *Song of Solomon*: Milkman's Limited Moral Development." *Journal of English Language and Literature* 41, no. 1 (1995): 125–47.

Kim, Aeju. "Destructive Mythmaking in Toni Morrison's *Song of Solomon* and *Tar Baby*." *Journal of English Language and Literature* 42, no. 2 (1995): 381–95.

Kubitschek, Missy Dehn. *Toni Morrison: A Critical Companion*. Westport, Conn.: Greenwood, 1998.

Kolmerten, Carol A., Stephen M. Ross, and Judith Bryant Wittenberg, eds. *Unflinching Gaze: Morrison and Faulkner Re-envisioned*. Jackson: University Press of Mississippi, 1997.

Mason, Theodore O., Jr. "The Novelist as Conservator: Stories and Comprehension in Toni Morrison's *Song of Solomon.*" *Contemporary Literature* 29 (1988): 564–81.

McKay, Nellie Y., ed. *Critical Essays on Toni Morrison.* Boston: Hall, 1988.

Middleton, David. *Toni Morrison's Fiction: Contemporary Criticism.* New York: Garland, 1997.

Mobley, Marilyn Sanders. *Folk Roots and Mythic Wings in Sarah Orne Jewett and Toni Morrison: The Cultural Function of Narrative.* Baton Rouge: Louisiana State University Press, 1991.

Moraru, Christian. "Reading the Onomastic Text: 'The Politics of the Proper Name' in Toni Morrison's *Song of Solomon.*" *Names: A Journal of Onomastics* 44, no. 3 (September 1996): 189–204.

Morrison, Toni. "Rootedness: The Ancestor as Foundation." In *Black Women Writers (1950–1980): A Critical Evaluation,* edited by Mari Evans, 339–45. New York: Doubleday, 1984.

———. "Unspeakable Things Unspoken: The Afro-American Presence in American Literature." *Michigan Quarterly Review* (Winter 1989): 1–34.

O'Shaughnessy, Kathleen. " 'Life Life Life Life': The Community Chorus in *Song of Solomon.*" In *Critical Essays on Toni Morrison,* edited by Nellie Y. McKay, 125–33. Boston: Hall, 1988.

Otten, Terry. *The Crime of Innocence in the Fiction of Toni Morrison.* Columbia: University of Missouri Press, 1989.

Peterson, Nancy J., ed. *Toni Morrison: Critical and Theoretical Approaches.* Jackson: University Press of Mississippi, 1997.

Rubinowitz, Paula. "Naming, Magic, and Documentary: The Subversion of Narrative in *Song of Solomon, Ceremony,* and *China Men.*" In *Feminist Re-Vision: What Has Been and Might Be,* edited by Vivian Patrake and Louise A Tilly, 26–42. Ann Arbor: Women's Studies Program, University of Michigan, 1983.

Scruggs, Charles. "The Nature of Desire in Toni Morrison's *Song of Solomon.*" *Arizona Quarterly* 38 (Winter 1982): 311–35.

Smith, Valerie. *New Essays on "Song of Solomon."* New York: Cambridge University Press, 1995.

Story, Ralph. "An Excursion into the Black World: The 'Seven Days' in Toni Morrison's *Song of Solomon.*" *Black American Literature Forum* (Spring 1989): 149–59.

Stryz, Jan. "Inscribing an Origin in *Song of Solomon.*" *Studies in American Fiction* 19, no. 1 (Spring 1991): 31–40.

Taylor-Guthrie, Danille, ed. *Conversation with Toni Morrison.* Jackson: University Press of Mississippi, 1994.

Weinstein, Philip M. *What Else but Love? The Ordeal of Race in Faulkner and Morrison.* New York: Columbia University Press, 1996.

Willis, Susan. "Eruptions of Funk: Historicizing Toni Morrison." *Black American Literature Forum* 16, no. 1 (Spring 1982): 34–42.